W9-CNB-965

Ask!

Also by Mark Victor Hansen

Books

Audios

How to Think Bigger Than You Ever Thought You Could Think
Dreams Don't Have Deadlines
Visualizing Is Realizing
Sell Yourself Rich
Chicken Soup for the Soul series
The One Minute Millionaire
Cracking the Millionaire Code

Also by Crystal Dwyer Hansen

Books

Skinny Life: The Secret to Spiritual, Physical, and Emotional Fitness
Pure Thoughts for Pure Results:
How Messy Thinking Can Make or Break Your Life

Audios

Freedom from Anxiety
Overcoming Insomnia
Garden of New Beginnings
Healing Meditation
Living Free of Depression
Learn to Make Life Happen for You
Weight Loss I
Weight Loss II
Purge Your Messy Thinking Forever

Ask!

THE BRIDGE FROM YOUR
DREAMS
TO YOUR
DESTINY

Mark Victor Hansen
and Crystal Dwyer Hansen

Post Hill
PRESS

A POST HILL PRESS BOOK

Ask!:
The Bridge from Your Dreams to Your Destiny
© 2020 by Mark Victor Hansen and Crystal Dwyer Hansen
All Rights Reserved

ISBN: 978-1-64293-495-3
ISBN (eBook): 978-1-64293-496-0

Cover art by Cody Corcoran
Interior design and composition by Greg Johnson, Textbook Perfect

Post Hill Press
New York • Nashville
posthillpress.com

Published in the United States of America

To all those who have bravely asked,
especially when they were feeling scared,
uncertain, and unworthy…

And to our parents who allowed us to ask
and who nurtured our respective journeys
toward fulfilling our destinies.
Heartfelt thanks to Una and Paul Hansen,
and Beverly and Reed Bowen.

Table of Contents

PROLOGUE

The Fable of Micaela

To prepare your heart and mind for the miracles that lie ahead,
we begin with a fable....

You were born with a destiny. Your job is to discover it. Once you discover your destiny and start to move toward it, you can manifest innumerable blessings for yourself and others.

Most people have beautiful dreams deep inside the things they would like to have, the relationships they'd love to enjoy, and the wellness and well-being that would help them express their best. But often those dreams lie dormant inside. Hidden by fear or unworthiness or a lack of awareness of what *could* be.

The Golden Destiny Bridge

Micaela's life was miserable. She was doomed to toil and labor all the days of her life. Her clothes were shabby, her stomach never full, and her only shelter from the harsh winds was a thick grove of trees she called home. She missed her mother and father terribly. From the local villagers all she got each day was silence, as she was generally ignored other than the occasional angry stare or impatient shove. She kept to herself mostly, trying to avoid the threatening bill collectors who had tried to find her to intimidate her into paying them for the bills remaining from her mother's illness. It wasn't enough they had already taken her home from her. In spite of her father's spending everything he had to get mother well, the relentless illness and the grief over her husband's sudden and tragic death had finally drained every ounce of life from her mother. Within a thirty-day period, Micaela had lost both of her parents. They had been the light of her world, and now everything felt heavy and dark. One night, after a long day's work, she lay her weary body on the bed of leaves in her grove. She dropped into an exhausted sleep and began to dream.

Micaela's First Dream: The Being Appears

In the middle of a deep and dreamless sleep, she heard a voice. He said, "Micaela, come with me."

Micaela was suspicious of strangers and mostly stayed away from them. But this was no stranger. His warmth and familiarity left her defenseless as she readily agreed, "Okay." Immediately, as her mind said that word, she was lifted up and soaring soundlessly across a beautiful night sky, alongside this…Being. Somehow, it didn't seem strange at all to be high above, effortlessly passing through the night sky, watching the lights below, guided by this warm, loving presence whom her mind couldn't recall knowing but with whom her soul felt so comfortable. Soaring along through air that was neither warm nor cold she felt both calm and exhilarated, as if everything was right.

After a time, she found they were suddenly hovering above a large bridge. It appeared to be daytime now, but even through the morning light, the magnificent bridge below seemed to shimmer and sparkle with golden radiance. She watched from above as people moved about, not seeming to notice the existence of Micaela and her guide as they gazed down upon them with the being on her left side. It never occurred to her to look at him next to her. In fact, it seemed as if she knew she wasn't supposed to gaze directly at him, but that was okay. Micaela watched the people below. Some seemed to be eagerly entering the opening of the bridge and others journeying across its great expanse. Those people had looks of hope, excitement, and anticipation on their faces. But others seemed to walk past the bridge as if they didn't see it. They seemed preoccupied, sad, or distracted, and because of that, unable to even notice this beautiful bridge before them. As she watched, the Being spoke. *Be careful what you choose, Micaela. Everything you think and do is a choice. Your decisions are powerful and will decide your path. Certain choices will lead you to your destiny and others far from it. The key is to ask. To ask again and again and never stop asking.*

Micaela fully understood his meaning, even beyond the words he spoke. As she said *okay* after each of his admonitions, and to affirm she knew what he was telling her, she realized they were speaking through their minds, not their lips. Still looking down at the people, she realized the tragedy of those who missed the bridge. She felt sad for them. At the same time, she felt the happiness and hopefulness of those making their journey across.

Suddenly, Micaela's eyes flew open. She was once again on her bed of leaves in the grove. She sat up quickly. What had just happened? Was it a dream? It didn't feel like a dream. It felt *real*. Who was this being? Why did he care so much? Why her? Why did she deserve such grace and kindness?

Her heart was lighter as she jumped up and pulled the quill and parchment from her old bag. It had been so long since she had used them, since Mother had died, and she had been indentured to the quarry owner to pay off the debt they owed from her mother's sickness. The tiny bit of ink she had left was almost dry, so she quickly wrote down everything she could remember about the encounter. She finished with these words that rang in her ears all day, over and over: *The key is to ask. To ask again and again and never stop asking.*

Several weeks had passed, and ever since her encounter with the Being, Micaela had not been quite the same. Her step was lighter each day as she walked to the quarry to do her work. Now she looked at people differently. What did they think? What did they know? Is there something she might learn if she opened up and asked? That word...*ask*...*ask*...*ask*...kept running through her mind throughout the day. As she was loading her rocks in her cart a few days later, she looked up at the middle-aged woman working next to her who had a pock-marked face and a missing finger. The woman always seemed to be happier than she should be.

When Micaela made eye contact with her for the first time, she gazed back with a smile and said, "At least when I do my work, I can say I'm working for the King!"

Normally Micaela would have turned away and ignored her. Instead, she looked at her and asked, "What do you mean? This quarry is owned by heartless men who don't care about anyone."

"No, young one, the King needs these stones to build the buildings that store the food for the villagers and to build the buildings to house the soldiers that protect us from harm. He needs the stones to build the walls that keep out the invaders who are ill-intentioned and want to steal from and pillage our community."

"Are you saying the King is kind and cares about us?"

"Oh yes, dear girl. Good things sometimes take hard work. Not everyone likes to do it. But if you understand the work is for something bigger than yourself, it becomes easier. Not everyone stays here forever like me," the woman said chuckling.

"I see," said Micaela, "but don't you want to get out of here at some point and do something better?"

The woman laughed. "This is where I like to be," she said with eyes shining. "I enjoy giving my help to the ones who've had it the hardest. This is where they usually end up. I'm here for them, and that's what makes me happy. It's what I was made for. What is your name, dear?"

"It's Micaela. And what is yours?"

"My name is Bekkie."

After talking to Bekkie, the day went so fast for Micaela. She started to notice for the first time, that when Bekkie would go to take a dip of water from the dipper by the well, she would also bring a drink to the older workers. Men and women who didn't move quite as fast anymore. Bekkie also left them with a cheerful word and a happy smile. If their carts weren't full enough to meet the minimum, she added more rocks to make them fuller. As Micaela began noticing these acts of kindness carried out by her new friend each day, some of the sadness Micaela had carried for so long started to melt away. Over the next days, she continued to watch and learn, paying careful attention to Bekkie. When she left the quarry at the end of each day, she didn't feel so tired. She noticed that her back wasn't aching like it used to as she walked home to her grove on her familiar path. Even now as she was walking home, thoughts of Bekkie made her smile. She felt thankful for her new friend and looked forward to learning something new from her each day.

Micaela was relieved that finally the hot days of summer were waning. The days had become a bit cooler and more comfortable. She yawned, feeling restful as she cleaned up the remains of her simple supper. She started to settle into her leafy bed to get ready for sleep. Beyond all the grief she had suffered, she was finally feeling there was more for her. She thought about the dream she'd had a couple of months ago. Since then she had begun to feel there might be a purpose for her life. But what was it? She still couldn't figure it all out—why did the Being care so much about her? Why did he bother? But since then she hadn't felt the same. Or been the same. That beautiful bridge! What did it mean for her? What was on the other side? She felt hopeful—even a little excited about what might be waiting for her. The changes were already happening, and she could feel them and see them each day. She had started wondering about everything. She felt a new curiosity inside that was telling her maybe things weren't as she had thought they were. Maybe they didn't have to be. Maybe if she started questioning everything, she could discover something completely different. She knew she had already stepped onto that sparkling bridge. She could see the bridge in her mind as she drifted off to sleep, and the sparkles became stars of light on a calm, peaceful night.

Ask Yourself—The Amethyst Gift

Micaela's Second Dream: The Angel Woman

Micaela was walking through a dark forest being pulled toward a light. She kept walking hurriedly to get to the light. As she entered a clearing, she saw a magnificent bonfire lighting up the night. Next to the bonfire, she saw a beautiful older woman with white hair. Everything about the woman was light and bright. The woman was holding out loving arms to her. A soft gentle white light surrounded the woman, and she shone with the same light. As she stepped in front of her, Micaela knew she was looking at an angel. With a glorious smile, the angel woman extended her hands to give Micaela a gift. It looked like a beautiful, purple, shiny amethyst. As Micaela reached out to take the gift, she suddenly felt the light fill the center of her body.

The woman spoke:

Your inner wisdom has already been seeded by your Creator. To find it, you must learn to find the awareness of that gem inside of you and keep calling on it. It is the center inside of you through which the wisdom of God pours. Ask yourself, "What are my gifts? What do I love to do?" Asking yourself will allow you to tap into the inner wisdom of the Creator. It is already inside of you. Through this, you will become the scribe who will write your own future.

As the sun pulled Micaela out of sleep, she realized she was still in the grove, but she had been given another important message through her dreams. She sat up and tried to recall every single part of what she had just seen so that she could understand it better. She felt inside like she had been called to something bigger. Again, she quickly grabbed her writing set and recorded it all. She didn't ever want to forget. She knew it was special. Thank goodness she had taken some of her coins from work and bought fresh ink. She ate a roll, dressed quickly, and rushed off to work.

Each day seemed to get a little better. Micaela thought often about the angel woman and the gift she had given her in the dream. She wondered if she was just imagining it, but she noticed she felt light and bright on the inside since then. Like the woman spoke the truth about her gifts. Now she just needed to figure out what they were. She started paying a lot of attention to the others around her. For the first time, she started to wonder about their stories. Why were they here? Did they have other people in their lives whom they loved? Were they happy or miserable here? She'd been so mired in her own misery she'd never thought of anyone else. Until now. Just today the supervisors placed a sign that all workers needed to be at the south end of the quarry. She looked up and saw a young man who looked just a few years older than her, get hauled over by the scruff of his neck to the south end of the quarry as the angry supervisor yelled to him, "Pay attention and *read the sign* next time!" The young man landed near Micaela's feet. The humiliation in his eyes as he looked up at her moved her heart.

She asked him, "What happened to you? Did you not see the sign posted over there?"

He looked at the ground as he replied, "I've never learned to read. There are quite a few of us here who don't. They just rely on others to tell them what to do. I haven't made any friends yet because I just got here last week."

Micaela felt truly sorry for the man. She wondered what it must be like to not even be able to read a sign. A warm glow started in the center of her belly as asked herself, "Is there something I can do to help this man and others like him? What gifts do I have that I could share?"

"Would you like to learn?" she asked.

"Ha! Me? Learn to read? How in the world would I do that? You think these rocks are going to teach me to read?"

"No, but I will."

The man's brow furrowed as he looked back at her suspiciously. "Why would you do that?"

"Because I can. Because I want to," said Micaela.

Trying not to look too hopeful, the man replied, "Even if you wanted to, and I'm not too stupid to learn, when would we find the time to do it?"

"What is your name?"

"Jack. My name is Jack."

"Okay, Jack, I'm Micaela. Every day when we take our lunch, I will teach you another letter and its sound. That will take twenty-six days. Then we will begin to put the letters and sounds together in small words each day. As you learn small words each day, tied together in a short sentence, you will begin to understand how it all comes together. Very soon you will understand longer words in longer sentences. Before you know it, you'll be reading!"

A huge smile that couldn't disguise his excitement or gratitude erupted on Jack's face. "Really? Is it that simple? I'd be so grateful. I...don't know what to say. I honestly don't know why I deserve your kindness."

"Well, just know that you do," she said with a smile. "Everyone does. If you're okay with it, we'll get started tomorrow."

"Yes. Good. I'm okay. No, I mean I'm more than okay. I'm...I'm so...ready. I...uh, don't know how to thank you for this," he said as he hung his head in humility.

"You can thank me by doing the same for someone else. Just promise me you will."

He jumped up off the ground with his arms outstretched. "I...of course! I will! If you teach me, I'll share it with everyone!"

With a beautiful smile, Micaela said, "Tomorrow it is, then. Meet me by the well right at the lunch break and don't be late. We've got work to do!"

"Don't worry! I'll be there!"

When Micaela turned to go, Jack jumped up thanking the heavens, then fell to his knees with tears in his eyes. Wiping them away, he stood and rushed back to his cart. He felt so strong; at the end of the day his cart was piled higher than ever with stones as he wheeled them happily to the collection area where they would be hitched to the donkeys for transfer.

Sixty days later Jack and Micaela were finishing their lesson and their lunches, and an older man named Gus squatted down next to them. He said with a twinkle in his eye. "I've been watching you the last couple of months. She's really got you reading, hasn't she?"

Jack responded by ceremoniously holding the parchment up high in front of him and reading, "I see the tin cup. I can fill up the cup. I can drink the ale." He looked at the old man with a huge grin. "What do you think?"

"I think you found yourself an angel there to care about you that much. No one's ever cared about me like that," he said with a chuckle. "You should thank your lucky stars."

Jack's face was full of sympathy for Gus.

"Do you want to learn to read?" asked Micaela.

"Maybe I'm just an old fool who can't learn. It's too late for me anyway."

"Why is it too late, Gus?" asked Micaela. "You come here every day to work. Why wouldn't you use the lunch time here like Jack has and learn to read?"

"Ah…no one ever offered to teach me."

"Did you ask?" said Micaela.

"Ahem…uh…okay…um…would you teach me? To read?"

Jack jumped up and said, "I will, Gus! I can teach you the things Micaela has taught me. But I want to ask something. Micaela, if I teach Gus to read, would you be willing to teach my young cousins to read? They live near the grove by you. Maybe after work or on a day off, you could go there just for an hour at a time. They are a good family, but the eldest child, my cousin Charles, is crippled. My aunt and uncle fear if he doesn't learn reading, he will be useless to anyone, and his life could be in peril as he gets older, once they are gone. I have new skills that you've taught me, but this is too important, Micaela. They need someone like you who truly knows how to teach so Charles's future is safe. If I promise to keep teaching Gus, will you teach them? I know it's a lot to ask, but I know this will change their future for the better, just like you've changed mine. Please?"

Micaela knew what her answer to Jack's heartfelt question needed to be. "Of course, I will, Jack. I can leave work each day and go directly to their house before I go home. I'll just have to take my supper later some days. Give me the directions to their house and tell them we'll begin next week!"

Ask Others—The Emerald Journey

Micaela's Third Dream: The Pond

Micaela was in a beautiful carriage riding along through a jungle. She bounced a bit on the padded velvet seat as she looked through the windows at the thick growth of rubbery trees and bushes she'd never seen before. She felt exhilarated and reached out to touch the thick rubbery plants with her hand. She felt a lovely excitement to the depth of her being. Like everything in the world was perfect. Like she lived an extraordinary life. Like there were magnificent things waiting for her. Suddenly the carriage came to a stop. She jumped out and called up to the driver, "Please wait. I won't be long. I'll be right back."

She walked with purpose into a large, beautifully designed building, with a different design she hadn't seen before. As if it were designed to fit into the surrounding jungle. She stepped into the soothing space inside but immediately looked beyond the large room to a pond just past the large openings on the other side of the room.

She moved toward the openings and beyond to the pond. The water looked so soothing. She kicked her shoes off to step into the pond and looked up as she did, noticing for the first time that the edges of the pond were filled with people both standing on the edges and wading into the water. She realized they were all looking at her. Not just looking at her, looking *to* her. For what?

As she looked from face to face at each one, questions began to run through her mind. Each one had something to learn. A part to play. Something to contribute. She knew they were all waiting for her to ask them. Ask about them. Ask to learn. Ask to grow. Ask to change everything. As she continued to look from person to person, there were so many questions to be asked and answered that she suddenly felt overwhelmed. As she exited the water into the building, all eyes were still on her. She felt a rare combination of honor, responsibility, and self-consciousness all at the same time. She moved into the cool, calming building and walked down a hallway to an open door. As she stepped into the room there were two beautiful, fresh-faced young women standing there. They seemed so happy, so very pleased to see her. "Hi, I'm Micaela," she said to them.

"We know," one of the women answered. "Your name means God's Gift. We've been expecting you." She pointed to a beautiful upholstered chair. "Just wait until you see all that you're going to learn today. It's all in your destiny. You won't believe the things you're going to do."

As Micaela stepped toward the chair, she suddenly remembered she had left the carriage driver waiting. "Oh, I'm sorry. I've left someone waiting outside, but I promise I'll be back."

The young ladies just smiled and said, "We'll be waiting for you," as Micaela took off down the corridor and out to the entrance from which she had entered. She hurried toward the carriage, jumped back inside, and it lurched forward. She felt absolutely blissful as it moved ahead, gently rocking farther into the jungle.

Suddenly her cheek tickled, and as she woke up and brushed it, a beautiful butterfly flew off.

What was *that* dream about? She said out loud, "I need to write this down so that I can understand it!" As quickly as she could, she penned the details of the dream, including her feelings about all of it.

She hardly noticed the work she did that day even though she collected more rocks than she ever had. She couldn't stop thinking about how beautiful the jungle was in that dream. She had heard tales of the jungle before but had never imagined it contained such exotic beauty and peace, until now. She could still feel the exuberance she had felt riding in that beautiful carriage through the thick green growth of plants and flowers she'd never seen before. How she actually felt the rubbery leaves on her hand. The wonder of all those people around the pond looking to her for something so important. What was it? And the young women who wanted to tell her about her destiny. What did they want to share? And why had she left before they could? While she still had more questions than answers, she knew a remarkable message had been given to her. She felt different. She felt purposeful. She felt as if she was appointed for something very important. But what, exactly? She hadn't forgotten the guidance the Being had given her in the first dream. She would follow it. She would keep asking. She would keep moving across the bridge to find her destiny.

Another week had gone by. Jack had gone to his aunt and uncle's house after his conversation with Micaela the week before and told them the good news. Their eyes had filled with tears as he told them the young woman named Micaela, who had taught him to read, was willing to come to the house each week and teach their crippled son,

Charles, to read. Each day at work, Jack started meeting with Gus by the well at lunch break to start teaching him his letters. Already Gus looked a little happier, even a little younger as he and Jack put their heads together over the parchment each day, going through the lessons. Jack started to have fun with Gus, calling out letters while they were filling their rock carts, to see if Gus could pick out a word that started with that letter. The days flew by.

The first day Micaela showed up at Jack's aunt and uncle's home, they were almost speechless. She introduced herself, and after a moment, with tear-filled eyes, they said, "Nice to meet you, we're Edgar and Elene Holloway. Thank you. Thank you so much for coming here to help our Charles."

They invited her in, and there was Charles in a chair with wheels. She thought she might find a boy who was sad and sullen. Instead, Charles looked up with flashing warm brown eyes and a playful grin and said, "I've been waiting a really long time to meet someone like you!" Micaela liked him instantly! The small house had a large front room where they lived, ate, and prepared food, and three small back rooms where they slept and stored things. They all agreed the corner of the front room by the window would be the perfect place to start the lessons. Micaela pulled a sturdy stool up to Charles's wheeled chair, pulled her supplies out of her bag, and began the lessons.

From the first day, she found Charles to be eager and willing to learn. He had a keen sense of humor as well and would say things unexpectedly that made her laugh. She made sure that as she taught him to read the letters, he was also learning to write them. The first lesson flew by, and afterward, they insisted she join them for a supper of meat and vegetable stew and bread. It tasted delicious to her. As she walked home to her grove, which was very close to their home, her heart and her stomach felt warm and full.

Prologue

A few days later, when Micaela arrived at the Holloway's house after work, there were two other children in the front room. A boy who looked to be just younger than Charles, maybe eight years old, and a girl who looked to be only about six. Micaela was surprised but pleased to see them. Elene Holloway quickly introduced the children saying, "I hope you don't mind. My sister's children Annie and Gabe haven't learned to read either. They're young enough that I'm hoping they could just listen in on Charles's lesson and learn along with him." Micaela noticed that little Annie seemed shy and embarrassed. Gabe looked at her eagerly for her answer.

"Of course, they can join us!" she said. "It will be no trouble at all. But we may need to buy more supplies for them."

"No worries. I thought they would need them, so Mr. Holloway picked them up at the street market yesterday," said Elene.

The lesson went wonderfully well, and by the end of the day, shy little Annie was leaning on Micaela's shoulder as she finished reading back her first letters.

The word got out among the villagers, and little by little, more kids began to join the lessons. Micaela didn't mind. In fact, she looked forward to meeting these new young ones each week. She made sure she started back at the basics each time for the newcomers, and then Elene would practice with them while Micaela moved forward with those who were becoming more advanced. Micaela was proud of Elene. She was learning along with her son and had improved her reading skills along with his. Charles was a quick study. She couldn't teach him enough! He was so hungry to learn.

Soon enough, over the next months, the little house was so crowded with eager students they needed to find a new place for them to gather. One of the fathers whose son had been coming to learn had a building where he stored and sold grain. It had a large open floor in the center with lots of shelves and bags of grain lining the walls. He closed the business late in the afternoon each day, so he offered to let the lessons take place there. The bags of grain could be used as benches for the children to sit on. Everyone seemed very happy with the new arrangement. They were less crowded, and the parents whose children came for lessons brought buckets of water to drink in case the children got thirsty. Elene came rushing to the building, excited and out of breath, just before they started their first lesson there with her arms full of parchments. "I've just come from the local church. I told the pastor about the lessons you're giving to the village children, and he was so happy to give me these parchments for us to use for the writing of the letters and words!"

Each day as Micaela finished work at the quarry and hurried over to begin giving her lessons, she looked forward to what was ahead. It was truly enchanting to see the children grow and change so much. They came in looking scared and unsure. But after a few sessions they would begin to warm up, delighted by the magic of learning to read and the world it was opening up for them. The parents were all so grateful. While most of them didn't have extra money, they paid her in pieces of cloth, warm meals, fresh vegetables, or a bit of meat, and occasionally, a coin or two. Since only royalty had access to education, it meant so much to the people. Very soon she was becoming known around the village as Teacher—sometimes even referred to as Headmistress. People everywhere were learning to read. They grew to love Micaela.

One day, when a family she had been teaching found out she was living in the grove, they offered to give her a small dwelling that had been used as a grain shed long ago. They had built a bigger one closer to the granary a few years ago and had not used the small one since. Micaela thought it was far too generous of them, but they insisted, even helping her clean and sweep it out and set it up with a proper bed frame, a comfortable straw-filled mattress, and two chairs and a table where she could enjoy her meals. "We can't have our village teacher exposed to the elements!" they said. "We need to keep her safe and dry." Micaela had never been happier. She felt needed and so appreciated.

In fact, lately she had begun to reflect on her life. She had suffered terrible hardships, having endured the loss of her parents and the bill collectors taking so much from her. Yet she could now see how many things she had to be grateful for. She'd had a very fortunate childhood. Even though they hadn't been wealthy, her father and mother were unusual because they had served in noble households. Mother had learned to read from her kind mistress, for whom she had worked as a very young woman. She had also taught Mother to do numbers and figures so that she could help log the expenses and income of the estate. When Mother had married her father, she'd taught him to read and do mathematics that she knew. It had given her parents an advantage in running their small business for so many years and allowed them to have a comfortable house, plenty of food, and warm clothing.

Micaela's parents had known how much it mattered to have education and knowledge, so they had taken painstaking efforts to teach Micaela everything they knew, starting when she was very, very young. She hadn't really understood the value of the knowledge she had from their teachings, until now. These children she taught were so precious, many of them so bright and eager to learn. It pained her heart to think that all children couldn't have these opportunities. Knowing that made her more resilient and determined to continue to teach as many as she could, no matter how much effort it took. It was a life-changing gift she could give them. She felt deeply honored to be able to have the gift to share. Some of them were progressing so much they could read a full book. She did everything she could to get her hands on books that could be shared. They were hard to come by, so she began to encourage those who could to start to write their own little books on the parchments and put them together with strings pulled through holes they made in the sides of the pages.

Even though the group was quite large now, Micaela knew each one of them by name. As the children gained more knowledge, Micaela loved to question them to understand each person, their thoughts, and ideas. What were the things that mattered to them? What did they truly want in life? Because she had asked them about the dreams of their heart, she knew a lot about the things that were important to them.

One day a well-dressed, distinguished-looking gentleman came to the lessons. He approached Micaela at the end of the lesson saying, "Excuse me. You must be Mistress Micaela. May I speak with you?"

As Micaela looked up, she couldn't help but notice his deep blue eyes and the blend of rugged aristocracy of his face. "Yes, sir, how can I help you?"

"You've been teaching my son, and I wanted to come thank you personally. What I didn't know until recently is how many people in the village you've been helping. From what I hear, people are coming from other villages to learn from you. That is quite a feat to become the Headmistress to all of the villages in the kingdom."

"Well," said Micaela, blushing, "thank you for the acknowledgment. I'm not sure I'm quite as important as all of that, but I do know I enjoy helping people make their lives and daily tasks easier by helping them learn all that they can. Who is your son, sir?"

"I'm Conrad Eaton. Please call me Conrad. My son is Andrew. I work as a treasurer to the King. Even though Andrew has had access to teachers in his young life, he has never been able to learn to read. His best friend in the village convinced him to come here with him for your lessons, so he's been sneaking away to do so. I don't know what you've done or how you did it, but as I tucked him into bed last night, he wanted to show me what he could do. He pulled out his parchment, and for the first time ever, he read me the words on the page. I feel tremendous gratitude for you, Mistress Micaela. I feared my son would be severely scorned and overlooked as he got older, like other people who can't read. You have given my son a new beginning. How can I ever thank you for that?"

Micaela started to feel warm and a bit overwhelmed with the outpouring of praise this important man was giving her. "I…love Andrew," she said. "He is a very special boy. He sat at the back of the group the first day he came. I noticed he started crying and seemed very sad at the end of the first lesson. I sat down alone with him and asked him why he was crying. He said he can't see the words the way other people do because he's stupid. I told him no one is stupid; we sometimes have special ways of learning things. After he answered more of my questions, I realized he was seeing the words backwards. So, I devised a special way for him to look at the words, and we spent a little special time together during every lesson to practice that. He has been so excited as he realized he can learn to read he's been coming over on some Sunday afternoons to get extra help. After a while, he started being able to do it on his own. I didn't know his home was on the castle grounds or that his father worked for the King. When he showed up with a group of the poor village boys, I thought he was one of them."

"He feels those are the only true friends he has. The kids from parents of nobility make fun of him and tell him he is stupid. I've told him he can find friends anywhere, and he has found them outside of the castle. Even though the King has questioned my wisdom in allowing this, I know it's what makes Andrew happy, so I don't discourage it. His happiness is more important to me than traditions and protocols."

"Your son is one of the most kind, gentle, and intelligent children I've ever met. He's thoughtful and considerate to everyone. He also has a gift. He is a brilliant storyteller and has started to write his stories and do lovely drawings for them. They are very special, but I think he's waiting to show you. Maybe he wants to surprise you."

"Well, I'll look forward to that surprise. Mistress Micaela, I won't keep you any longer, but I want to thank you again and tell you that anything you should need to make your efforts in teaching the children easier, please do not hesitate to ask. And here is a small token of my appreciation." He placed a small, weighty leather bag in her palm, stepped back, took a quick bow, and said, "I'll be seeing you again very soon, I hope. Thank you for your time today."

As Micaela watched him walk away, her heart was racing for no apparent reason. She thought maybe it was because she was trying to take in everything she had just seen and heard. She peeked into the top of the small pouch and saw it was full of gold coins. Gold coins. Not silver. She hadn't seen a real gold coin since before Mother got sick. Father used to have one or two when he was making a big purchase.

Later that night in her little home, as she tucked away her dishes from supper, Conrad's words were still running through her mind. In those months he'd been coming for lessons, she'd had no idea little Andrew lived on the castle grounds! He was such a sweet, humble boy. And the entire village knew about her? People were coming from other villages? Finding out what the children needed and then teaching it to them was so important to her that she had never taken the time to wonder where the children were from. She only knew they needed her, that she could help them, and that she loved doing it. He worked for the King? So he talked to the King every day, and now he had just spoken to her! In fact, he made a special trip to speak with her! She fell to her knees by her bed, overwhelmed with gratitude. While she knew she had been guided to this place, she still didn't know why she deserved so much good. So much happiness. But she was deeply grateful for all of it. For this warm, wonderful house to live in. For the beautiful children who came to learn. For the dreams, the Being, for Bekkie, Jack, Gus, Elene, Edgar, Charles, for little Andrew and Andrew's father. Conrad....

She must get some sleep now. Life was so good, and there was so much more to do.

Ask God—The Pink Sapphire Light

Micaela's Fourth Dream: Conrad

Micaela dreamed she was walking down a village road with Conrad. There was a strong pull between them. The feeling that they were being pulled together to merge into one. As they approached the end of the road next to a beautiful wood-crafted house, Micaela saw a beautiful bright pink star shooting across the sky and descending. It was coming closer and closer to them—both of them staring at it because they couldn't look away. As it got closer it became larger. Finally, it was hovering in front of them, bigger than both of them. It was an enormous giant oval of soft pink light. As she looked into the center, it was as if the star had a beating heart and some kind of intelligence. Conrad stepped back in fear. Micaela reached for his hand and said, "Don't worry. It's just here to gather information about how you and I can help the world together."

Micaela woke with a jolt! She sat up feeling awake and energized. What was that? Why had she just had a dream about this man she only just met a few days ago? The pink star was so beautiful, and it seemed so…alive. She put her feet on the cool floor and hurried to the shelf, taking down her writing tools and sitting at her little table. She wrote down the whole dream, feeling the same feelings all over again. It was she who had reached out and grasped Conrad's hand in the dream! … *how you and I can help the world together…*. She had been so sure and so bold! She felt embarrassed just thinking about it! Where did all that boldness and certainty come from, and what did it all mean? She may never see the man again. They came from completely different worlds. He was just being kind and grateful for her help with his son's reading. Maybe it was just her imagination running wild. But it didn't feel like a strange imagining. It felt like something real. Like something was happening. Some strange destined connection.

"Ok, that's enough," she said to herself as she placed her things back on the shelf. "Time to get to the quarry." She was already running late, and she had a surprise for everyone.

All morning as she picked up the rocks and placed them in her cart, she had been thinking of the Being, wondering what he thought of last night's dream. He had become her spiritual lodestar since his first visit with her in the first dream. To her, it felt as if he was a personal representative to the Creator of all. She kept asking him in her heart: "Tell me, what does this mean? What am I to think about the dream? Is there something there I'm supposed to pay attention to, or is it nothing more than my silly imagination? Is this a clue to my destiny?"

As she asked these questions from her heart, and contemplated the answers, the morning flew by. She was working with such energy and exuberance, her cart was two-thirds full by lunchtime. She walked to the well to join her friends and set a bag of goodies on the ground with a big smile on her face. As each of them pulled out their meager portions of bread or a bun, she laid a cloth on the ground and spread out apples, dates, cheese, and bits of different kinds of dried meat and invited them to enjoy! She'd had so much fun at the market the day before, using one of her gold coins to buy the treats for her friends. By now, Jack had taught a dozen more people to read. They all joined in their happy feast. She had plenty so everyone nearby could enjoy.

"I have been so fortunate and blessed by all of you. I wanted to share some delicious things to celebrate how much we've grown together. How much we've learned from each other." After much eating and happy chatter, Micaela pulled something small out of the bag and looked right at Bekkie. As she held out a simple but beautiful pendant in the shape of a heart, handing it to her friend, she said, "Bekkie—watching you express yourself each day through your kind and gentle heart helped me find my heart, which I'd hidden away for so long. Thank you for being a true friend to me and to all of us. You make our lives so much better by being you. I had truly lost myself. Without your loving heart to show me the way, I'm not sure I would have found myself again. So thank you." The little group clapped and hugged right before the horn blew. The signal for everyone to get back to work.

She couldn't have been more buoyant as she finished her day at the quarry and headed to the grain building for teaching. She was thinking of those happy, eager faces that would be showing up for their lessons soon.

As she moved her feet along the path quickly, she was suddenly yanked back abruptly by the arm and spun around roughly. There right in front of her were the two nasty-looking bill collectors. Her heart dropped suddenly and started slamming in her chest. She felt like she couldn't breathe as the one with the scar across his eye said, "Ha, you think you can avoid us, Missy? Who do you think you are, running away from your debts?"

Micaela looked at the two men who had already taken everything from her. That familiar feeling of defenselessness started creeping over her. She began to stammer, "You…you've already taken everything I have. I've paid you again and again. I have no more to give you."

"You think we're stupid, Miss?" said the tall one covered with pock scars. "We hear the talk in the village. The high and mighty teacher who teaches all. Well that teacher better be sharing some of the spoils, or she might be losing one of her teaching fingers. In fact, we can make sure, if we don't get what we want, you lose everything."

"This nice little life you think you have. It all might just go away in a blink," the short, heavy one said, as they both pealed into fits of laughter.

Just then Micaela felt three little bodies throw themselves up against her in a tight hug. There were three boys she taught, one of whom was getting so tall he almost reached her shoulder. Micaela heard more noise behind her and glanced back to see more of her little students headed her way to get to their lessons. Her three little saviors stared at the two men with very intense looks on their faces.

"So, you think your little children are gonna save you, do ya? You'll find out you have your own lessons to learn if we don't get some payments from you soon." They turned back in the direction from which they'd come, saying to her, "Don't get too comfortable, little teacher. We'll be back before you know it."

Micaela and the children stood there holding their breath until the men were far enough away. "I hate those men, Mistress Micaela! Why are they trying to scare you?" asked the oldest boy.

Trying to control her shaking voice, Micaela said, "Oh, don't you worry. We're not going to let those mean people ruin our day. They're gone now. Let's forget about them and go have the best lesson ever!"

It took all her will to appear calm and cheerful during her lesson that afternoon. She was so relieved when it ended so she could be by herself and think and not worry the children. She kept looking over her shoulder as she made her way to her little house. For the first time, she was thankful her friends had insisted on installing bolts on the doors and window covers as she closed up the place tightly and sat down think. She looked up toward the ceiling, and thinking of the Being, she started asking, "Why is this happening again? Why won't they leave me alone? What is going to make them stop? What if I lose everything I have?"

Micaela had a fitful night's sleep, finally falling deeply into sleep a few hours before dawn. She slipped into another dream.

Destiny and Diamonds

Micaela's Fifth Dream: Treasures of Life

Micaela was at the grain store finishing the class and looked down for her satchel. It was gone. She knew she had set it there. It contained all her gold coins. It was all she had. She quickly ran out of the store and started running toward her home. She burst through the door and everything was gone: her table and chairs, her bed, her writing tools. Everything. Gone. She hurried out the door, racing ahead to try to find her things, and up in front of her, she saw a white house she'd never seen before. Maybe her things were in there! She ran toward the white house and opened the door. To her surprise, her mother, her father, and even her grandfather, who had died before she was born, yet she knew him somehow, were all sitting there in chairs that were lined up against the walls. There were other people there too. They were all smiling and seemed very happy to see her. They seemed to recognize her, like they were somehow connected to her family. Her mother stood up and said, "Welcome, Micaela, please take a chair. We have something to show you." Micaela looked around in wonder and then took a seat.

Suddenly, two young men who looked like servants from a castle came in bringing a very large trunk. They brought it and set it at her feet. "This is for you," they said as they opened the lid, and inside were miniature houses and carriages with people inside all of them, like a toy set of a large estate. She was awestruck as she looked at the beautiful things. After she looked carefully at all these beautiful things, they moved that trunk aside; then two more serving men came through the door bringing another large trunk. They placed it in front of her and opened the lid. Inside was the most beautiful clothing made of the most beautiful fabrics she had ever seen. She leaned over in amazement as she touched the most exquisite clothing made with beautiful fabrics, realizing all of this was for her. The trunk was once again moved aside, and two more serving men came through the door with yet another trunk. They opened the trunk and to her astonishment, there was her satchel with all the things she thought she had lost, including her gold coins. Micaela woke up.

Her eyes were wet in the corners as she tried to hold on to the faces of her mother and father. They had looked so beautiful. Like they glowed. They were so happy, and Mother was well! She had asked the Being to help her. Had he taken her there to see them? To some special place beyond this world? She felt humbled that all those gifts were for her. Instead of feeling like she was ready to lose everything again, she now knew that was not true. She knew she had been given a vision of something very different from that. She stopped feeling afraid. She knew in her heart no one could take anything away from her. As she finished writing about the dream, her last line on the parchment read, "I know now that the Being hears me and loves me. I know he has more in store for me than I've ever dreamed of." She turned her head upward in gratitude and uttered, "Thank you."

Everything went well over the next few days. Work at the quarry flew by. More people than ever were challenging themselves to read, and Jack was starting to become a teacher in his own right. He was a different man now than the one who had fallen at her feet that day many months ago. She had even seen him talking to the daughter of the butcher at their village stall a few times, and he seemed awfully happy to be there!

Some of the children were reading so well now, they were helping her tutor the younger or newer ones. Little Andrew was almost finished with his surprise for his father. He had written a story with beautiful illustrations. It had taken him a while, but as they tied the parchments together in a book, Micaela could only imagine the joy Conrad would feel when he opened it!

As if right on cue, she looked up to see Conrad walk in the door. They had just finished wrapping Andrew's book in a cloth to give to his father later that night after supper. The children were shuffling out the door, and Andrew scurried out to play tag with his friends. She and Conrad were suddenly alone together. Why did her cheeks suddenly feel too warm again as he approached her? She hoped he didn't notice it. "Well hello, Mister Eaton! What brings you here today?"

The closer he got, the more it felt like those deep blue eyes could see all the way inside her. She adjusted the parchments in her hand, trying to distract herself from it. He smiled broadly at her and said, "I've brought some good news for you. The King wants to see you!"

"Why? Why would he want to see me? What did you tell him?"

"I give him reports each week, but it's not what *I'm* telling him. It's what everyone in the village is talking about. Do you know how much you've changed the way people feel, Micaela? Do you realize you've given hope to the hopeless? That you've given people a reason to wake up and be happy each day? People have changed. They work harder. They're helping each other more. They're opening businesses now that they have more skills. You might think you've done a small thing by helping people read and do numbers, but, Micaela, it's so far beyond that. You've changed lives for the better. You've made our entire village better."

Micaela was aware that Conrad knew about her teaching the children. But how had he found out that on Saturdays she had been helping some of the businesspeople understand how to do numbers to keep logbooks for their businesses? It started with helping the Holloways with their logbooks and had spread to a dozen or so others who really needed help so they could keep better track of money coming in and going out to help make better decisions in their trades and, hopefully, make better profits. "Well, I guess the word gets around in this little village, doesn't it?" she said, feeling a bit self-conscious.

"And thank goodness it does!" he said with a smile. "The King has been looking for someone like you for a long time. His Queen is a very kind woman who insists that they do more for all the people. They want all the people in their kingdom to have prosperity and happiness. She's been trying to find a way to get lessons for reading and numbers to people who live outside the court, but they didn't have a way to do it…until now."

"You mean me?" Micaela started going from self-conscious to overwhelmed. "But how would I manage to do that for the whole kingdom? How could that possibly happen? We're so overcrowded *now*. I mean, I'm not ungrateful of his notice, but truly, I don't know if I can do any more with the time and space I have."

Conrad laughed out loud, completely enjoying her humble lack of awareness. "Micaela, the King and Queen will provide you everything you need. They want you to lead the teaching of all the kingdom. It's what you're already doing. It's what you do so well. They're going to make it easier for you and make sure that you can reach all our people."

"How will I have time to reach them all?" she asked meekly.

"You will groom the best learners into more teachers. You will make sure they are prepared with your skills and knowledge, and then you will assign them to different areas and villages of the kingdom. You will be the headmistress of all learning for the kingdom. I humbly ask you to join me on Saturday. I will have a carriage pick you up at your home, and we will go together to speak to the King and Queen."

Micaela's mind began racing. What would she wear in front of the royal couple? She had a few practical dresses, obtained with the coins he had given her and the cloth that others had provided, but nothing fit for a meeting with the King. As if he could read her mind, he summoned his driver, who immediately brought a package to him. He handed it to her and asked her to open it. As she pulled the package open, she gasped. She was looking at the most beautiful dress she had ever seen. The fabric was exquisite. She'd never had anything like it.

"Please accept this gift from the Queen herself," he told her. "She wants to thank you herself over a luncheon at the castle, and she wanted to make sure you felt very comfortable attending."

She looked up with moist eyes, "How can I refuse such a gift and invitation? It would be my great honor to come with you to the castle on Saturday to meet the King and Queen!"

"It's set, then!" Conrad said enthusiastically. "I will pick you up promptly at the eleventh hour. Please be ready!"

"Okay, I will…. Uh…don't you want me to tell you where I live?"

"Micaela," he said smiling, "I already know where you live. Everyone in the village knows!"

He took a quick bow, saying, "Okay, then. I'm off now, and I look forward to Saturday, Mistress Micaela!"

Micaela bowed her head with a quick curtsy and said, "Yes! Thank you! I'll be ready!"

As she watched him walk out of the building, she felt giddy. Completely exhilarated but nervous at the same time! Was she even worthy of such an honor? She wanted to shriek with excitement, but knowing the kids might be lingering outside, she instead threw her hands in the air, and jumping up and down, whispered, "Thank you, thank you, thank you!"

When the kids came for lessons the next day, she greeted Andrew at the door. Bending down to him, she said, "Andrew, what did your father say when you gave him your book last night after dinner?"

Andrew looked up with big sincere eyes and said, "After my father read the book, he started crying really hard. He cried when my mama died too. I thought the book made him sad at first, but then he told me those were happy tears. He said the book made him happier than any gift he's ever gotten. He told me happiness that makes you cry is the best kind of happy of all."

Micaela gave him a tight hug as she said, "Andrew, I'm so glad you were able to give such a special gift to your father. Your storytelling and drawings are a gift that could make so many people happy, so I hope you keep sharing your gift."

Andrew gleamed with pride. "I will, Miss Micaela. Now that you taught me to read and write, I'm gonna make so many people happy!" And he ran off toward the other boys who had just come in.

Over the next few days at work and teaching lessons, Micaela felt like she was floating on air. She kept pinching herself to make sure she was awake, and this wasn't all a dream. She threw herself happily into her work. She challenged the workers who were learning to read and write by asking them to spell words out loud. The quarry seemed like a different place now. People knew each other, helped each other, and took pride in one another's accomplishments. Even the grouchy supervisor had softened a bit. He wouldn't stoop down to their level to sit with them to learn, but she saw him hovering nearby and listening carefully. He wasn't quite so rough with people these days.

Finally, it was Friday. Micaela stayed a bit late at the granary to finish working with each of the kids. There was barely any light left as she rushed home. Suddenly she felt a chill, and the next second the bill collectors stepped out in front of her from a tree, behind which they had been hiding. She was filled with dread as she took a couple of steps backward.

"We told you we'd be back. Now where's our money, teacher? You didn't really think we were going to let you have all the spoils after everything we've done for you, did ya?" Suddenly an arrow shot past the man's ear, nicking it as it flew by. "What the...!" the man yelled, looking past Micaela with a shocked expression as three men rode up on horses. There were Conrad and two other men, one with a long sword drawn in front of him.

Conrad spoke up, "Micaela, these men aren't giving you a problem, are they? Because if they are, I can make sure it never, ever happens again."

Through a clenched grin, the pock-faced one said, "No, no, we just were makin' sure the teacher didn't need any help gettin' home."

"If I find out you're anywhere near Mistress Micaela again, I promise you it will be the last time. Are we clear?" Conrad said as his colleague moved closer until his sword touched each of their chests.

"Y…yes, we're clear," they mumbled as they tried to back away as carefully as possible.

"Good then!" Conrad said as he jumped off his horse and gave a hand to raise Micaela up on it. "We'll make sure our village teacher gets to her home safely tonight and every night."

When Conrad lifted Micaela down from his horse in front of her door, she was speechless as he walked her to the door. Finally, she said, "Thank you. You didn't have to do that, but I'm very grateful you were there. Those men took everything from me after the death of my parents to pay the bills for the money we owed due to my mother's illness when father couldn't work. I thought giving them everything I had, including our home, was enough to make them leave me alone, but now they're back, asking for more."

"I intend to find out a lot more about those men, and when I do, you'll be hearing back from me about it. You don't need to worry now. They won't be bothering you anytime soon. Get some good rest, and I'll see you tomorrow, then?"

"Yes, I promise I'll be ready on time," she said with a grateful smile. "See you then." She closed the door on her little house, locked the bolt, and drew in a huge sigh of relief. She had gone from giddy exhilaration to sheer terror all in a day, and suddenly she felt so tired.

It was all she could do to eat her small supper and drag herself to bed to fall into an exhausted sleep.

Someone was knocking rapidly on her door. She shot out of bed. The sun was high, and she had overslept. She opened the door to see Elene standing there. "I'm here to help you get ready for your big day!" Micaela was so happy to see her friend and gave her a big hug! Elene made a quick breakfast of eggs and berries she'd picked from her bushes. Then she started heating water on the fire for Micaela's big tub. She dumped lavender oil into the hot water. Smiling, she said, "You're going to the castle today, so today you will look and feel like a princess!" She laid out the beautiful dress Conrad had given to Micaela, smoothing it and making it ready for Micaela to step into. After scrubbing Micaela's hair and then brushing it until it dried and was gleaming, she helped her into the dress. When Micaela spun around, Elene gasped! The robin's-egg-blue gown was elegant on Micaela's graceful body. It brought out the blue-green of her eyes so they sparkled like jewels. Her bronze hair was pulled up on one side with a beautiful comb Mother had left for her. It was one thing she had hidden from the men because it was something that had looked so beautiful on Mother when she had worn it. Micaela put on the pretty little leather shoes she'd purchased from the village shoemaker. It was her biggest splurge in a long time. She was excited but so nervous! Elene looked into her eyes as she said, "Remember, Micaela, the only thing you have to do today is to be yourself. You've changed so many lives by doing just that. Don't try to be anything different. Just be you."

Elene was right. She had come so far by searching, asking, and finally finding herself and her Destiny Bridge. Now she was taking another step forward on the bridge. Above all, she must remember that her gifts lie in expressing all that she is. Nothing more. Suddenly, there was a gentle knock on the door. Elene peeked out the window and said, "He's here." She wrapped her arms around her friend for one more big hug.

Elene opened the door, and Conrad stepped inside. She heard him draw in a quick deep breath as he looked up at Micaela. He stood there a bit dumbfounded for a moment, then quickly gathered himself, saying, "Mistress Micaela, you look absolutely beautiful today. That dress suits you so well. I hope you like it."

"I love it—thank you," she said with a beautiful smile. "And I'll certainly thank the Queen when I see her."

"Shall we go, then?" He held out his arm for her. Taking it, he guided her out to the carriage. After helping her inside, he jumped up to the seat across from her, and off they went to the castle. Elene stood there until she could no longer see them, tears streaming down her cheeks. She felt like she was watching her own daughter go to the most important event of her life. She was so proud of Micaela. So happy for her.

Micaela's eyes were gigantic in her delicate face as she took in the beauty of the castle. Conrad had gone off on some business the minute they arrived, so she was seated on a comfortable chair as the servant brought her some tea in a sitting room. Happy to be alone for a few moments, she tried to gather herself and breathe deeply. She didn't know what to expect or how this was going to go. She kept thinking about what Elene said to her this morning: *Just be yourself.*

The double doors at the far end of the room were suddenly flung open. Conrad strode in looking very pleased. He held out his hand to her and said, "It is time for you to meet the King and Queen."

As they walked toward the thrones sitting side by side at the end of a long hall, time slowed down, and it seemed Micaela was watching the whole thing from outside herself. She was so glad she had Conrad's hand to keep her steady. When they reached the King and Queen, she made a deep curtsy along with Conrad's bow and looked up again as he began to introduce her. "May I present the Mistress Micaela, who is known throughout our lands as the one who is willing to teach all the people."

Micaela looked up into the faces of the King and Queen. The kindness each of their faces showed instantly put her at ease. The King spoke first. "Micaela, you are here today because you have created quite a reputation for yourself, not only in our small village, but in most of the villages in the kingdom, people know your name and the work you've been doing to teach all those who desire to learn."

Just be yourself.

Micaela looked earnestly into the King's eyes and said, "Your Majesty, I have done nothing more than to try to share any gifts I might have with those who have a desire to learn. It is truly my honor to be able to answer the needs of others. There is nothing more rewarding than being able to grant someone's wish to learn by helping them through the process. Knowing that I have answered another's most heartfelt requests has brought me more joy than any gold or precious jewels."

"That is why we have chosen you to be here today, Micaela," said the Queen in a voice born of gentleness and strength. "Your generosity and humility are a rare combination that has caused us to take notice of you."

"Those qualities, along with your fast-thinking mind and tireless work ethic, have all been noticed and repeatedly reported back to me and the Queen. You single-handedly have changed everything in our kingdom, Micaela. People are happier, they're working harder, they are more productive and feel more valuable…more hopeful."

"Your Majesties, I deeply appreciate your generosity of praise, but I was simply doing my best with the gifts I've been given."

"And that is what makes a great leader, Micaela. One who doesn't seek praise or glory but instead utilizes their gifts and talents to lift and glorify others. In this way everyone rises and becomes better. You are a natural leader, Mistress Micaela. Because of that, the Queen and I are inviting you to take a position with the Royal Court, as the Head Mistress of Teaching for the entire Kingdom. We will give you the resources you need to teach a group of people who can be sent across the land to teach in every village. Our desire is that learning reading and numbers is no longer saved only for nobility, but that every person learns those skills to better themselves. In this way we will bring great strength, prosperity, and happiness to our Kingdom."

Micaela looked at them with a radiant smile and answered, "Of course, it would be my greatest honor to take this position, Your Highness. I promise to do my very best and not let you and the Queen down."

"We have no concerns about you letting us down, Micaela," the King answered with a jovial chuckle. "Hopefully we can keep up with you as you continue your movement for teaching and learning across the villages."

"Your work has come to us at a most auspicious time, Micaela," said the Queen. "The time has come for all people to rise to their best because that makes all of us stronger. We know that you are a divine gift to the entire kingdom. Thank you for being all that you are and teaching all of us exactly what we needed to learn. Now let's celebrate our new Headmistress!"

The luncheon banquet was a sublime feast with many toasts and accolades given. Conrad was especially jovial as he sat next to her, leaning in to explain who people were and what their roles were in the royal court. Her heart and mind were alive with anticipation of all that was ahead of her.

When she returned back to her home, she spent all evening chatting with Elene about her magnificent day! Elene had been waiting for her when she arrived back at her home very late in the day after her adventure at the castle. They sipped tea and giggled together like two young girls!

Now it was Monday afternoon, and she was walking home after teaching lessons to the children. As she neared her house, Conrad came galloping up on his horse. Could he see how much she lit up when she saw him? She hoped she didn't give herself away too much. He slid off his horse and asked if he could speak to her. "Of course," she said.

They pulled two chairs outside to watch the last of the sunset. "The Queen asked me to ask you if you could start next week at your new position."

Suddenly, reality set in for Micaela. How was she going to get out of her contract at the quarry? Someone owned her contract. They might as well have owned her. Why hadn't she thought of that?

Conrad saw her face cloud over and asked, "What? Something is wrong, I can feel it."

She hung her head in shame and said, "I haven't told you, Conrad. I work every day at the quarry as an indentured worker. I don't think I can work for the court. I don't know how to get out of that."

Conrad tipped her chin upward and said, "Do you not think I know that, lovely Micaela? The men who indentured you are very bad men. I followed up on them and found they have carried out much corruption throughout the kingdom. They've done great harm to many people. I brought your contract before the King's solicitors, and the King signed your release from it. Those men are now being held in a prisoner camp so they can no longer destroy lives. The King was very relieved this was brought to his attention. You are free, Micaela."

She could hardly believe what he was saying. She didn't mean to, but she began to cry. Conrad reached over and held her as relief from the past two years of dread slowly flowed out of her body. After a long while, she finally looked up with a wet, red face and said, "What about my friends at the quarry?"

"They'll always be your friends, Micaela. This is clearly going to take some getting used to, but you are free to do as you wish."

Micaela stepped out into her little garden outside her lovely little house. Her new home was a cozy cottage, inside the higher town near the castle so she could easily meet weekly with the Queen to report the learning progress in the Kingdom. After several months of living there, she was beginning to love her new surroundings and becoming more comfortable each day with the authority she had over so many important things. As she snipped flowers from her garden for her dinner table, she smiled thinking about her life. She had hired Jack, Gus, and Elene as her first teachers. More were being trained each week. She had her own little house of learning in the village, a school that had plenty of tables and chairs for children to sit upon and writing supplies for everyone. She was starting to amass quite a good collection of books for the students to use and borrow, as well. Classes for the children began earlier in the day now. The adults came later in the afternoons to learn to read and write, followed by a supplementary hour for those who wanted to learn the methods of teaching. Charles now came with the adults because he had decided, as soon as he turned seventeen years of age, he would become a teacher!

Once a month, Micaela brought lunch to her friends at the quarry. She missed Bekkie so much and looked forward to the time they spent together. Little Andrew came by every day to spend time with her now that they lived so close. He was a happy, confident boy now. So different from the scared, shy little boy who showed up for his first lesson. When Conrad finished his busy workdays, he would come by and the three of them would enjoy dinner or strolling through the town together.

One late Saturday afternoon, Conrad stopped by in an open carriage. He had invited her to go for a ride to the cliffs for a picnic. She expected to see Andrew, but when she asked, he said Andrew was staying behind to play with his friends. After riding along for a while, enjoying the beautiful green landscape surrounding them, they stopped by a waterfall near a cliff that overlooked a panoramic expanse of the kingdom. Every once in a while, they would see a wild bunny or a deer peek through the foliage. They laughed; ate cheese, dried meats, and fruit; and reminisced over the past year. Everything that had happened. All the delightful changes that had taken place in both their lives. Micaela knew her life had begun to turn that night the Being had come to her. She had started to ask and had never stopped.

The day was drawing to a close, and they stood to watch as the sun was dropping low in the sky. Conrad reached over and, squeezing her hand, he suddenly dropped down on one knee and asked her one of the most important questions she'd ever been asked: "Micaela, will you marry me?"

The light from the sunset was shining a soft halo around her as she threw herself into Conrad's arms and answered, "Yes. Yes, I will marry you!"

ASK!

After a marriage celebration that was fit for a prince and princess, Micaela and Conrad held hands and walked toward the beautiful carriage that would carry them on their wedding holiday. They looked deeply into each other's eyes just before he lifted her in. Micaela knew she had crossed the bridge. Her hopes and dreams had become her most beautiful destiny.

PREFACE

Innocent Enough to Ask

Everett's Story

At Christmas time our precious six-year-old grandson, Everett, received a Gizmo Watch from Santa Claus. He called us, enamored with his new "Dick Tracy" watch equivalent that was a good-looking wrist-wearable and allowed him to make phone calls to a very limited number of people his parents had preapproved, including us. The main purpose for the watch was his safety, as it had a tracking device his parents had connected to his grandparents' cell phones so that any of us could step in if there was an emergency.

This was a year where the grandchildren would spend Christmas with the other grandparents in California, as we took turns each year having the kids on alternating Thanksgiving and Christmas celebrations. In the late afternoon that same day, I received a call from an unknown number. I answered it and realized with a grin—I got my first secret call from Everett.

ASK!

A precocious first grader who loves life and learning, he was already reading at a third-grade level and learning Spanish. I answered the unusual call, and happily discovered it was Everett's enthusiastic young voice that responded to my "hello."

"Hi Grampy, it's me, Everett. Can I talk to you privately? I stepped into a quiet place so we could talk."

"Where are you?"

"In my closet. I needed it to be quiet, and the family is being too noisy in the family room. So Grampy, can I ask you an important question?"

"Of course, Everett, we can discuss whatever is on your mind, now and forever."

"Grampy, you know your Chicken Soup for the Soul *books?"*

"Yes, I do." At this point I'm smiling from ear to ear.

"Well, I like them a lot. Are you and Mimi going to write any more books?"

"Yes, Mimi and I are writing a book called *ASK! The Bridge from Your Dreams to Your Destiny*."

There was a moment of silence, then, in a boldly earnest voice he asked, *"Okay, then can I write it with you and Mimi?"*

Smiling from my heart and soul, I answered, "Well, that would certainly give us a brilliant, original, youthful perspective. And I think that would make our book better. Yes, I think we could use your help on this book."

"Okay, then, I will start today working on my part."

And so, one of the youngest writers in history commences his journey and adventure into learning about the difference-making impact that asking generates for individuals of all ages.

Everett asked a question I would never expect any six-year-old to ask. We lovingly answered, but it caused Crystal and me to reflect on the power of asking. In his young life, this little boy hadn't experienced the rejection, self-doubt, or feelings of unworthiness that cause so many of us to shut down our hopes and dreams and never dare to ask to participate in the pieces of life that call to our hearts. We were reminded, once again, how powerful it is just to ask. If our little guy hadn't asked, we most likely wouldn't have realized what he truly wanted or how important it was to him. We didn't honestly know that he knew much about the *Chicken Soup for the Soul* books or how much they meant to him. That small but bold question opened up many subsequent conversations we've had with Everett, and we're watching his love for reading, writing, and using his imagination blossom into lovely stories that could someday become part of a book that someone cherishes.

Asking is a powerful tool in life that too few of us utilize. Why? Because we have to put ourselves out there to ask, and frankly, it can feel like we give up a measure of control if we're depending on an answer from someone else. We believe asking is different than that.

Asking for what we want can be honed into an art form, if you start by understanding the three things it requires of you: clear communication, commitment to what you want, and detachment from the outcome.

Everett knew what he wanted, and after this discussion was opened through his request, we found out from his mother that he had been writing little "books" that consisted of pieces of paper stapled together, with stories he had created himself. He had accumulated quite a nice little stack of these books by the time we got to see them. Starting about age three, as soon as this little guy learned to write letters, and then the letters became words, and then the words became new adventures he could experience on a page, he knew in his young heart he had to be a part of this glorious world of writing books that people could read and enjoy. He knew what he wanted, but he didn't know what our answer would be. We might have said, "*You're too young, you need more practice, or let's talk about that when you're ten or twelve.*" If we had responded to him in any of those ways, we're certain he would have kept going with his plan to write books and not have taken the rejection personally. Kids are resilient askers. One or two *nos* seem to do very little to shut down their determination to get what they want. Their communication when asking for what they want tends to be clear and unambiguous. "*This is what I want, and I'm comfortable asking you for it*" kind of a thing. They are very committed once they decide what it is they want. They all seem to naturally excel in finding multiple ways to have their request heard. And talk about a remarkable level of detachment! When you say no, it doesn't seem to bruise their self-esteem or deter them from launching future requests. They're fully ready to ask again next time!

It takes the courage of a child to ask
and keep asking until your answer arrives.

Ask, and it shall be given to you;
seek and ye shall find;
knock and it shall be opened unto you.
For everyone that asketh, receiveth;
And he that seeketh, findeth;
And to him that knocketh
It shall be opened.
—MATTHEW 7:7–8

To achieve your ultimate destiny, ask boldly but humbly, one question at a time, just as little Everett did.

INTRODUCTION

Asking Is the Answer

Look for the answer inside your question.

—RUMI

Crystal and I love questions, because every day, we find that we live in a remarkably well-orchestrated Universe that seems to conspire in helping us discover answers. Asking stimulates the possibility of having a dream come true that makes life deliciously interesting.

With the ability to ask we can add dimensionality to our experience and life expression. In the animal kingdom, only humans have the ability to ask. Human beings are the exception for their ability to perform critical thinking. The art of asking questions is the tool that brings us a higher excellence of thought and an ever-higher experience of life.

We like to think of *Asking* as a language that binds together all of human relationships because it is through asking that we realize new understandings with others.

Asking is the only language to which the Universe can deliver a **solution, understanding, illumination,** or **plan**. Asking is a cultivated art, science, and talent. In fact, there is no mechanism that has the ability to reveal what is hidden like *Asking*.

Everyone is quick to say how others should lead their lives, but only a few ask, "How should I lead mine?" Every question ignored can become a curse; every question to which you pay attention reaps a blessing.

Before you decide to go any further in your asking journey, let's test that theory right now. Are you getting better, smarter, wiser, faster, and stronger in your life? If not, why not?

When we *Ask*, the answers cause us to strive to become better than we are. When we strive to become better than we are, everything around us becomes better too.

Questioning helps us discover, and then transcend, our human limitations.

There are three distinct channels through which we can ask:

Ask Yourself
Ask Others
Ask God

When you embrace the asking journey, it will give you an opportunity to review your life day by day to discover:

1. **What your expectations are for your life**

   - Your own potential and success and your ability to draw it to you
   - The areas of your life that are truly satisfying and those that are not

- How your own integrity enhances your life or the lack of it is causing you pain
- If you're courageous enough to ask others to help you reach your desires
- The habits you think would enhance your life if you got rid of them
- The habits you think would enhance your life if you began integrating them

2. **What your expectations are for others**

- If you're open to someone else providing solutions and assistance to you
- The belief, or lack thereof, that people are each other's greatest resource
- If you have you embraced and implemented healthy boundaries or not
- Your willingness to accept that no single person has all the answers
- If your heart and emotions are in alignment to foster healthy, happy relationships
- Your own vulnerability, or lack of it, when asking for your needs to be met in relationships
- If you look for ways to succeed in relationships or brace yourself for failure

3. **Your highest potential and service to humanity**
- That there may be limitations you've put on yourself
- That your ultimate destiny might go far beyond what you've ever imagined

- That your ability to create your most amazing life lies ahead of you
- That your impact on humanity may be far greater than you've ever realized
- That your best days and years are yet to come

We've found, in our collective journeys through life, that we learn the most through a connection to other people. There is a lesson in every person's story. Throughout this book we have shared stories of pieces of people's lives with you. Some of those people are well known; some are not. Some have created great levels of wealth and abundance; others have chosen the joy of living simply. In each story, with each person, lies tremendous value in their personal journey of questions and answers and where those led. Human beings learn in patterns. Our brains are wired that way. Stories all have patterns. The emotions of our stories are what bind us together and help us learn from each other's experiences. We connect to the situation and circumstance and experience the pattern in our minds and heart, thus borrowing the benefits of the difficulties, joy, tragedies, triumphs, and successes of each other's lives. As you read the stories, imagine yourself and your own life. As you do so, you will begin to feel and know the great benefit of understanding the lives and worlds of others.

How to Use This Book

We want you to grow to become the master of this asking process. So much so that you notice your own life improving and the lives of the people around you beginning to improve along with you. We'd like to suggest a few tips to help you get the greatest benefit as you travel through these pages. Please know that our hearts are holding yours as you begin your journey across the asking bridge to achieve your ultimate destiny.

1. Opening this book and reading these words is the launch of your asking journey.
2. Take a minute, draw a deep breath, and get centered and calm each time you read this book, so that you can feel the way the words are speaking to your own life.
3. Highlight the thoughts and ideas that speak to you.
4. Remember, this is about your potential to improve your life in a dramatic way. Take time to pause and reflect, as you read the stories of what other people have asked for and think of those experiences as many portals that are open for you to take.
5. Summarize your *ah-ha* moments in a separate journal. Include the questions, inquiries, and requests that blossom in your heart and mind as you integrate your asking methods into your day-to-day life.
6. Challenge yourself to connect to others in a brand-new way that integrates your new-found asking skills and begins to build a beautiful and more sturdy bridge to your ultimate destiny!
7. Periodically review your progress and give yourself plenty of high fives along the way!
   - If you want greater love
   - If you want happier relationships
   - If you want to know how to connect with people better
   - If you want things to work out in your favor
   - If you want more sales or business success
   - If you want to get the job or career of your dreams
   - If you want overflowing abundance

ASK!

- If you want more fruitful results from your efforts
- If you want to have a greater impact on the world

Keep reading. Get ready for your world to open up in ways never before imagined. Your destiny is waiting for you.

PART I

The Seven Roadblocks to Asking

It's pretty much a universal truth. Nobody likes to be told "no." The fear of rejection is a powerful moderator, causing us to hold our tongue, be quiet, sit back, and wait for something to come to us on its own. The problem with that pattern is that the things we desire will continue to elude us, and we'll stay stuck in our box until we decide to break the pattern. The key to breaking the pattern is to always remember this: if you don't ask—the answer is already an automatic *no*.

Asking is an age-old artform. We begin to ask probably before we can talk. Our six grandkids were each taught basic sign language to communicate their requests, before they could speak. Research shows that thinking is stimulated by asking questions. Preschoolers develop their cognitive abilities as they ask about how to solve a problem or they need targeted information on a subject or area of interest. In other words, as humans *we must ask* to learn and develop in a healthy normal way.

Once children can talk, they begin to ask Mom and Dad for everything. As they evolve, they ask why, why, why. But then eventually that pattern of curiosity and learning can start to shut down. Parents get worn out; the child is told that's enough, don't ask again; and he or she feels emotionally cut off. As they go to school and exhibit curiosity, children are told you can ask only when you are told you can ask; so again, basically we are told to zip it up. It has the effect of stifling our inborn curiosity and natural thinking reflexes.

Research shows the **three reasons** this dynamic in education begins are:

1. Teachers are considered the almighty vessel of knowledge with the ability to impart that knowledge by teaching.

2. Teachers usually are uncomfortable saying, "I do not know; let's look it up together."

3. With state-mandated curricula, there is little, if any, time to deviate from the script. The ability to ask a question, research the answer, and present it to the class requires some degree of flexibility in the weekly lesson plan. Most teachers, particularly in state-run schools, do not have that luxury. At the root of all three obstacles is the lack of time in K–12 education for in-depth investigation by students or teachers.

Educators could solve the problem by reducing the amount of required material in their curricula to allow more time for in-depth learning, teacher initiative and professional development, and exploration of questions. Finland is adopting such asking strategies and, according to their research, is experiencing substantially better educational outcomes than the United States.

Unfortunately, this ability to ask, and the environments that nurture curiosity and question-asking, continues to become scarcer as we get older.

In university classes, and especially online and in mega-classrooms, there is no time for question-asking, only output by the professor. If you join the military, you are told, "Do as you are told and don't ask any questions." Most company leaders do not want to hear workers' questions; they only want productivity and results, with the rare exception of great leaders who do ask for questions. These iconic business leaders, like Jack Welch, formerly CEO of General Electric; Bill Gates, Founder and CEO of Microsoft; and Jeff Bezos, Founder and CEO of Amazon, have all understood that the curiosity of their employees, and their willingness to question everything, is what causes a company to stay on the cutting edge in ultracompetitive business environments.

Good question-asking takes mentorship, learning, and practice to be mastered, just like building up the pectoral muscles to do a hundred push-ups. No one can do it on the first try. In an encouraging environment a child or an adult can learn this skill and make it an active practice of mind.

A simple but profound question that changed the history of photography was the one asked in 1943 by young Jennifer Land. Jennifer was only three years old when she asked her daddy, Dr. Edwin Land, a Harvard student studying physics and chemistry and an avid photographer, "Why do we have to wait for picture, Papa?" It got Land thinking, and he threw himself into deep studying that led to the creation of the Polaroid Land Camera that took instant pictures. This freed users from needing a dark room to develop their pictures.

When Steve Jobs of Apple Computer thought of the brilliance of Dr. Land and saw that Kodak had developed but not patented a breakthrough in digital photography, he asked himself if this technology was applicable to the evolving iPhone. The answer to that question changed the world of photography. Because of Jobs's endless curiosity and understanding of commercializing photographic innovation, over eight trillion photos are taken each year.

Our minds are brilliantly structured with a tendency toward unlimited and ever-evolving questions. We must pay attention to ourselves to discover if we've been stifled, stopped, or detoured from utilizing the greatest stimulator of thinking, innovation, and life advancement ever given to any life form. As far as scientists can tell, only humans have the capacity to ask, think, store insights from asking, and continue to ask until the answer shows up in their experience one way or another.

Effective asking becomes its own language that is both art and science. It's time to figure out how you've utilized the language of asking in the past, starting from your childhood, to discover if your asking skills were honed or shut down in your personal past, and how you can rekindle the art of asking to create a massive shift and ever greater fulfillment in your life.

We all come from different families with different norms, traditions, and family patterns. Without laying blame on those who came before us, it is important to understand how our childhood opportunities to ask and be answered might have been encouraged or shut down. That's not to judge our background harshly because little good usually comes of that. It is only to understand what our upbringing taught or did not teach us in terms of asking skills and what we need to learn going forward as we integrate the art of asking more easily into our lives.

Which of these seven roadblocks stand in the way of your asking?

1. Unworthiness/Insecurity: Conditioning from our childhood or past experiences that tells us we don't deserve better.

Too Insecure to Ask: Bob Proctor's Story

As a kid growing up, I was always too afraid to ask. I didn't want anyone to know that I didn't know. This continued on into my adulthood. I never asked anyone for anything. I was too insecure to ask. You have to be reasonably secure to ask, and I wasn't. I think when you ask, you have to realize you don't know it all, and you have to acknowledge you need other people. I was not comfortable with that.

I grew up in Canada during the Depression. My mother raised me by herself during the war, where I was surrounded by lack and limitation and not a lot of guidance. Because I grew up with very little belief in myself, I learned to expect very little. I didn't know myself, and I didn't like myself. I didn't have enough confidence to ask anybody anything.

In my early twenties, I was working at the fire department, and it was there that I met Ray Stanford. He was the guy who woke me up. He saw something in me, so he started talking to me and asking me questions.

Ray started asking me things that I'd never dared think of. At one point, he asked me what I wanted. I said all I wanted was some money. I didn't have any, and I figured if I had some, all my problems would go away.

When he told me I could have *anything* I wanted, I didn't believe it. But I believed *he* believed, so it caused me to start asking *myself* questions....

"Why is he doing this?"

"Why don't I listen to him?"

"Why does he think I'm capable of more?"

"What does he see in me that I don't?"

Even those questions started giving me a glimmer of hope that there was perhaps something better for me.

ASK!

I'll never forget the time Ray said to me, "I'm happy, healthy, and wealthy, and you're not. Why don't you try doing it my way?" He told me to start by reading *Think and Grow Rich* by Napoleon Hill. It's the only book I still read to this day, every day. This book, coupled with Ray's coaching and mentorship, helped me gain new awareness. I was on a new path.

One day, Ray asked me, "How much money do you really want?"

"I want twenty-five thousand dollars," I told him. That was an enormous amount of money at that time, in 1961. He had me write it on a card and read it every day. He's the one I credit to this day for my writing my goals on cards and carrying them around.

Ray caused me to look at how I was living. I started questioning everything, and I began to live my life differently. I started to think about earning money when, prior to that point, I only thought of the debt I had.

Shortly thereafter, I met a gentleman who told me there was good money in cleaning offices. I borrowed money from a relative to buy my first cleaning supplies, and I managed to get my first office cleaning account. Suddenly, I was in the cleaning business.

I figured the answer to making more money was to get another office to clean, and another, and another. Soon I was cleaning as many offices as I could; I was working around the clock. I got so many offices to clean that I wore myself out. One day, I actually passed out on the street. I woke up with a cop looking at me, some ambulance guys hovering above me, and a crowd of people gathered nearby. They thought I'd dropped dead, and looking up at all those people, I thought they might be right.

I was just plain exhausted.

They were going to take me to the hospital, but I talked them out of it and walked to a quiet place by myself. While I was standing there, trying to process what had happened, a voice in my head said, "If you can't clean all of them, don't clean any of them." I'll never forget that.

So, a day or two later, I got all dressed up, went out, and started finding other people to work for me cleaning offices. This plan worked very well for me, and I started making a lot of money while working fewer hours. When people asked what I did for a living, I simply said, "I clean up."

That turning point in my life occurred when I finally acknowledged I needed help. We all do. To get that help, we need to ask. I was afraid to ask, so my results were a mess. I went from being all screwed up, afraid, and not knowing anything—to finally realizing that my biggest gains came from asking myself questions and asking others for their help and insight.

I also discovered that the quality of the question defines the answer. A lot of people ask the wrong question. Are you asking the right question of yourself? For example, don't ask, "How do I get out of debt?" Instead ask, "How do I create abundance?" Are your questions moving you in the direction you want to go? If the answer is "no," then it's time to ask different questions!

Many years ago, I learned to simply ask, "How can I get what I want?" The perfection of our being causes us to want things, to move to an ever-higher experience of life. We are always evolving because we are always wanting more. *Want* is spirit jabbing you in the consciousness to move you to a better place, a higher level of expression. We always want more than we've got, and this isn't necessarily to have "it" but to experience the growth within ourselves. We're created to expand and grow.

The other morning, I was sitting in the kitchen with my wife, Linda. She was looking on her phone at something, and she asked me a brand-new question. "Bob, have you ever thought of becoming a billionaire?"

I was fairly surprised to admit that I hadn't. "No," I said, "I never, ever have. I've never thought of being a billionaire!"

Linda's question triggered something new in my mind. For me, that trigger wasn't about just having a billion dollars, but how we could actually *get* there. If we had a hundred thousand Proctor-Gallagher consultants teaching our material, we could actually reach that goal.

Once I arrived at this solution, it suddenly didn't seem to be an insurmountable goal, and the money part just faded away. I know everyone needs what we have. Our job is to help people become aware that they need this life-changing material, just as Ray Stanford helped me become aware many decades ago. So...that's what we're doing now. We're going to get a hundred thousand people to teach what we're teaching! If I become a billionaire on the way, that's okay, too!

See how just *one* question shifted my perspective? See how just one question created a viable solution? Jesus once noted, "Ask and it shall be given to you, seek and ye shall find. Knock and it will be opened to you." It really can be that easy...and it all starts with the ask.

2. Naïveté: Unaware of what is possible. Grew up with limited possibilities.

Imelda and the Mangos

When my children were very young, I (Crystal) hired a lovely Filipina woman to be a mother's helper to me. Our whole family soon fell in love with Imelda, who always had a joyful smile on her face. She quickly became lovingly attached to my nine-year-old son and my two baby girls, who were sixteen months apart in age. Imelda loved taking over dinner preparation duties, often surprising us with yummy-tasting dishes from her homeland. One morning she showed up with a fruit I'd never seen before. She cut open this oval-shaped fruit, slicing it in perfect peachy-colored crescents, and told me to try it. As I bit into this juicy, perfectly sweet, perfectly textured fruit, I asked, "What is this?"

"It's a mango," she replied. I considered myself a fairly worldly person and had traveled a fair amount, but somehow, I had never encountered a mango. I knew *of* them, but always imagined them to be found in exotic places. In fact, she told me she had gotten it at the grocery store! How had I missed that? I didn't realize this delicious fruity wonder was available to me every week if I wanted it. I wasn't aware of it, so I never noticed it. Never asked the grocer where to find it. It made me stop and reflect on what else I was missing out on in life, simply because I wasn't slowing down enough to be more curious, to find out what I didn't know, to notice and inquire about something wonderful I might pass by each day! In addition to mangos, what other things, people, and experiences were missing from my life because of my own lack of awareness or naiveté of what else was out there for me that I might enjoy and even love?

We all grow up with a certain set of people, who live with certain traditions, beliefs, and varying ways of life. I grew up in Idaho, where you'll find oodles of potatoes but no mangos! We're all limited by what we know. Often those limitations don't reveal to us what is possible. Asking begins to open us up to possibilities, big and small, of which we had no previous awareness. Through the asking process we can grow and learn, and life becomes a whole lot sweeter.

3. Doubt: We're not sure how to ask. It wasn't encouraged in our childhoods.

How Does a Young Girl Ask for Love?

My oldest and dearest friend, Janet, and I (Crystal) were headed up to Sedona, Arizona, which is one of our favorite moms-getaway spots. We love spending a few days together unwinding and catching up while hiking through one of nature's most dramatic red-rocked scenescapes. As two women who met at the beginning of fourth grade, there's not much we don't understand about each other, and it makes conversations—about life, kids, spouses, where we've come from, and where we're going—extremely rich and enjoyable. It was during one of those conversations, as we logged the miles past the saguaro-adorned Arizona landscape, that she told me something I never knew.

We were sharing our emotions of my dad's passing away just a few years before, and she said, "I used to sit in the back seat of the sedan your dad drove while you or your sister Teresa rode in the front with him. I would watch how he talked to you and said such sweet and kind things to each of you. He always seemed so happy to be with you. I used to watch the way he'd hold your hand as we drove along, and I wished so much that my dad would hold my hand like that."

When we really got deep into this topic, I asked Janet how all that made her feel. She said, "I'm ashamed to say, but I felt jealous, hurt, and just a deep longing to have my dad love me like yours did. Your relationship with your dad was so much more loving. So much happier. My eldest sister, Laura, was involved in school organizations and civic clubs and excelled in everything to get my dad's approval. My middle sister, Linda, was stubborn and tough and fought back with Dad, so he always engaged her in some way. He was just worn out when I came along, so he basically didn't deal with me. He didn't like to talk to me. Growing up, I was a lost little girl looking for love. I think he thought I got enough from my mom. I know that's one of the reasons I accepted such bad relationships with men. Until I met Walt, my sweet husband, pretty much all my relationships with men were disrespectful or abusive."

"Did you ever feel like you could ask your dad for something?" I asked her. "Ask him to spend time with you or have more fun together? Maybe even hold your hand?"

"No. I could never ask him for anything. I was afraid to ask because I had a constant fear of rejection from him. I truly doubted that he would want to accommodate any request I had. That anything I asked for would only make him mad. For example, I remember I needed new school shoes when I was in eighth grade. I went to his law office, which was downtown, close to Hudson Shoes, where I had picked out the perfect shoes. I was in total doubt when I asked, but I needed those shoes, so I asked anyway. It was awful. He couldn't even verbalize his anger with me. He would just stare at me and give me the silent treatment. Anything I asked for was wrong. It wasn't important. I was undervalued and unimportant to him.

"My father was a depressed person, and I didn't know that during my childhood. He was angry all the time. I felt like my presence made him mad. I think by the time I came along, as his third daughter, seven years after my older sister, he just wanted a son. He didn't want me. That's why he always seemed angry. My dad rarely talked to me or shared anything with me. I didn't find out that he was a World War II POW until I was in my thirties. I didn't know many of the details of that experience until his funeral. I found out that his plane had been shot down, and he had watched one of his buddies, who was sitting right next to him in the plane, get blown up. He also watched his friends flying in the plane just off their wing get blown out of the sky. He and his remaining service comrades ejected from the flight, and as several of them hit the ground before him, German soldiers shot some of them on the spot. By some miracle my dad's parachute was caught in a tree. As he hung there waiting to be shot, for some reason they decided to bring him down and take him as a prisoner. Fortunately, the war ended a few months later, so he was released.

"I know now those experiences caused him a tremendous amount grief and anger. Survival guilt probably haunted him each and every day of his life. In my adult years we started being able to talk more and to try to understand each other better. I think he finally started appreciating how I lived my life and started respecting me more. I realized he liked to take walks and talk. It seems like those were the times he seemed most relaxed with me and began to open up and have something close to a real conversation. I'm glad we got to that point. Later, as Dad saw me navigate through some difficult health and life issues in my adult years, my relationship with him completely changed. He began to view me as a person, a loving daughter, and finally recognized me for the strength I possessed. I am very grateful that for the last three years of his life he and I were actually very close, and he mellowed in his attitude toward all his daughters. My poor dad. He was an amazing man, but a challenged father."

4. Excuses: Too stubborn or proud to reach out to someone and be vulnerable.

Brother Bailey's Story

A few years after the death of his beloved life partner and wife, Priscilla, my (Mark) eldest brother, Bailey, came to visit and enjoy a holiday with us in Arizona. We had a gloriously happy time of festivities, family discussions, and hiking through the cactuses at McDowell Mountain Preserve. Bay is a dedicated hobbyist wood carver. So, we invested an afternoon making a bow out of raw wood, inspired and guided by my survivalist teacher and friend, John "Bluebird" Classman. If you asked Bay, I believe he would have said that the best-spent couple of hours in Arizona were carving and creating something great and useful out of a large oak tree branch. We carved it with vigor together. When it was complete, he said in his gruff way, when he didn't want to express his emotions: "Little brother, I taught you archery, bow and arrow hunting, when you were a teenager. Now, you keep it as a memento of our efforts together."

On the morning of his departure, we rose at five o'clock because Bay had an early flight with several connections to get back home to Tennessee. We had a quick breakfast and headed faithfully to the Phoenix airport with plenty of time for him to comfortably get to the gate and get a snack.

Having flown over six million miles, I am deeply aware of airport and airline protocols. Because Bay and Pris had done a lot of vacationing around the world, I assumed he was too. It never dawned on me that before her recent passing, Priscilla had guided him effortlessly through airports and the respective procedures. I asked, when we arrived, if he needed help. He assured me that he did not, that he was at the right airline; he had his luggage, which he would hand carry; and he was just fine. We hugged and appreciated each other, and he went into the airport. I drove off figuring he was perfectly okay.

Hours later, just to be sure he was safely back home in Tennessee, I called his daughter, Jodi, who had planned to meet him on the other end and pick him up, and asked, "Did your dad get home safely?"

Her response floored me. "Didn't you know? He missed his plane. He had to sit in that airport for hours waiting for the next flight. He won't be home until after midnight. He is distressed and angry!"

Feeling defensive, I said, "I got him there in plenty of time. What happened?"

"Dad doesn't know his way around airports," Jodi said. "He couldn't find his gate. He was utterly dependent on Priscilla to get him around."

"I didn't know. I am so familiar with airports and moving quickly through them, that with all of his travels, I thought he'd be fine. I asked him multiple times if he needed help. He said no."

"It's not your fault, Uncle Mark," she said. "You know Dad. He is too darn stubborn to ask for help. His pride won't let him do it. Now, I have to pick him up about midnight, and neither of us will make it home until three o'clock or later."

Let me unpack this. If my brother had just asked me for help, I would have parked my SUV, walked with him to the gate, gotten him safely to security, and pointed out the directions to gate three, and all the distress, anger, disappointment, finger-pointing, waste-of-time, hassle, and bad memory could have easily been avoided. These frustrating incidents could have been missed, and a great weekend would have been packaged with a delightful bon-voyage bow.

Option number two was, once Bay was in the airport, he could have asked any number of airport employees, security guards, or airline employees for the right direction or protocol. He refused to ask anyone.

Option three: he could have called me once he knew he had missed his flight and asked if I could come to his assistance, and I would have gotten him through or picked him up and gladly had him as a houseguest for another day.

So, instead of employing any of those options and asking for help, information, or assistance—Bailey instead missed his flight and, as a result, spent a wretched day alone in the airport. To make matters worse, the cold he was coming down with worsened greatly, and a touch of pneumonia he thought was gone came back over the next couple of days. Most likely because of the stress and long hours spent traveling.

Bailey recently passed on, and it caused me to reflect back on his life. My brother was one of the most helpful, giving guys you'd ever meet. But he had also expressed a lifelong pattern of stubbornness. I had never stopped to think about the complications it could effectuate until that trip to Arizona. I could clearly see the numerous times that Bailey had refused to ask for help, choosing instead to gut out tough situations on his own. Asking for a simple direction, advice on how to do or accomplish something, or insightful guidance on relationship skills was something he rarely, if ever, did. This could have saved him from mountains of hassles, uncomfortable situations, and a lot of personal grief that was much more serious than a miserable travel experience. The only thing standing in the way of navigating life in a more stress-free fashion was his own stubborn pride. The really crazy part of that is, the people in his life, including me, would have been so happy to help in a multitude of ways.

5. Fear: The underlying feeling we'll lose something by asking—usually love, approval, or our dignity.

The Unflappable Pat Burns

The fear of asking for something can thwart a person's success in every area of life. Pat Burns is not one of those people. Pat, a superstar sales-woman, says fear is not part of her DNA. When we asked Pat what one of the most important questions asked of her during her career was, she said there were a few times when working with would-be clients that they would question her bold comments or promises. She never forgot one particular time when the client began their own interrogation and asked point-blank, "Who do you think you are to promise this or that?"

With a smile, a strong dose of self-generated self-confidence, and a doubt-free attitude, she would respond: "I am somebody who can get the job done—how about you? Are you prepared to commit the same?" Pat learned years ago that you must be a fearless asker to achieve your best.

As a young, brand-new, and eager real estate salesperson she saw an opportunity to sell a nostalgic Palm Springs property to a celebrity billionaire that Pat thought would be perfect for their well-known, iconic empire.

Though she had no connections to anyone in the company, she desperately wanted to get to the top decision maker and ask for the opportunity of presenting the property, writing up a contract, and converting the deserted estate to an elite private club. A lot of young salespeople (with *zero* experience) would talk themselves out of such a goal because they knew nothing about preparing such a contract and harbored feelings of unworthiness.

Fearless, Pat called the executive offices. The chairman's secretary listened to her request for an appointment and, without missing a beat, suddenly said, "Thank you for calling, Pat, but they are perfectly happy with the mansion and have no further need of any property."

Pat immediately jumped back in and asked, "But how can you say no when I haven't even told you about it?"

The secretary was not used to such instant and bold feedback and said, "Okay, Pat, then tell me." Pat did. She presented to the secretary, and the secretary presented the information to the chairman. Two weeks later, Pat was showing the property and ultimately was under contract with the property, with one more added twist: the client not only wanted the existing property but also told Pat he wanted the entire neighborhood. Pat made a fortune and became salesperson of the year from one giant courageously made ask.

Pat's success from her unflappable confidence and her fearless willingness to ask is a living testament that inspires us to release our own fears. After all, why would we hold on to our fear? It really serves no good purpose in achieving our ultimate destiny!

6. Pattern Paralysis: Brain conditioning/habits keep us repeating the same disappointing patterns.

My Uncle Dean: Jonathan Westley's Story

I grew up knowing my uncle Dean very well. He was a likable, talkative individual who seemed to get along with everyone he came across. He presented himself as a top leader in his industry and to the people he was around. He talked a lot; he had a lot of opinions and promises of things he was going to do, but his words did not lead to action. They did not lead to the grand results that were spoken in these words because, in reality, he was held back by a pattern of paralysis that led to increasing problems in his life. Pattern paralysis is not always easy to see or obvious to the carrier of the pattern. It is often a blind spot they cannot see. Their blindness comes from blaming the world outside of themselves, rather than asking what role they are playing in their results. The paralyzing behavior becomes the fuel for the future to continue down a path of endless, self-created problems.

Dean was married at a young age to an even younger woman, who gave birth to a son, my cousin Chase. Several years after Chase's birth, they went through a divorce. Instead of asking for help in getting through the difficult time, Dean became bitter and held on to whatever pain he felt, renewing his pain each and every day. It didn't matter that the two were only twenty-two and eighteen years old when they married and the likelihood of such a young couple staying together was very slim. It didn't matter that he still had his whole life ahead of him and could move on to anything he chose.

Instead, this difficulty became the first brick in a large fortress of protective layers he created. A fortress that kept in his painful experiences and shut out anything new or redemptive that would create a better future. This paralyzing pattern continued with every new challenge that came up in his life. Instead of asking how he could improve, asking for help from so many who cared about him, or asking God to give him strength to be and do something new, he just fortified his fortress of misery and blamed the growing content of experiences for not being who he really wanted to be.

Uncle Dean could be really great to me and my cousin Chase, and to our other friends. As I grew up, we all liked him, and he could really make us all feel like he had it all together. Through the years we realized he could put on a good front, but behind the scenes he wasn't in a good place. He refused let go of the negative feelings he had from his past challenges and experiences. Instead of letting things go and moving on with his life, he replayed those difficulties like a recording in his mind, day after day, so they became a burden he put himself through each day. By not letting these challenges go, he became the biggest obstacle in his own life: living a life of fear, hiding, and self-doubt.

In certain situations, Dean outwardly acted like he was just fine, but he was anything but fine. The more he held on tightly to his negative experiences, the more dysfunctional he became. He began to screen his phone calls, avoid people, and layer the barriers of separation from others in his life to make sure people could not connect with him. He would not answer the door when people would visit his home, even though they knew he was there. It was a total pattern of paralysis, which prevented him from asking anything of anyone, even himself. I could see how frustrated Chase would feel at times when he just wanted his dad to let go of the past, move on, be functional, and create a better life for them. So often, I felt really bad for my cousin because he felt trapped by his dad's behavior patterns. It created a lot of unnecessary drama for Chase and our whole family. Embarrassing, painful drama.

Dean went through terrible financial struggles because he would never fully give himself to a job, never ask for feedback nor welcome it.

Because of this, he never achieved the success he hoped for. He would tell himself stories to avoid any truthful self-examination. He would say things like, "I am so good at what I do that I don't need to work with clients like that," or "I only take this type of client; I only work on this type of job," when actually he had no paying jobs and was living out of a storage unit with no air conditioning or at friends' houses.

As life went on and his son grew older, Dean was able to get the courage to get out of his shell, start dating again, and eventually marry another woman. Wendy seemed like the right woman for him, and he seemed to feel great about it. He was finally moving on in his life. Like buried patterns always do, however, his pattern started revealing itself in his new marriage. This new relationship forced him to take new people into his life, and he went right back into the old pattern because it was so entrenched.

He didn't trust anyone and behind their backs demeaned them as wrong or different. He went to great lengths to isolate the individuals in his now-larger family to keep them separate and try to control and manipulate the relationships between them.

The problem got even worse when Chase got married. Because his dad held on to everything from his past, he would conveniently pull it out and impose his anger or bitterness onto someone new who had never done anything to hurt him. He constantly attempted to drive a wedge of separation between Chase and his new wife, because his only son was the last thing he could hold on to from his past.

He could not stand to be around his own son's wife, even though she was (and is) an amazing girl, because his pattern paralyzed him from taking a fresh new look at anything. It prevented him from accurately assessing my cousin and his wife's relationship together. He searched for any negative in every situation and hung on to those moments, never to forgive them. These were small things that most people would stop and question, saying, "Should I really be this angry over something so small?" One time, about eight months after Chase's wife had given birth to their first beautiful son, I remember she was concerned Dean hadn't seen his grandchild in several months, even though he lived close by. She called and simply said, "It's been a long time since you've seen your grandchild. Do you want to come to dinner and see him?" Uncle Dean went nuts, accusing her of implying he was a bad grandfather. His bitterness toward Chase's wife became so hateful Chase finally had to cut off communications with his dad.

Dean was born naturally intelligent, talented, and good looking. He had come from a family whose members, as with any family, weren't perfect, but they loved him and loved each other. I started to realize that as much as my uncle started out with great potential, this pattern controlled him and really destroyed his life. His decision to hold on to anger from every situation and to justify his bitterness daily had prevented him from ever being able to ask for anything new. This retention of anger is the poison that continues to paralyze his life, his happiness, and his success. It has stopped him, blocked him, and provided excuses to demean good people, cut them out of his life. It has truly prevented his every success and happiness.

I learned so much about how *not* to be from my years of experience with Uncle Dean. What a valuable lesson. There's no reason to accept anything less from life than to become the person we want to be. If your past controls you, that simply can't happen. If you can recognize the self-defeating pattern you're stuck in and be willing to let it go, the sky is the limit for what you can accomplish in life. Holding on to baggage and old patterns takes up all the space that you need to create any great thing in life. It's yours for the asking. If you want a good marriage, ask for a good marriage. If you want success in life, ask for success in life; if you want to be the best parent you can be, ask to be the best parent you can be. Ask yourself and ask around you. Ask for things that are beyond you, bigger than you, bigger than anyone you know, and bigger than anything you've accomplished so far. Then make sure you're humble enough to listen for the answers and take the necessary actions because no one is responsible for your happiness but you!

7. Disconnection: We've become numb to our inner truth. Out of touch with our own sense of unworthiness. Given up on the real desires of our heart.

Margot Danley Story

I couldn't believe this was happening to me. I had fought it for so long. I went to my friend's house to tell her the news that I had only just admitted to myself. I was miserable in my marriage, and I was calling it quits. After I had spent years glossing over my husband's violations of trust and fidelity, a final straw had broken the camel's back. The reality of what I had gone through during my years of marriage was suddenly weighing in on me like a mountain-sized boulder. How had I stayed so disconnected from the truth for so many years? How had I continued to be the supportive wife, loving mother, and willing helpmate? How had I continued to play double duty as mom and co-breadwinner? How had I enthusiastically thrown great parties, cooking wonderful foods that my husband and all our friends enjoyed? How had I continued to throw myself into my marriage and my life with dutiful determination and never asked for what I deserved?

It became clear from the beginning that my husband didn't have fidelity to our marital vows. It started with him sneaking off with a girl he met at a bar here and there when we lived and worked overseas in the beginning of our marriage. When he would come home the next day, he would explain that it wasn't anything that was going to last. That he was just experimenting and having fun since we were young, and he wouldn't do this kind of thing when we returned to the US and settled down. But we did return to the US. We did settle down. We started a family and still, after having two children, I continued to see the sneaking, lying, and evidence that he was not faithful. But I stayed and carried on with a smile and determination, until that fateful day when it finally hit me that I had somehow, for so many years, successfully disconnected from my own truth. Why had I never asked my husband for the respect I deserved? Why had I never asked for fidelity? For him to honor our marriage vows? For him to be considerate of my thoughts, my feelings, and my heart? How did I take this trip so far away from my inner being? These questions were so tough for me to face, but I knew some of the answers could be found by examining my early life.

I grew up in middle-class family with two working parents. Mom worked night shifts and split up her sleeping schedule to be able to take care of her six children. Because Mom was often gone or sleeping during the day, a lot was expected of all of us kids.

My mother definitely had a favorite child, and it wasn't me. In fact, I truly believed my entire life she disliked me. She made it obvious in just about every way she could. Mom's favorite was my sister Susie. Susie was a world-class runner. An Olympic hopeful. A champion. Someone who lived up to my mother's insistence on perfection and achievement. Someone she could brag to her friends about. In spite of the fact that I was a straight A student, was active in clubs and sports, held a part-time job, did housework, cooked and baked for the family—in essence was an overachiever—in my mother's eyes I was flawed.

I had really bad knees from the time I was young. My joints were hypermobile, and as a result, they were prone to injury. By the time I was nine years old, I had already had multiple injuries and many appointments with an orthopedist. By age sixteen, I'd had two surgeries to try to correct my injuries. Even with all my ongoing issues, pain, and rejection that went on much of my childhood through my teenage years, I never gave up on sports or being active.

In spite of all my mom's animosity toward me, my dad totally adored me, and I knew it. In fact, I felt I was his favorite. He loved my intelligence, sense of humor, loyalty, and hardworking, can-do, positive attitude. I often thought one of the reasons my mom disliked me so much was because of my dad's love for me. Dad was such a kind man—you might say the complete opposite of my mom. He was playful, positive, happy, and would do anything for you, and my friends all loved him. I knew which of my parents I wanted to be like. I wanted to be as little like my mother as possible. I did my best to be a nice person. I helped at home any way I could, cooking meals for the family, packing lunches for my younger sisters and helping to take care of them, sewing clothes to help save money, and mowing the lawn as well as my normal household duties.

Mom wasn't mean just to me. She was mean to everybody except Susie. Just meaner with me. My friends were scared of my mom and didn't like hanging out at my house because they didn't want to be confronted by her.

You would think I would be resentful of my older sister Susie because of her monumental achievements in sports, her international fame, and the fact that my mom thought she walked on water. It was just the opposite. Susie and I were very close. I loved her so much and was so proud of her accomplishments, and she loved me. Since she traveled internationally often, I was more than willing to take over her commitments required for the high school office of student body treasurer she held, do extra babysitting for my younger sisters, and make sure everything was taken care of while she was away. I cheered her on and would wait with giant congratulatory banners at the airport when she would arrive home from a national or international race or event.

Now, as I faced this collapse of my marriage, and the uncertainty of my life ahead, I could see how much my family dynamic had shaped me. Had shaped even the way I was determined to have a happy marriage and be the nice wife, at the cost of my own inner dignity and truth.

I discovered that, for so long, I had gone overboard in my determination to be a nice, happy, and helpful person, to the point that I didn't have healthy boundaries. I didn't want to be someone who was difficult or unsympathetic. I didn't want that mean person who lived inside my mother to ever come out in me.

But in trying to take care of everyone's needs and demands with a smile, I didn't protect or honor my own needs. In allowing my husband to follow his heart wherever it led, I didn't remember to protect my own heart. My dad had been such a sweetheart. He had absorbed so much of my mom's wrath and hatred. As much as I wanted to be more like my dad than my mom, I knew the stress he took on, being so kind and understanding of my mother, had contributed to cutting his life short. He died at the young age of fifty-seven. I wasn't willing to give up my well-being any longer in order to let my husband happily walk all over me. I was done. In confronting these issues, I knew I needed to reclaim myself. I needed to connect to my deepest truth and to ask for each and every thing I knew I deserved. It was tough. At first, I felt wistful; a bit regretful of losing the naiveté that had kept me blissfully ignorant of some very ugly truths. Ignoring them had allowed me to always be a sweet and thoughtful person regardless of how I had been treated. I knew that not only would I never be that person again, but I didn't want to be! I wanted to go forward with knowledge and boundaries that would bring a more fulfilling and balanced life.

That was twenty-six years ago, and through a lot of personal work on myself, I'm a much different person today than I was all those years ago. I run my own business, have wonderful relationships with healthy boundaries, and spend time doing the things I enjoy like art, sports, and travel. A few years ago, after a multiyear journey of my siblings and me overseeing her care from a retirement home, my mother died at age ninety-one. I got the call at 11:00 p.m. that she was slipping away. I raced through the night to get to her side. I just missed her. She was gone. The nurse told me she'd had an unusually free shift that night and had sat by my mother's side for about three hours as Mom chatted away about her life. She said toward the end my mother started talking about me, and minutes before she died, she had said to the nurse, "Yeah, she's the best of the bunch." That was an emotional moment for me. I knew that those years of learning to stay in my truth and clearly communicate healthy boundaries, even to my mother, had completely changed our relationship. She had finally begun to see me for who I am.

Do any of the **seven roadblocks to asking** to seem familiar to you? As you continue on this reading journey, you'll begin to identify exactly what is standing in the way of living your best life. Can you imagine the greatest challenges you've always experienced being absent from the picture? Are you able to form a mental picture of a life for yourself that includes happiness, success, vibrant health, and well-being? Can you begin to picture yourself being free of destructive habits? Can you envision yourself in a passionate, fulfilling relationship with someone you love and worship? Can you capture a picture of yourself in a dynamic, successful career doing work you love to do: a job you embrace with enthusiasm each and every day? As the sun rises each day, new questions will rise to the top of your mind demanding answers. As you approach your day with brave new questions, you will see yourself writing a new story for your own life. How glorious, adventurous, and noble will that story be? Keep asking.

If I had an hour to solve a problem
and my life depended on the solution,
I would spend the first fifty-five minutes
determining the proper question to ask...
for once I know the proper question,
I could solve the problem in less than five minutes.

—DR. ALBERT EINSTEIN

Ask Gold Nuggets

- There are three channels through which to ask: Ask Yourself, Ask Others, Ask God.
- It takes the courage of a child to keep asking.
- Good question-asking takes mentorship, learning, and practice to be mastered.
- Effective asking becomes its own language that is both art and science.
- The Seven Roadblocks to asking are: Unworthiness, Naïveté, Doubt, Stubbornness/Pride, Fear, Pattern Paralysis, and Disconnection. Don't let these keep you from asking the questions that lead to your destiny!

PART II

Pivot Your Destiny by Asking

1. Pivot Your Life Direction

You play the lead role in creating the life you desire.

Sometimes the best question you can ask is the one you ask yourself because usually it signifies an acknowledgment that you are rejecting the status quo. That you want to explore better options for yourself and you're willing to risk seeing yourself clearly.

The Question that Pivoted My Life Direction

I (Crystal) was one of those kids who found school and homework to be easy and unstimulating, which led me to accelerating my high school curriculum and graduating from high school when I was only sixteen years old. I believed I was on a quest to seek a more fulfilling and interesting life. I felt mature and independent and ready to make my own big decisions. Just one week after my seventeenth birthday, I wed a twenty-one-year-old kid who had no more business getting married than I did. We were both too young and immature to succeed. Three and a half years later I found myself trying to work through my own divorce, with a two-year-old baby boy on my hip, residing in a new city where I had no job, no friends or family around me, and no real plan of what to do next.

I was too proud to ask for help from my parents. The only option I left myself was to figure it out alone. At one point, I applied for food stamps so I could buy diapers and food. But when I stood in the grocery line the first time I used them, I suddenly felt sick inside. Something inside me was repulsed by the idea of accepting help because I equated it with incompetence. I had been raised in a family with a decades-old pioneering spirit, which relentlessly taught that you work hard and create your own breaks. There was a part of me that couldn't accept the situation I was in. Suddenly, I heard a voice in my mind asking, *"Are you really trying to tap into your own skills and talents to resolve this situation, or are you taking the easy way out?"* The answer to that question caused a complete pivot inside me. I knew immediately that instead of using my energy to find ways to barely survive, I needed to try harder to find ways to thrive. I made a vow to myself, in that moment, that I would finish the food stamps I had for the month and never reapply. Even as I was handing the food stamps over to the cashier in exchange for milk and diapers, I was saying to myself, *"This will not be in my future."* I knew that if I would just dig deeper inside myself, I would find the resources to make my life happen the way I wanted it to. I was twenty-one by then and ready to step into my adulthood and make better decisions in my life.

The next day, I scanned the job ads again and called three temporary service agencies. I asked to register with all of them, so that I would have a constant stream of options for jobs. I did everything from clerical work and receptionist work to setting up display booths at malls. I was learning a lot about many different kinds of businesses, working with many different kinds of people and enjoying the variety. I would be assigned to some jobs for up to several months, and some for only a few days. I was happy to be able to pay my bills, buy food, take good care of my little boy, and still have a little fun.

During this period, several people approached me to see if I would consider doing some modeling. I decided I had nothing to lose, so I investigated various agencies, made appointments to meet them, and ended up signing a management contract with one of the top modeling agencies in my town. It didn't take long before I was hired as a model for some well-paying print ads and television commercials. Life began to get a bit easier for my little guy and me once I had this new stream of income with full insurance benefits from Screen Actors Guild.

The money I made in modeling and TV commercials allowed me to put myself through a real estate school and certification program and begin a career selling real estate. Right after I finished the program and got my real estate license, I started working for the top homebuilder in our valley. In a short time, I was salesperson of the month. I was making great money and enjoyed being in charge of my life for the first time. Over time, I began investing in my own real estate, and to this day, my intuition for buying and renovating properties for a profit continues to be an important part of our family investment portfolio.

From time to time, I've wondered what my life would now look like had I not faced my situation with honest, gut-wrenching questions at that very difficult time in my life. It would have been easy to feel sorry for myself and take all the free assistance I could get. I believe God had a better path for me than the one I had begun to take, but without those questions that forced me to hold up a mirror and look into it, where would I be today? My father used to say, "There are many paths you can take that appear to exist side by side. But choose carefully which one you take because the further you get down the path, the further apart those paths are. Eventually they lead to destinies that are worlds apart."

Asking delivered an illumination, and the revectoring that took place in my life through that process wasn't just that I started making some money or achieved some success in modeling or the real estate business. It set me off on a path that is, truly, worlds apart from the one I was on.

It doesn't matter at what stage of life we are; most of us have untapped potential or unfulfilled dreams that lie dormant. As we traverse down life's various roads and become immersed in the people, places, problems, dramas, and emotions of each day, we begin to settle in and think, *This is it. This is my life.* But is it? What if this is only the second or third act of a five- or six-act play? It's funny because, when we ask the people I work with those questions, we find it's not that someone else has put a limitation on them, and it certainly isn't the Creator of the Universe who puts any limitations on any of us. Instead, our perceived limitations mostly come from a lack of curiosity about what else might be there for us or a fear that we're not capable of achieving what we want.

Could you rekindle your love for art or music and do something amazing with it? Could you learn a new skill or language? Do you have an unusual ability to organize or lead? What if that led to a new opportunity or career? If you really took away the well-groomed borders you've put around your life, might you find the life you're living could be enlarged or lived in a bolder or more inspiring way?

If you reached a little deeper inside and began to ask those probing questions, where might it lead? Have you fully crossed the bridge to your destiny, are you halfway there, or are you just now finally seeing that bridge calling to you?

Mind Mastery through Asking

Asking the right questions requires really looking at yourself in a deep and honest way. Too often when we're not happy with the way things are going, we ignore what's happening inside us and refuse to look deeper. If you let your mind run amok with negative thinking, worries, and negative memories of your past experiences, before you know it your mind is on autopilot: regurgitating negativity that dominates your mental space. You have to be determined to deliberately intervene in this useless cycle on behalf of yourself to master your mind to your greatest benefit. Remember, asking takes courage and conviction, and never is that truer than when we use the **"Holding Up the Mirror Questions."** These are the questions that challenge the foundations of your life and your beliefs about yourself and everything around you.

Holding Up the Mirror Questions

We recommend writing these questions and answers in your Ask journal. Go back to them from time to time and see how your answers are changing and the growth you're experiencing.

- "In what areas of my life does it seem as if I just keep missing the target?"
- "Am I able to challenge my current issues and believe things could be different, or have I accepted that this is how life *is*? Or that this is who I *am*?"

31

- "Do I believe that even if I resolve my current problems, more will come up and I'll never really get ahead of them?"
- "Am I living my ideal life?" (Circle your answer.) Yes No
- "In which areas do I feel the least fulfilled?" (Rank each area from 1–10.)

Money/Career _____   Relationships _____

Health _____   Weight and Fitness _____

Spirituality _____   Life Purpose/Contribution _____

- "Does my life feel out of my own control?" (Circle your answer.) Yes No
- "Do I sometimes feel like something is standing in the way of my living my ideal life?" (Circle your answer.) Yes No
- "Do I often feel powerless to change things?" (Circle your answer.) Yes No
- "At times does it seem that others have more control over the decisions I make than I do?" (Circle your answer.) Yes No
- "Do I feel powerful and resourceful enough, right now, if I wanted to change things?" (Circle your answer.) Yes No
- "How long have I felt this way about the questions above?" (In your own words.)
- "What would my ideal life look like, feel like, *be like*?"

Where your questions are, there will be your answer. Questions can open a closed mind and transform the way you think. When you're going through your **Holding Up the Mirror Questions**, ask fearlessly and be willing to listen for the answers with your heart *and* mind. Sometimes answers come to us in the form of a feeling or knowing.

When you feel stuck in your life or relationships and it seems like there is no way out of the mess, always go back to the **Holding Up the Mirror Questions**.

What Are You Best At? Brad Rotter's Story

"What are you best at?" That great question was first asked of me by my granddad, starting when I was about nine years old. My mother's father was the man who influenced me the most in my life. Granddad was a renaissance man. He practiced yoga, kept bees, made his own yogurt, gave me books to read on spiritual topics like Zen, and asked me the above question incessantly. It was his boxing lessons that led me to understand and contemplate inner self-mastery...and how to take a punch. Growing up on a farm in Iowa, he was definitely a farmer futurist.

His one question—*"what are you best at?"*—has defined my life. He got me to look at what I was best at and explore my future path every day by reasking it of myself. My entire life, I have repeated that question in my mind and thought: *What does my future hold, and how can I mold it better for me and everyone else?*

"What are you best at?" is an important question for each of us to ask periodically throughout the year. If you can figure out what you are best at and do that, typically that makes everything in your life become quite a bit easier. The answers will change over time, because you are changing, growing, and becoming more yourself.

At ten years old, I announced to Grandpa Cook that because of my love of animals, I would become a veterinarian. I had goats, sheep, cattle, ponies, chickens, rabbits, squirrels, and a bevy of young pet skunks. As I was active in 4-H with my animal projects, I pursued my veterinary plans, and because of my school leadership experience and tireless focus on academics, at age sixteen, I earned a full scholarship to Iowa State University, which was the premier vet school in the country.

Unexpectedly, the answer to that question would change. Being politically active was especially fun in Iowa, and I was appointed as page in the Iowa Senate in Des Moines. Des Moines was conveniently located six hours away from our family's hay fields. I had my own apartment at the YMCA in Des Moines while learning about the legislature and working as the chief page.

It was just a magical time. I was really into the daily workings of the government and legislation. At night, I had another job. When a couple of senators were out carousing with the lobbyists at night, I was invited to tag along. Since I reported directly to the secretary of the senate, I knew the senate calendar cold; so, having me at the table benefitted the senators. At the end of the night, I was to safely drive them all home after they'd been drinking. One night, I'm driving home Senator Kennedy from Columbus Junction, Iowa. It was just the two of us. While driving, I asked: "Senator, I've really been looking forward to this one-on-one time with you. I've read all your bills, looked at all your statements, but you're a hard man to figure out. Can you help me?"

Being a bit relaxed from a few cocktails, the senator looked at me and said, "Boy, my job as an Iowa senator is to take money from the rich, get votes from the poor, and then protect them from one another." That night, I decided not to go into politics. I knew I could never be good at that.

As a result of my state-level political activity, I was asked to help manage a House campaign for a congressman named Fred Schwengel. He had served many terms and was considered a lock for reelection.

On the campaign trail, I met the guy we were running against: Edward Mezvinsky, who had no experience, but who was messaging new ideas with the stamina of youth. Back then, it was a different world in politics. I liked the opponent and alerted him to events he probably would have missed otherwise. When the young upstart won the election, against my five-term incumbent, it was a surprise to everyone.

Six weeks later the congressman-elect, Ed Mezvinsky, called me out of the blue on our home party line (a "party" line was a telephone line shared by four or five families in the neighborhood). After talking for a while and joking with each other, I asked, "Why did you call me?"

"I watched you operate during the campaign and decided to appoint you to West Point."

"Wow! That's amazing! I don't know what to say. I appreciate that magnanimous gesture very much, but I must decline. I have a full veterinarian scholarship to Iowa State."

"Well, that's okay—you probably couldn't have gotten into West Point anyway."

That rattled, humbled, and challenged me. Yet that was a great day. I asked my favorite question to myself. What am I best at? The answer was clear. West Point was, at its very core, a leadership school. I knew because of the experience and skills I had gained through my role as the chief page that the notion of trying to lead others with the persuasion of good ideas had kindled a new passion inside me. I enjoyed leading and being out front. I applied to the US Military Academy, and after a lengthy interview and strenuous physical tests, I received the appointment and acceptance into West Point. Talk about a change in my trajectory. It was at the Academy that I saw my first mainframe computers, and I learned to program with trays of program cards that would run in batches. It was at West Point when it occurred to me that computers would be fundamental to all the branches of the service, and when that happened, that strength would be our vulnerability. That spiked a lifelong passion for cybersecurity, and I have often spoke on "Web War One: The First War in History That Cannot End."

It was at West Point that I developed an important corollary to my "grandfather" question. Yes, of course, doing something you're good at is usually more enjoyable and often fruitful. However, it becomes of paramount importance that you get the broad strokes as correct as possible. That means finding what you are good at that will have *relevance* and *utility*. You might have been called to helping people arrange their travel, but if you became a travel agent at the time the browser was invented, you are regretting that decision.

I imagine I first began honing my skills in predicting the future, with futures!

I didn't start trading commodities until I was sixteen. Growing up on a farm made one painfully aware of the swings in commodity prices. We raised corn and cows, and I was in charge of hedging the prices of our modest output. It became obvious to me that the time to sell was not when everyone else was trying to do so. Bing! Granddad's question popped into my head! The answer told me that trading was a challenge that would never get old, and I found myself on a steep but enjoyable learning curve.

After the Army, I raced back to Chicago for two reasons. That was the center of the universe for commodity trading, and it also was the location of the top business school (at the time), which had just accepted me. While working on my MBA at the University of Chicago at night, I spent my every free moment of the day trading commodities on the Chicago Board of Trade. Grown men yelling, kicking, screaming, shouting, sweating, and swearing at one another...it was fabulous!

With Granddad's question in mind, I was determined to develop those skills that might be used to anticipate important future trends. That answer was clear. There were initial discussions of trading futures contracts on financial instruments. This was surprisingly controversial but not to me. Money is the largest commodity of all. I dove in headfirst and helped pioneer the concept of financial futures trading futures contracts, helping the exchange design and market these new products and transacting the first transactions on the floor in the new contracts as they were rolled out. I got thrown out of some of the finest banks in New York trying to educate them on these new instruments to trade and hedge interest rates. Financial futures exploded, easily surpassing trading volumes from the other commodities and are now an integral part of international capital markets. As one of the few traders who had traded on both exchanges, I advocated a combination of the Board of Trade and the Chicago Mercantile Exchange to capture obvious efficiencies. That would later occur and would only do so as a result of their exploding businesses in financial instruments.

Alas, another prediction I was vocal about was the sunset of open outcry. Walking onto the Board of Trade as a member was one of the proudest moments of my life. The scene was accurately portrayed in the movie *Trading Places*. Mayhem. Pit trading was the epitome of capital markets, but it was inefficient and not exactly fair. I had a strong vision that open outcry would be supplanted by computer servers. When invited to dinner at Gene & Georgetti with the chairman of the Chicago Mercantile Exchange, Leo Melamed, I was most excited. Leo was a godlike figure in Chicago and was the revered leader of a burgeoning exchange. After a couple of bottles of wine, I exclaimed, "Leo, your Chicago Mercantile Exchange will someday be a large, rather irregularly shaped museum."

"Not in my lifetime, sonny," Leo retorted. "Not in my lifetime."

I was so convinced of that thesis, that I left the floor and moved to San Francisco to be closer to technology. My prediction was right. The floors are now all gone, and all the world's exchanges are basically a server farm.

Because I had traded on Wall Street, LaSalle Street, and Montgomery Street, I knew about as many traders and risk-takers as anyone. As a method of personal diversification, I began pulling money out of my trading account and allocating capital to other traders who were specialists in their own fields. I'm generally known for pioneering a new asset class that would become known as hedge funds. It turns out that one thing I was "good at" was picking risk-takers. Because I was one, and most of my entire circle of friends were trading something, I was able to do my "investment research" in the normal course of the way I ran my life.

That go-to question I learned from Granddad gave me a continually evolving worldview and helped me move into the things I was destined to do. Thanks to him, I view the world now as an ever-expanding opportunity to use your best talent in the best place and at the right time.

Asking will pave a sure and steady road to the achievement of your desires.

Entrepreneur and Dad

Greg Hague is a fascinating man who uses questions to reinvent himself again and again. I (Mark) met and spoke for Greg Hague's original real estate company over forty years ago. I knew he was successful as an entrepreneur, attorney, author, motivational speaker, pilot, world motorcycle traveler, and a radio host teaching entrepreneurship on KTAR radio in Phoenix, Arizona. However, if you ask him, he is first and foremost a dad, who so deeply loved his dad that he wrote a book about him as the greatest of fathers. Currently, he is building a new empire in real estate called *Sell Your Home in 72 Hours*, and as usual, his business is booming.

What Is Your Definition of Happiness? Greg Hague's Story

I was super successful and had exceeded all my dreams. But suddenly I found that I just didn't feel as happy as before and started feeling bored. I had a big, beautiful home; nine motorcycles; and two airplanes. I traveled everywhere, and yet something was bothering me. Fortunately, I went to lunch with an extremely successful friend. The smartest man

I know other than my father. His name is Bruce Redding. Bruce and I shared the love of motorcycling, business success, and life. He asked me the most important question I had ever heard (which I now repeat to myself often): *"What is your definition of happiness?"* I didn't know. I really couldn't answer. So, he gave me his.

"Greg, happiness is a deep sense of satisfaction that comes from a pursuit of worthwhile goals of your own choosing. What's happening is that you have confused pleasure and purpose. You are trying to get happiness through the pleasure of buying stuff and taking trips, and that does not work. Happiness is waking up every day with purpose. It can be about building a business, seeing the world, learning everything about the world; it can be about making a nonprofit amazingly successful; but you've got to have purpose, or you won't be happy. What is wrong with you is that you have lost your purpose! Purpose is the cake, and pleasure is the icing on the cake."

That question and his guiding answer changed my thinking and my life. I now know that I have to have a purpose to be a happy guy. Daily I ask myself: "What is my purpose? What am I trying to accomplish today that is bigger than just me, that drives me?"

People ask why I've been so successful in each business I've created. My answer is all business success is achieved by great marketing. And great marketing is about asking the right questions. I learned from Bill Bartmann, a billionaire and friend who was called "The Comeback Kid," that I needed to do what he called "sliver marketing" to a very specific demographic. I needed to market and speak specifically to a customer's exact pain point. That's what I am using in my *Sell Your Home Your Home in 72 Hours* campaign, and it is starting to sweep the nation.

I started it in my home area of Paradise Valley and Scottsdale, Arizona. I proved that it works with minimal viable testing that was inexpensive, and yet the results were phenomenal. Now, I have expanded my marketing into Tucson, Arizona; Las Vegas, Nevada; and San Diego, California. My system works, and I plan to offer it to all the 1,300,000 licensed realtors in America. Because, for the most part, agents are starving. I want to help make a difference for those people. I teach every one of my agents to ask themselves, "What is my purpose?" That you've got to have a purpose. You've got to have a purpose of accomplishing something bigger than just making a lot of money. My purpose right now is not building a real estate firm; rather it is showing the world that with my seventy-two-hour selling systems, I have developed a watershed system that transcends the hundred-year-old system we have been using to create more success for every realtor!

Most people make a product and then think through the marketing. I always start with the marketing and test that first. It's like asking the market, "Do you like this or not?" If it works, with minimal viable testing, then, and only then, I complete the product or service. Whenever I have a business idea, I quickly run it through my system of dimensional thinking to be a creative marketer. My questions are: "Can it be bigger or smaller?" "Bigger budget or smaller budget?" "Faster or slower?" "What is the opposite way that it's currently being done?" "What if I did it a different way from the traditional way?"

Years ago, after college, I went to law school in Ohio and passed the bar exam. But in the eighties I moved to Arizona and started successfully selling real estate, and so I put my law license into inactive status. Then the 2008 crash hit, and no one was buying or selling real estate. The values had dropped over 25 percent, everyone was miserable, and I was without purpose—and I'm a purpose guy. For me, that means redefining it as life changes. So, I returned to my question. My answer this time was to reactivate my law license; I had always wanted to practice law, which was why I had gone to law school in the first place. The law bar exam is second hardest after the medical exam. Only 65 percent pass, and those are younger people who just finished three or more years of school. I was sixty years old at the time, and I hadn't been to law school in what seemed like forever, so I bought fifteen hundred dollars' worth of books and study guides and enrolled at the law school to take the four-and-a-half-month bar exam cram course in order to just brush up and see if I could pass the exam course.

Mind you, the rest of the people in this course were like twenty-two years old. After the second week into it, Jo Hudson, the instructor who's also a prosecutor in town and one of nicest people in the world, called me and very respectfully said, "Greg, you are such a nice older guy, but you have no chance. You can't learn everything you need in four months. It's impossible. You will never pass the exam. Don't go; don't waste your time. I looked you up. You have a history of success. Don't beat your brains out. I am just being courteous to you."

I was pretty depressed that night, but after mulling it over, I thought, *Bull crap! I'm not just gonna give up!* But I knew she was right about a couple of things. I was getting killed in the practice exams. Even by the second week, I was not even in the realm of where you needed to be. So, I took a few days away from it, and I developed a new study system that I called the four-X system of accelerated study. It consisted of five different ways to learn twice as much in half the time and remember it better. It was my goal to develop something that would work for me, that would accelerate my learning, to see if that would get me a pass on the exam. So, I outlined the whole thing and started studying that way. I went back to Jo and said, "I'm hanging in there!

"Okay," she said, "it's all good." Lo and behold, about a month later she called me and said, "I gotta tell you, whatever you're doing might actually be working. You have a chance. Just keep at it because you're starting to test a lot better."

I studied fourteen hours a day. All I did was study day and night; even while I was working out; during breakfast, lunch, and dinner, I just studied, studied, studied using my system. I only went to two movies and out to dinner three times in four months—my only social activities during that time.

By the time I took the exam, I was burned out. I finished taking it and went for a one-month motorcycle ride around Africa, while I had to impatiently await the results. I was sweating bullets when I went to the Arizona Supreme Court website after I returned from Africa to view my results. Out of three hundred and fifty who took the exam, I was number one. I started crying. I got huge publicity, and I was awarded a job at the top law firm in town. I was flooded with legal business. I loved it and practiced law for two and half years. It was a great chapter in my life.

After successfully practicing law for those few years, I found a new purpose to drive me. My purpose was to write the best book on fathering ever. The book is called *How Fathers Change Lives* and is a collection of fifty-two examples of doing it right that are fun, inspiring, and heart-touching life lessons.

I was so inspired by talking about these life lessons that I became a motivational speaker. I taught that it is important to be well educated and it is more important to be smart. So, I built another company called RapidFire Books to help individuals become smart in the shortest amount of time possible. I read and digested the best business books ever written. I recorded three two-minute audios of the wisest takeaways from each book. My smart "sliver marketing" tagline was: "When you're hungry for knowledge but starved for time—RapidFire Books delivers three times a week, two minutes at a time, directly into your phone, a smart condensation of easily digested sound bites on Monday, Tuesday, and Wednesday. In one year, you drink in fifty-two different great business books." I gave it away free. It was super popular. I had a hundred thousand subscribers virtually overnight.

The bottom line is that asking and answering my question gives me clarity of purpose. For me, my purpose is always tied to not just making myself better but also everyone around me better. I love new ideas and challenges. I love niche ideas. I work with sublime intensity, focusing continuously on what I'm doing. I am dependable, and I try to set the highest work ethic for everyone around me. I make it all fun! The key is to remember to ask yourself what your definition of happiness is so that you stay connected to your purpose!

> *Some men see things as they are and ask, "Why?"*
> *I dream things that never were and ask, "Why not?"*
> —ROBERT F. KENNEDY

Too Isolated to Ask?

As the internet and social media have increasingly "connected" people from around the world, it seems that people are feeling lonelier than ever. This is something that is puzzling in so many ways. When we were young the only chance you had of connecting with someone, if it wasn't in person, was to attempt to call them on a telephone land line—hoping that they would be near the phone at the precise time you called and that they wouldn't be too busy to get to the phone or too far away from it to hear it. Often, to get ahold of your friends, you would run down the street or hop on your bike to go find them. You would either knock on the door and make plans to get together later, or hopefully you were both finished with your chores and could run off to play.

Even as preschoolers Mark and I (Crystal) each have clear memories of our lives as youngsters—feeling bored because elder siblings weren't home and telling our mothers we were going to walk to a friend's house to see if they could play. As young as age four, we had to put ourselves out there and bravely toddle down the street to see if there was someone to socialize with. Most of the time, to connect with someone, you had to physically be in their presence because there weren't any digital or virtual options to do so. This lack of virtual connecting or entertainment forced us to come together and to really get to know each other. There was nothing else to do. With no screens to look at, we had to look at each other. We had to try to understand each other. What was important? What made us happy or sad or caused us to laugh or cry? We couldn't friend or unfriend each other with a touch of a button. To have a friend, you had to invest in another human being. You had to explore each other's personalities and experiences, ask the thousands of questions and care about the answers in order to build something called real friendship. Because we were up close so much of the time, it was difficult to be artificial in your presentation of you. For example, as one of nine siblings, my mom had strict rules about doing your share of the chores. If my best friend, Janet, showed up in the middle of that, often she got stuck working beside me to finish faster so we could take off and have some fun. In Mark's case, after one of his best buddies would eat at their kitchen table, his father would often think of a task that needed to be done. As much as he loved hosting the young men for a warm meal, he also loved sharing the same lessons of responsibility he expected his own sons to learn. As soon as lunch was finished, he would put his hands on their shoulders and say, "It's time to go mow the lawn." They were happy to help.

There was nothing glamourous about doing other people's chores. But those are the things we did for each other because we knew there was a price to friendship, which we were happy to pay.

Being a real part of each other's lives allowed us to ask more of each other. We could ask each other to keep one another's tender secrets and to believe in each other's dreams. We provided the feedback and support that all young humans need to prop each other up and navigate our way through to adulthood.

It's sad that people are so isolated these days. We're not gathering as a society like we have done in the past. Civic clubs like Rotary, Kiwanis, and Lions clubs, that in earlier days were the heart of the social community, are reporting such declining membership numbers they don't know if they can survive. Church membership for all religions is down drastically. In the past twenty years the drop-off has accelerated, with a 20-percentage-point decline since 1999 and more than half of that change occurring since the start of the year 2000. Belonging to clubs and churches used to give us an instant community with whom we shared common beliefs, interests, and a shared sense of concern for each other and the community. As we move away from that kind of real-life sharing and caring, our levels of depression are rising.

NBC News published an article on May 11, 2018, that covered recently published findings from health insurance provider Blue Cross Blue Shield regarding depression. The findings showed that major depression is on the rise in all age groups. The data doesn't even include unreported depression or those without a commercial health plan, which means the problem is way underestimated, but the statistics are startling. Why are so many people suffering in this way? Dr. Laurel Williams, chief of psychiatry at Texas Children's Hospital, says, "There is a lack of community. There's the amount of time we spend in front of screens and not in front of real people. If you don't have a community to reach out to, there's no place for your hopelessness to go."

Unplug to Bond

One of our goals with each other and our family is to try to unplug as much as possible. While we're all on the digital hamster wheel, there's nothing that says that we can't jump off as often as possible. When we're really feeling burned out, one of our favorite things to do is to take a cruise. Why a cruise? Because when you're out in the middle of the ocean, internet service is terrible. They say they have it, but you know what? It doesn't really work because you're not close enough to any infrastructure to make it work well. The first time I realized my internet wouldn't work on a cruise I was irritated. Then I realized it was exactly what we needed. We needed to unshackle ourselves from the handcuffs and ankle chains called our cell phone and computer. Just for a week. It's amazing how relaxed you become when you do it.

The last cruise we took was a ten-day sail through the Greek Isles and the southern tip of Italy. There was a collection of couples and families on board from all over the world. One afternoon we walked to the outdoor café at the back of the ship to get an iced tea and a snack while enjoying the endless ocean views. As we passed one of the salons, people were lined up for a bingo tournament. There were husbands, wives, kids, grandmothers, aunts, and cousins all coming together to play. We started taking note of the many collections of family and friends all over the ship, sitting at tables playing cards, laughing over stories, eating, playing basketball, strategizing over giant chess on the deck, or lounging by the pool. They were connecting in the way that families connected before the digital age. On the tender boat from the ship to the port in Santorini, Greece, we started chatting with one family that had twenty-nine members on the cruise from ages ten to fifty-five. They were celebrating one of their family member's fiftieth birthday. There were a dozen teenage cousins who had come on this two-week-long venture to hang out together in ten different countries. What a joy it was to see them laughing, bonding, and hanging out together, as they navigated through their Mediterranean adventure.

There is truly nothing more important to your happiness and success than being with other individuals or groups of people. It is through our sense of connection and belonging that all these other experiences and breakthroughs can occur. Find out where there are network gatherings that you can join. Search for a place of worship where you feel comfortable and safe. Keep in mind that others need you too, so never hesitate to reach out to foster new relationships or rekindle old ones. We need each other as we bring our dreams to life. You never know what person or people are meant to be part of your destiny unless you open your heart and mind to that possibility.

No man is an island
No man stands alone...

David Webb is a SiriusXM talk show host, Fox News host and contributor, columnist, journalist, and commentator. He has done appearances on CNBC, CNN International, BBC Radio, BBC TV, NDTV India, Dutch National TV, and KSA2 Saudi Arabia. He has also been featured in media outlets in Germany, Italy, Spain, Japan, France, Australia, Brazil, and Canada.

A Journalist's Way of Asking Better Questions: David Webb's Story

I'm a journalist, so asking questions is what my life and career are all about. I think the most important thing I learned was from a man who helped guide my journalism career. He told me something that is a skill to be used for all good question-asking. He taught me to open up with an initial question, but rather than having a preset question list, let the person's answer dictate your next question. As a journalist, if you really want to get it right and really tell the story, you have to connect to the person or people you're interviewing and let yourself feel and understand the impact of their answers, because *that* is the story. Whether in journalism or business, or just life, often we have preconceived ideas about what people are about, or how a business transaction should go, but if we're only answering our own questions and not listening for a deeper question inside the answer, we're not going to get the same authenticity in the story, the same business result, or the same understanding in our personal relationships.

I deal with crazy events, disasters, earthquakes—all kinds of scenarios that can rattle a person. To stay grounded, I always try to look for the question that wasn't asked or what the situation is that really needs to be presented to the people watching and listening.

For example, several years ago, I was covering the Ferguson riots in Missouri. Chaos had broken out, tear gas was everywhere, and people were rioting; I kept hearing the sound of windows breaking. There were anger and destruction all over the city. And that's the story you usually get from the questions reporters pose: "Here's what's happening; here's how bad it is." I like to go in during the aftermath and talk to the people. The experience of the people involved is what matters. I like to ask them what it's like to be them. I don't want to say, "This is Mohammed at Sam's Meat Market, and his store is ruined. What a tragedy."

I sat down with people in Ferguson and looked a little deeper into their lives. I asked questions like, "How did you build this store? How long have you had it?" Or like the conversation I had with Jeniece Andrews, who lost her business in the riots. When I started asking about her experience, she told me how hard they'd saved up for a long time to build that business. How they were still dealing with the stress and grief of having just lost her father, who had recently passed away. How overwhelming it felt to lose so much in such a short time. Using a deeper kind of questioning, the real story unfolded. These were the humans behind the regular news story, and it was their experience I was after. It was not just about people going crazy and angry over a verdict they didn't agree with. It was about every person who had built lives there and what their lives would look like now.

I look for the stories that tie people together. I ask the questions that aren't being covered by others but that reveal our humanity. And when you ask questions, it's important to keep your eyes and ears open. You learn so much from seeing and hearing their responses. As a journalist I also pay close attention to try to hear and see what my colleagues are doing. When you do this, you get a picture that is bigger than a list of questions. Your mind opens up to a bigger story or a different potential story. One that's not being told but one that people really want to hear. The story that's really being lived out in the lives of the people who are in the middle of it all.

> *He who asks a question is a fool for five minutes;*
> *he who does not ask a question remains a fool forever.*
> —CHINESE PROVERB

An International Game Changer

Internationally renowned marine life artist Wyland is one of the most celebrated and recognized artists of our time. An innovative painter, sculpture, writer, photographer, philanthropist, and filmmaker, Wyland captured the imagination of people everywhere by completing over one hundred monumental marine life murals around the world from 1981 to 2008. The project, known as the Whaling Walls, remains one of the largest public arts projects in history and continues to be seen by an estimated one billion people each year. Wyland has been my (Mark) good buddy for many years. We've painted together, traveled together, and written a book together (*Chicken Soup for the Ocean Lover's Soul*). I have had the great pleasure of scuba diving with him at some of the most beautiful diving spots on the planet. Crystal and I enjoy lingering over meals with Wyland, while we brainstorm about ways to keep our oceans clean and pristine. I happily serve on the board of the Wyland Foundation, which is dedicated to sea life preservation and the cleanliness of our oceans.

Challenge Yourself with Ever Bigger Questions: Wyland's Story

The goal in life is to challenge myself with ever bigger questions, never feel like I have done well enough. I drive myself with questions that drive me to become better as an artist, communicator, visionary, clean water conservationist, and the man to help uninvent plastics.

My art is in the homes of over a million art collectors, in every one of the fifty states and over one hundred countries. My 101 giant Whaling Walls are seen annually by over a billion people.

The biggest challenge question I ask myself each day is, *"How do I use my art to raise awareness of conservation to the entire 7.5 billion people on our beloved Earth?"* My Wyland Foundation creates new projects every year. Our motto is: *Let's Make Every Drop of Water a Clean Drop.* I am planning to build the Wyland Museum of Art and Science on forty acres and help save the planet's water, which is the source of all life.

I find inspiration by challenging myself with questions that require gigantic visionary answers. I asked myself, "How can I engage the entire world to love and protect the oceans?" I knew the answer would be found through art and science. The answer came to me in a vision. I would paint one hundred ocean murals around the world. I completed my goal in twenty-seven years, by 2008. One of those was a canvas over two thousand feet long in China during the 2008 Beijing Olympics. I invited children from all 212 Olympic countries, from Afghanistan to Zimbabwe, to paint parts of the nearly half-mile-long canvas. We called it *Hands Across the Ocean*, signifying that water connects all the people in all the countries around the world. The very next day, after we dedicated the giant mural, Whaling Wall 100, I unveiled the first of one hundred monumental sculptures called *Faster, Higher, Stronger* at the Beijing International Sculpture Park. It was the official sculpture for the Olympics, featuring three life-size dolphins riding the energy of an epic wave in bronze.

I was born in Detroit, Michigan, at a time when many people my age became factory workers. I didn't like the idea; I wanted to become an artist. My first-grade teacher said, "Wyland, you have great artistic talent. You could become a great artist." I was so pumped up to hear her in belief me.

In junior high school I had art expositions, inviting my teachers, neighbors, friends, and everyone to buy my original oils for twenty-five dollars, and fifty years ago, that was a lot of money for a kid. In my home city, I was asked to paint a mural on the Dairy Queen, so I painted a snowy Alps scene on a wall. After I did the mural, it inspired people to become hungry for ice cream. They thought it would take three weeks—I finished in three days and got one hundred dollars. It ultimately inspired my vision to paint my first Whaling Wall mural in Laguna Beach, California, in 1981.

My new vision is to finish one hundred monumental sculptures in major cities around the world. Ten of them will be underwater, so you'll have to dive or snorkel to view and appreciate them. Each sculpture will feature endangered species from the UN red list. The one hundred sculptures will be monumental, some larger than life size in bronze, marble, or stainless steel and other materials. These public art sculptures will hopefully inspire a generation to see the animals in a new way and to take action to ensure their survival. I am just finishing a twenty-five-foot orca whale for the City of Seattle, Washington.

One of the most troubling issues about which I ask the question daily is, "How do I help uninvent plastic?" In the world's food chain, small fish eat plastic and are eaten by bigger fish. Ultimately, we consume those fish and the plastic in them. Research is now showing that humans have way too many plastic chemicals in their bodies. There are plastic islands in the ocean as big as the state of Texas. I have started a grassroots movement to get people to change from plastic to glass, aluminum, and organic materials, or to use reusable, rather than disposable, items. I am working with companies and encountering great cooperation. I've asked myself, "How can I build bridges not walls?" We all need to work together for a healthy planet. The seeds are planted with this idea, and it is quickly taking root.

My art promotes itself not just because of its quality but also the importance of its message. Every day, tens of thousands of people visit Wyland.com, which tells me people really do care about these issues. I want to inspire everyone to become water wise and aware of all the life on Earth. I want every citizen of the planet to get on board to clean and save the water of the Earth—it is the only water we have. We don't get one drop more.

I bring art and conservation together and invite kids everywhere to paint with me and listen to me speak about why we need to clean and save the oceans and the species that live there. So far, I have had over one million children paint with me while doing these bigger-than-life projects. When asked, I teach the kids that the pinnacle of success is doing what you love to do, whether you're paid or not, appreciated or not, and respected or not.

I constantly ask myself, "How can I think bigger, do more good, and inspire others to do the same?" I truly believe that if you put good out, it comes back tenfold. I am sixty-three and just beginning. I'm going to keep asking the challenging questions that will ensure our future looks ever brighter. My biggest focus is on our youth. It's up to us to mentor and inspire them to change the world with our support!

> *People travel to wonder*
> *at the height of the mountains,*
> *at the huge waves of the seas,*
> *at the long course of the rivers,*
> *at the vast compass of the ocean,*
> *at the circular motion of the stars,*
> *and yet they pass by themselves*
> *without wondering.*
>
> —St. Augustine of Hippo

The Creative Power of Asking

Asking has creative power. Whenever we are asking for something that is either good or bad, we give life and possibility to our asking. Many people ask negatively, saying things like: "Flu season is coming; I wonder if I'll get the flu?" "I haven't gotten any business breaks. I wonder if my business is doomed to fail?" They are asking negatively and thus receiving negatively.

Asking prophesizes your future. Prophesize something good through the way you ask because life's provisions, in all forms, come from asking.

You've got to ask in the direction that you want to go in life. You can't ask "what if I go bankrupt?" and expect to get rich. You can't talk sickness and get health. You produce whatever you ask for. The right kinds of questions to ask yourself are things like: "Five years from now, who do I want to be? What do I want to do? What do I want to have in my life?"

There are an infinite number of asking possibilities. Here are some thought stimulators that will evoke your thinking. We ask you to write your own. Put them in your journal to start weaving them into your future reality. When you own the idea and embed it deep within your mind, it manifests as your chosen destiny.

I ask for complete blessings over my entire life and future.
I ask for financial abundance and prosperity.
I ask to make my great dreams a reality.
I ask to be creative and original.
I ask for passionate purposefulness.
I ask for great plans for my future.
I ask to know my own value system.
I ask to be delivered from lack, limitation, and shortage.
I ask for forgiveness.
I ask for love.
I ask for joy.
I ask to be happy and make others happy too.
I ask for windows of opportunity.
I ask for accomplishments and achievements.
I ask to be a wealth builder.
I ask to thrive and prosper.
I ask for the right breaks.
I ask to become debt free, stress free, and set free.
I ask for favor in my future.
I ask for the right relationships.
I ask to be a people builder.
I ask to feel good about my life.

I ask to be calm and peaceful.

I ask for faithful friends.

I ask to fulfill my destiny.

I ask to discover my hidden talents, skills, and abilities.

I ask to be a great contributor.

I ask to be philanthropic with 10 percent or more of my wealth.

I ask to be victorious in all that I do.

I ask big, think big, and receive big.

I ask for God's help and get it.

Speaker and author Mitzi Perdue is a businesswoman, a master storyteller and an accomplished artist. She holds degrees from Harvard University and George Washington University, is a past president of the 35,000-member American Agri-Women and was one of the U.S. Delegates to the United Nations Conference on Women in Nairobi. She currently writes for the Academy of Women's Health, and *GEN, Genetic Engineering & Biotechnology News.* Mitzi is the daughter of one family business titan (her father founded the Sheraton Hotel Chain) and the widow of another (her late husband was the poultry magnate, Frank Perdue), and she is also a businesswoman in her own right. She started the family wine grape business, now one of the larger suppliers of wine grapes in California.

Mitzi likes nothing better than to share insider tips for successful family businesses. Her family of origin (the one that started the Sheraton Hotels) began with the family business, Henderson Estate Company, in 1890, and her Perdue family started in 1920 in the poultry business. These two families have a combined tradition of 222 years of staying together as a family. Mitzi also speaks on how to make your family business last across the generations.

We met Mitzi through one of our close friends and from the first time we all got on the phone together, we knew we were kindred spirits. It was delightful to discover that we share common values and are dedicated to many of the same initiatives. We're already making plans to combine our collective visions and efforts to make the world a better place in every way that we can.

Illuminating Questions from a Family of Business Titans:
Mitzi Perdue's Story

My father, Ernest Henderson, was the co-founder of the Sheraton Hotel chain. I think my father particularly enjoyed the realization that as the youngest of his five children, I was absolutely fascinated by his success. It was exciting to me as a child to grow up with a family in the hotel business. Being the daughter of somebody who was the co-founder of a hotel chain meant that wherever we went, we stayed in presidential suites and were treated wonderfully. People paid deference to my father that I thought was extraordinary, so I was endlessly curious about what led to that much success.

My father was very kind to me and very patient with my curiosity. He would fully answer every question I had. There would be variations on it but actually, all the questions boiled down to the same question. That question was, "What made you successful?" I remember in one such discussion, he said that he felt his competitors in the hotel industry would go for a deal that came available if the odds were one in twenty or maybe even one in forty. They may or may not take it, but somewhere around one in forty when the odds became greater, he felt his competitors in the business would drop out. His risk/opportunity philosophy was different than theirs. He told me that if the reward was big enough, he'd go for odds that were one in a hundred.

That influenced me the rest of my life because numerous times, I have tried things that were real long shots and very often they didn't work. But once in a while, dear heaven, they *did* work. So, I try my best, as a result of that conversation, not to be discouraged by long shots if the reward is big enough. Another question I would ask my father was, "What made Sheraton grow?" He told me that he had the equivalent to the "secret sauce" for success, which was: He was obviously very good management and he was extraordinarily good at selecting excellent people who worked under him. In fact, he said that that Sheraton success at every level came from the people who worked for the company. But the part that I memorized, and it's influenced me for the rest of my life, was when he told me that Sheraton grew in part because as a negotiator he never wanted to be "a shark."

He said when he was negotiating with somebody, he would always leave something on the table. He wouldn't drive the hardest bargain. That his goal was for both sides to the negotiation to walk away not just content, not just happy, but ideally, they would be ecstatic. So, I asked about that and he said, "In every negotiation you can drive the hardest bargain possible, and you can make more money short term. But long term, it's different." Developing a reputation of being somebody who is eminently fair and generous meant long-term success. That meant he would be the first choice when an attractive hotel property came up for sale. To give an example, suppose there's a widow and maybe she's inherited two or three hotels. She's gotten on in years and she doesn't want to run it herself. She asks her lawyer or whomever her agent is to handle it for her. Whoever was on the other side of the table from my father probably chose him first because they knew that he was going to be generous and fair. That meant, as he told me, that he regularly got first pick of all the best properties. So, a short-term sacrifice of not driving the hardest bargain was probably one of the most important ingredients in his secret sauce.

At the time of his death in in 1967, our family owned four hundred hotels. People sometimes want to know why Sheraton was picked for a name. I like this question and the answer to it because it reveals something about my father. When he bought his third hotel it was clear to him that he needed one name for advertising purposes. He had just bought a hotel in Springfield, Massachusetts that had a ten-thousand-dollar neon sign, which back in the nineteen-thirties was a lot of money and it was also the most current technology. As a good New England Yankee, he didn't want to tear down the neon Sheraton sign, so that's how the Sheraton chain got its name!

When I was thirty-four I had a Harvard degree, I had a father who was incredibly successful as co-founder of the Sheraton hotel corporation, and yet with that kind of background, both resources and education, I looked around my life and I realized I wasn't doing anything with it. I had always wanted to be a writer. I had always wanted to be in television. The question that was kind of rolling around in the back of my mind was, "Why am I not doing anything with my education and background?" At this time, I was growing rice in northern California. I'd done it for years. A tenant farmer on my rice farm had an unusually extraordinary background. He had an IQ of over two hundred points. That puts him twenty points above Einstein! We know that he truly had that high IQ because *Psychology Today* even wrote a story that included a mention of him. I knew that his life plan was to write a great book because he was aware of his most unusual IQ and he felt he owed it to the world to give back in some way. The best way he could think of doing it was to write a book. He even had a title for it. It was going to be called *Life—An Owner's Manual*.

He had been collecting information for the book since his early twenties but at that time he thought, "I'm too wet behind the ears. It would just be too presumptuous for me to write a book called *Life—An Owner's Manual* at age twenty." At age thirty he felt the same way. At forty he felt the same way. At fifty he felt the same way. Suddenly now at sixty-eight he hasn't written his great book, even though he has a whole garage full of file cabinets with information for what was going to be the great book. Well, at sixty-eight he was diagnosed as having terminal heart disease. Then one day he was told by his doctor that his arteries were so occluded that they didn't think they could get him to the Mayo Clinic in time to have quadruple bypass surgery. So as far as he was concerned that was a death sentence. By wonderful coincidence, I had heard of something called the Pritikin Clinic which has a great record for dealing with people who are very ill with heart disease. I persuaded him to go there for a month. An amazing thing happened. At the end of the month, this man who was dying lost twenty pounds and he was now able to walk four miles without pain. His doctor said, "This is a miracle!" Once he came back, he told me that as far as he was concerned, he was cured! I said to Peter, "This is the most wonderful news I've ever heard in my life! Write your book!" And his answer was, "I'm almost ready to do it. I just have to do a little more studying." And at that point, I realized I was talking to the world's greatest under-achiever, because he never was going to write this book and he never did, even though he lived another twenty years.

I began wondering what held Peter Smith back. And I came up with an answer and I knew him well enough, I'd stake my life on the accuracy of what I'm about to describe. I think he never even started writing the great book because he was afraid of failure. He was afraid that if he put his whole soul into writing this book and it didn't work out well that he couldn't stand it.

The result?

He did the one thing that guaranteed failure. He didn't try.

That experience brought me to *the* question that turned my life around. I started asking myself, "Am I the same as Peter Smith?" "Am I so paralyzed by the fear of failure that I'm not trying to do the things I'd most like to do?" Well the answer was a great big resounding capital Y-E-S! I determined that fear of failure had kept me from auditioning for television or just sending in articles to local newspapers or magazines. I decided at that point, the question was certainly, "Am I afraid of failure?" and since the answer was definitely *yes*, what do I do about it?

I decided to redefine failure. I made a conscious decision that every time I got turned down, I wouldn't say "Oh, I've failed." No! I'd say, "I'm paying my dues. This is a badge of honor that I've tried." So, I redefined my fear of failure. Failure for me up to that point in my life was getting turned down. Instead, I redefined failure to be, *You didn't try as hard as you could. You didn't put yourself out on a limb. You didn't give it everything you've got.*

Let me tell you what happened within the space of one year of having reversed my definition of what failure was. I started out immediately submitting articles to the local newspaper. They got published. I submitted articles to the local inflight magazines. Those got me to be invited to be on the local farm show at the CBS affiliate in Sacramento. Normally I would have been too terrified to appear. But having redefined failure, failure would be *not* trying. So, I had the equivalent of an audition and at the end of it, the station manager at the CBS affiliate in Sacramento asked, "Would you like a job in television?" I went from being somebody who was actually so shy that it was hard for me to use the telephone, to somebody who became a broadcaster all in the space of one year.

At one point I realized that what I really wanted to do was public speaking in addition to doing television, but I didn't have a preparation for it. So, I began taking courses. I took The National Federation of Business and Professional Women's Club's course called the Individual

Development Class. After that I took the Dale Carnegie public speaking course. I took the Dale Carnegie salesmanship class. I took the Dale Carnegie management class. Eventually, between preparation and being willing to go out on a limb, I not only got a job in television, a job at Capital News in California, but it also led to my having my own show on the Coast to Coast radio network. These were all things that I never would have tried before if I had allowed my fear of failure to guide me. With this new philosophy, my successes continued to add up. I had always been a somewhat ambitious person, but now I was willing to put myself out there in a new way. I decided to run for office with our oldest and largest farm women's organization, American Agri-Women. It had thirty-five-thousand members at the time. First, I ran for second vice-president, then first vice-president, and eventually I became president. These are situations in which you can fall flat on your face. Along the way I actually did fall flat on my face numerous times, but the end result was success beyond anything I've ever dreamed of because finally I dared to ask people for what I wanted. I dared to go out on a limb, I dared to follow through. I dared to learn the skills I would need for the positions I wanted. I would describe my life right now as one that's satisfying, one that I'm happy with. But I wouldn't be in that position today if I hadn't dared to redefine failure.

In 1988 I met my husband Frank Perdue. I was living in California growing rice and he was living in Maryland growing chickens. Perdue is the largest producer of organic, antibiotic-free chicken today. We were both invited to a party in Washington DC. I had to leave the party early and he arrived late. We met and introduced ourselves, but our time there together overlapped by only ten minutes. During that ten minutes we quickly established that I was in rice and he was chicken. That was funny to us. We got on an unlikely subject in the first five minutes, about why we would never consider the possibility of marriage again because both of us had been unhappy in our previous marriages. Both of us felt that marriage was an institution designed to make people miserable and we would never ever do it again. Then we began discussing how this is unfortunate because companionship would be nice, love would be nice, but neither of us could ever trust anybody again. Then he looked down at me and he said, "I believe I could trust you." I looked up at that beautiful, handsome face and blurted out, "I believe I could trust you." Then in the next four minutes we're talking about what our marriage would be like. It would be supportive and not competitive. We would be there for each other for the good times and the bad.

At that time, I was president of American Agri-Women and I had a whole speaking tour scheduled between Washington DC and California, so I wouldn't get back to California for ten days. This was before cell phones. When I got back to California there were all these "While you Were Out" slips saying that Frank Perdue had called. He called again when I returned and we both agreed that we'd never been more serious in our lives. That we were going to marry. I went back to see him several weeks later. When I had known him something like five hours, he gave me my engagement ring which is a large near-perfect emerald from the ship Atocha, which was a treasure ship that sank in 1622. Frank was one of the financial backers for recovering it and that's how he came into possession of this amazing emerald.

I went back to California. I had to wind up my television show, my radio show, my newspaper, and my farming business. Then I came back to see him. This was the third time I've seen this man in my life. Our church had a six weeks prenuptial counseling period and we wanted to start the clock ticking. One of my favorite moments in life was when we agreed to meet at Reverend Draesel's rectory. We both arrived at the rectory and Reverend Draesel looked at us and he said, "Oh, I'm so happy for both of you! How long have you known each other?" I said, "Well, do you mean in person? He said, "Well, yes," and I looked at my watch and I said, "Thirty-six hours."

Although we'd known each other in person for only thirty-six hours, we had talked on the phone an hour or two every night for about three or four months. I think I'd recommend that to all couples. It gave us quality time to just talk and get to know each other. We both made up our minds we were going to be as honest as we could conceivably imagine being. To tell the bad things as well as the good things because we'd both had previous unhappy marriages and we didn't want any surprises. So, through these deep phone conversations, we actually got to know each other pretty well by the time we met in Reverend Draesel's office. Six weeks later, we married. It makes me question what the whole universe is about because how could we know that we could trust each other so quickly? I don't understand that but nevertheless it was the right choice. My seventeen years with Frank were just the happiest time of my life!

After my marriage to Frank, my two sons, who are both amazingly competent people, took over the rice farms. Once Frank and I were settled into our marriage I missed writing. Once again, I went out on a limb and applied for writing jobs. The one that accepted me first was Scripps Howard. Before, I had been writing on food and agriculture, but the idea I sold to Scripps Howard was to write about the environment. This being early in the environmental movement. Focus on the environment hadn't taken off the way it has since then, so I didn't have a whole lot of competition. I proposed to Scripps Howard that I would create a niche in which I would never write gloom and doom but instead, I would write environmental success stories. Things that would help people feel encouraged or uplifted, or perhaps that they could copy. That formula worked because my boss told me that I was in the top ten out of four hundred, for being picked up by newspapers throughout the country.

I don't think I'm that great of a writer but as far as I know, I didn't have a whole lot of competition. People who would read me would know at the end of an article that they were going to hear about somebody doing something fantastic.

If they were a student, they were going to have some ideas for careers. Not only a career in the environment, but the fields that support the environmental studies and technologies. As an example, when I would ask mister famous scientist, "What's enjoyable about your career and what do you have to study to get that kind of job?" part of my theory was that a lot of environmental problems are going to take a science component to deal with them. So, I thought that would serve in helping to encourage kids to study science. I'm told that many science classes at the high school level would assign my articles for the student to learn about these exciting things that were happening in the world of environmental studies and technology breakthroughs.

Today, in support of the family business, I also write a monthly newsletter for our employees at Perdue Chicken. I visit different parts of the company and tell all the amazing things that they're doing. There are twenty-two thousand Perdue associates or employees at the company. I will interview somebody who is doing something amazing. It might be something that they're doing on the volunteer level or it might be something that they're doing professionally. For example, I interviewed the person who was responsible for steering the company into getting awards for Leadership in Energy and Environmental Design (LEEDS). That's a very rare and difficult achievement when you have an operation the size and scale of ours. It was really impressive for me to interview the guy who shepherded that monumental task through to success.

I did another recent article for the newsletter about Perdue being the largest producer of organic chickens in the world. That means that the chickens are fed grains that are non-GMO. No antibiotics are ever given, and instead they are given a healthy important probiotic formula. They're allowed to go outside in paddocks to get sunshine and peck around. It's a pretty wonderful enterprise but it took us somewhere between ten and twelve years to achieve this because if you don't have the right biosecurity it will fail. The head veterinarian involved told me you need a hundred things to go right or the chickens will die. So, if you are a backyard farmer you can do it much more easily, but if you're growing chickens on this scale it takes extraordinary measures to get it right and I love that we got it right! This was largely because of Jim Perdue, Frank's son. Jim has a doctorate in marine biology, so he knows how important this is to the health of people and to the environment. He just soldiered on and today we are the largest producer of organic chicken in the world!

In recent years, I've taken on a project that I believe is critical to the wellness of civilization. That is the effort to end human trafficking. It's easy to think that slavery only existed in the past, but according to the UN, there are 40 million people living in slavery today. Many of these are children in sex slavery. A twelve-year-old girl may be forced to have sex with strangers ten times a day, 365 days a year, whether she's sick or having her period. Her life expectancy is roughly seven years. Unless she's rescued, she's going to die of an overdose, suicide, disease, or murder. The suffering is so cruel and unrelenting and horrible! I want to spend the rest of my life combating this problem.

The idea came to me that people often have valuable items like art or jewelry in storage that they wouldn't mind giving up. I asked myself, "What if we could have an auction in which people could convert possessions into cash, and they could designate that their favorite anti-trafficking organization would be the recipient of this cash?" I began asking for these items from people who were willing to listen. I started getting some fabulous donations.

The auction house Sotheby's liked the idea of a high-end anti-trafficking auction and agreed to forego their usual seller's fee. When PBS heard about some of the high-end donations we were getting, such as a 69.7 carat ruby or twelve historic dinner plates that belonged to Tsar Alexander II of Russia, Burt Wolf from PBS created a half-hour documentary on the Auction that he expects 100 million people worldwide will see.

The Sotheby's auction is planned for 2021. The high-end auction is wonderful because it will get fabulous amounts of money and attention for combating trafficking, but we also want to have an auction that everyone, everywhere can participate in, whether as a donor or buyer. It will have the same approach as the Sotheby's auction, but it will be an online auction. Everyone who either donates or buys can have the satisfaction, maybe even joy, of knowing that they're doing something about one of the ugliest, most horrible scourges that's going on in the world today.

Sometimes people ask me why I'm working on this anti-trafficking effort. After all, I'm a senior citizen and I could be sitting home relaxing instead of traveling this year to Hong Kong, China, Taiwan, Colombia, Tel Aviv, Monaco, and Germany to speak about this issue and to recruit volunteers and donors.

My answer is, I have a purpose in life. It can be summed up in two very simple statements. Increase happiness. Decrease misery.

Throughout my life, I've always tried to follow that dictum. I know if I hadn't come to the point where I faced those two questions that turned my life around, I would have been powerless to do the things I was meant to do. Confronting those life-changing questions: *Am I afraid of failure?* and *What am I going to do about it?* allowed me to challenge myself and redefine what failure was. Because of that I removed the barriers that stood in the way of success and happiness, which allowed me to express all of those things I had previously held back, and to unlock the dreams that were waiting for me to manifest.

Everything you want, you are already that.
—RUMI

Dan Clark is an internationally recognized Speaker, Entertainer, Songwriter/Recording Artist and *New York Times* Bestselling Author. Since 1982, Dan has spoken to more than 3 million people in over 4,000 audiences, in all 50 states, and in 30 foreign countries. Achievers North America and Achievers Europe named Dan one of the Top Ten Speakers in the World. Dan is a contributing author to the *Chicken Soup for the Soul* series and author of twenty of his own bestselling books, including "Puppies for Sale" which was made into a film at Paramount Studios starring the late Jack Lemmon. Dan has been published in more than 30 million books in 30 languages worldwide.

What Is the Punchline? Dan Clark's Story

"What is the punchline?" That is the question I always ask myself, whether I am writing one of my motivational speeches or bestselling books or composing one of my gold-record-winning country songs.

In the world of medicine, we know that prescription before diagnosis is malpractice. Which means that in order to get a better answer, we must ask a better question—life is not about answers; it's about asking a string of the right questions that reveal the right answers. And so it is in writing stories and songs. The punchline is what sells it and drives home the point. It's most easily illustrated in humor. What makes a joke funny is the punchline. What makes the punchline funny is the "setup" that takes you in one direction and then blindsides you by suddenly taking you in the opposite direction. For example: "When my mother was sixty-three years old, she started walking five miles a day. Now she is ninety-one, and we don't know where she is!" Ha! In music: "My wife ran off with my best friend, and I'm going to miss him dearly." Ha-ha! All my compositions, whether they are jokes, song lyrics, or stories, start by first asking a question that reveals and/or inspires a powerful punchline that is so compelling that it begs for a riveting storyline to bring it to life. Most often, this is an entire message captured in a single phrase that pulls on your heartstrings and places in your mind an unforgettable, catchy quote.

In this way you not only begin writing a story or song with the end in mind that focuses on the destination, but more importantly, you begin with the "why" in mind that focuses on the journey and storyline. As a professional speaker the goal is to bless, not impress—so listeners remember how they feel more than what they hear. Yes, knowledge is power, but it has no heart. Reason leads to conclusions, but it is emotion that leads to action. Let me illustrate by sharing my most well-known story called "Puppies for Sale," which I wrote at thirteen years of age. Although it was first published by my family in 1968 and was again published in two of my first three books (1982 and again in 1985), I was thrilled when it was accepted into the very first *Chicken Soup for the Soul* book in 1993. I wrote it as an entry for a speech contest to teach the universal principles of empathy and unconditional love. The punchline is set up by the story of a young boy seeing a sign in the window of a pet store that advertised Puppies for Sale. As he walked in, seven puppies came running out, with one little dog badly limping and lagging behind. Immediately the boy asked what was wrong with that one. The storeowner explained that it was crippled and would never run, jump, and play like the other puppies. To which, the lad raises his pant leg and shows that he too is crippled and has a metal brace going down each side of his leg. The boy's heart is full of compassion and will love the little dog in a way no one else could. Heroically and valiantly, he responds to the storeowner, stating, "I don't run so well myself, and the little puppy will need someone who understands."

Bam! This is the punchline! And the boy pays for the puppy with every cent he has in his pocket. The story evokes deep feelings each of us have has felt of being rejected, not feeling good enough, or being chosen last in sports, work, or life. The story gives each of us hope that there is someone out there who feels like we feel and will love us and want us in spite of any imperfection. Some of my other punchlines that make my stories memorable include: "I didn't know how to fix the doll; I just stayed to help her cry!" "It was the sickness that made me well." "I like me best when I'm with you." "I want to see you again." "No matter what your past has been, you have a spotless future!"

Without sounding like I'm throwing my parents under the bus, I grew up in a family where I was raised with conditional love. My parents didn't do that on purpose. My older brother was a genius. He is six foot one and has four degrees from major universities. My sister is five foot seven and also a super-achiever genius. She graduated in fashion merchandising design from a university, so she sells real estate. Ha! My younger brother is six foot one with a prestigious MBA and is a superstar investment banker. They all have dark hair and dark eyes. Then I come along as a six foot five blond, blue-eyed athlete. I was always compared to my brothers and my sister, and so I grew up in an environment where I was the different one. I was never good enough. I always carried the mindset that I had to prove myself. I know it's still a demon inside me. My feelings of inferiority spilled over into my relationships. As I got into my dating years, I would talk myself out of asking beautiful women for a date, thinking, *Why would they ever want to go out with somebody like me?* It didn't help that in high school, I was so skinny I had to jump around in the shower to get wet. I had so many pimples that when I fell asleep in my math class, the kids played connect-the-dots on my face. Ha!

Fortunately, I started growing and became bigger, faster, and stronger, and was recruited to play football and baseball by several major universities, including UCLA, Oregon, Arizona State, Colorado, Missouri, and Nebraska. But I ended up at the University of Utah because I followed a girl there. Eventually we broke up, but it worked out for me as I had an invitation tryout with the Kansas City Royals baseball team as a pitcher, and as a starting defensive end I became a projected number-one draft pick by the Oakland Raiders. However, one day in a practice tackling drill, I suffered an injury that left me paralyzed for fourteen months, which cut short my career. Fifteen doctors told me I would not recover, but recover I did. Now that I'm healthy, the two most frequently asked questions I get asked are: "Why did you go to so many different doctors?" and "Why did you stay paralyzed for so long?" The answers? I kept going from doctor to doctor until I found one who believed I would get better (number sixteen). And the reason I stayed paralyzed was because I was asking the wrong questions. I was asking the doctors "how" to get better, when I should have been asking myself "why?" Once we answer "why," figuring out the "how to" becomes clear and simple.

In retrospect, I find it intriguing that although I have been injured multiple times in my life—physically, mentally, spiritually, emotionally, and socially—my resiliency and ability to turn every setback into a comeback are predicated on my lifelong mission to do whatever it takes to get better. Spending my entire life believing I was not ever whole and complete is what gave me the drive and perseverance to keep keeping on. Because of my life experience, not only can I write emotionally stirring stories and songs, but it also has allowed me to raise my four children with the understanding that the only person they need to be better than is the person they were yesterday! One of my favorite quotes is:

"Everybody is a genius. But if you judge a fish by its ability to climb a tree it will spend its entire life believing it is stupid!"

This mindset has definitely infiltrated every aspect of my being, especially as a songwriter. What turns a song into a hit is the punchline, which in music we call the "hook." As a writer, I find music the most difficult to write and yet the most rewarding, both emotionally and financially, because it combines a melody with the spoken word. And to complicate things, there are only twelve notes from which to write songs. Every song ever written was written with the same twelve notes. The only difference between one song and another is the order in which the twelve notes fall and the timing and spacing between them. When we write in English, we only have twenty-six letters in the alphabet from which to work. The same three letters G, O, and D can represent God or dog. And with only three minutes and forty seconds allocated wherein we must start and finish a song, we must edit so "every word pays its own way." Consequently, I have learned economy of words and to be extremely selective and use only emotional and provocative words that evoke feelings and memories and validate the Trisha Yearwood lyric, "The song remembers when." It is for this reason that people use songs, stories, and poems to mark, connect with, and commemorate important milestones in their lives, to keep the memories alive.

As mentioned, the breakthrough to my writing started when I was thirteen years old. My English teacher liked my writing, and she was kind enough and attentive enough to make sure I knew it. She believed in me in such a new and unusual way that it instilled something in me that I didn't see in myself. She continually encouraged me to write stories and made me believe I could become a master storyteller. During the seventh and eighth grades, I wrote "The Circus," "Broken Doll," and "Croak." That ignited the passion and perspective to continue writing through high school and college. During that time, I produced my story

"The Greatest," which was turned into a country hit recorded by Kenny Rogers, and wrote my popular kissing poem, "Mathematical Love."

My "punchline" here is revealed in the question: "What's the difference between a great story writer and a lousy story writer—they have access to the same twenty-six letters in the alphabet?" The answer is: passion, creativity, and imagination. When we ask the compelling question that illuminates "why" a particular message matters, it automatically inspires a punchline that changes the world one song, one poem, and one story at a time!

Life is funny. Just when we think we've got it all figured out, we find ourselves in the middle of an uncomfortable or distressing dilemma or struggle. Here's the truth about life. You never stop learning. You're never finished evolving. Just like you graduate kindergarten, then move on to middle school. Graduate middle school and then move on to high school. Graduate high school and finally perhaps move on to college or technical training. Life will continue to provide you an endless education in stages from which you'll feel fully graduated. Until you start the next part of your education. While you're alive, you're always in training. That is why it's so important to tuck these tools tightly into your tool belt and pull them out often. You're going to need them for the rest of your life. They will help you take another step when it otherwise would seem like there's not one to take. They will help turn up the light in your mind to help clear out the fog. They will provide a step-by-step path to unwind your confusion until you can see the truth in front of you.

Ask Gold Nuggets

- Are you really trying to tap into your own skills and talents to resolve this situation, or are you taking the easy way out?
- What are you best at?
- What is your definition of happiness?
- Are you too isolated to ask?
- To get to the heart of the real story, let people's answers determine the next question.
- Challenge yourself with bigger questions.
- If you're afraid of failure, redefine what failure means to you.
- What is the punchline? Where are you ultimately going with your life story?

2. Ask to Enhance Your Personal Relationships

Having healthy, dynamic relationships with others is crucial to our happiness and well-being. Simply put, we need each other. Without plenty of love, friendship, and social interaction, human beings cannot become all they were meant to be. Certainly, the highest path to our destiny includes life-enhancing, joy-filled relationships!

Boundless Benefits to Asking

- Fewer disappointments and misunderstandings
- Clarification of your own value system
- Shift in awareness from lack, limitation, and shortage
- Forgiveness
- More love
- More joy

- Being happy and making others happier
- Opening windows of opportunity
- Greater accomplishments and achievements
- Becoming a better wealth and business builder
- Thriving and prospering at greater levels
- Getting the right breaks
- Receiving favor in your future
- Fostering the right relationships
- Feeling good about your life
- Feeling calmer and more peaceful
- Meeting more faithful friends
- Fulfilling your destiny
- Discovering your hidden talents, skills, and abilities
- Becoming a great contributor
- Living more victoriously in all that you do
- Receiving more awareness of God's blessings

Connecting to Others through Asking

Asking something of someone requires them to engage. It invites them to share your curiosity, to help understand or solve your problem or confusion, and perhaps even help you form a solution. In other words, the process of asking creates an *immediate bond* between two people. If you have memories as a child of having your questions and requests shut down, it's more important than ever to practice your asking skills. Understanding that our parents and their parents did the best they could from their own state of consciousness, and maybe their questions and curiosities weren't nurtured, so they didn't understand how to nurture yours. It's never too late to sculpt the life that is *your* creation, not another's. Honing your asking skills at any stage of life will help you do just that!

Have you ever been out doing your thing, wrapped up in your own world—just minding your own business—and suddenly someone is there and insists on sucking you into a conversation you didn't want to have? You're reluctant at first, but suddenly you find yourself enjoying it. I (Crystal) can't tell you how many times, in my determination not to deviate from my to-do list, I've braced myself to dismiss someone, so I don't have to spend the time or energy to engage, and suddenly I'm…well, engaged and actually really enjoying the conversation. Ultimately, you walk away and realize that time you spent with that person was worth it. Whether it made you feel a little lighter, made that person's day a bit better, gave you an idea, or just made you smile, there was value in that exchange. I continue to remind myself that no matter how busy I am, or how important it is for me to finish my agenda or accomplish my tasks—people are important. Everyone is important. I've learned so many times, the more I stay open to that reality, the more I'm surprised and delighted by the gift of each person.

My Home Depot Helper

I (Crystal) had just finished a flurried round of shopping through Home Depot—gathering a list of things I needed for my handyman, who was coming later that day. I exited the store with a full cart and pressed my cart across the parking lot to my car. As I popped the lift gate on my SUV, a woman approached me and said, "Can I help you unload those bags, ma'am? It looks like you have your hands full there." I was immediately thankful for her kind offer because my cart was loaded with some heavy items and I was in quite a hurry to get home. I was feeling lucky that one of the workers from the store just happened to be in the parking lot where my car was to give me a hand.

She was chatty in a friendly way, and I instantly sensed her warmth and natural intelligence as she seemed to know just what I needed her to say. She told me her name was Anita. Because I was taken in by her engaging personality, it took me a couple of minutes to realize she wasn't a Home Depot worker. She was a homeless woman. After we got the car loaded together, I thanked her for her help. Then she asked me, "Ma'am, is there any cash you could spare for me? I have a baby in my belly and nowhere to go." I felt her sincerity and felt instant compassion for her dilemma. At the same time, I was fully aware of this common cycle. Street people who beg for money often use it for drugs or alcohol and are in exactly the same place the next day, never advancing themselves beyond this vicious cycle.

When I answered her, I said, "Anita, I'm going to give you twenty dollars right now. But I want to ask you something. What is going to change tomorrow? How is this money going to do you any good if you don't do something different in your life? If you don't make a different decision right now, when you leave me, you will be doing the same thing again tomorrow, and nothing will ever change. Nothing will get better for you. I also want to ask you, what do you want for this little baby you're carrying? Don't you want something better? Doesn't your baby deserve something better than this?"

Anita got teary and started gushing out a very emotional response to me. "I know, I know. This isn't right. I need to change. It's just been so hard, and I'm all alone. Thank you for talking to me. No one ever talks to me. I know I'm doing bad with my life, and I really want to do better."

I told her there was help for her right now at Phoenix Rescue Mission. If she would take one of those dollars and take the bus there, they would help her work out a better plan for her life, if she was willing. She promised me she would do that. She thanked me again and again for taking the time to talk to her. I'll never know for sure what happened to Anita, but I remember to say a prayer for her whenever I think about her. I do know that her question to me that day opened up an opportunity to create a bond between two women who were very unlikely to ever meet. When Anita asked with a combination of humility and boldness if she could help me, I couldn't resist her request. Asking if she could serve me first, softened my heart to fulfill her more important request, which was money to feed herself and the baby growing in her womb. I know by her response that I fulfilled her request beyond her expectations. When she asked to serve me and did so, the bond was formed, and my heart and mind were touched to help Anita find her answers.

Human Beings Are Wired to Help

Human beings are wired to want to help when they can. But people also tend to not want to overstep boundaries in offering help. The difference in the outcome between expecting someone to automatically help you or provide an answer or service and *asking* them to help you is like day and night. Usually, if you don't ask, they won't know what you want and won't want to cross a boundary or impose their help.

Researcher Thomas Moriarty conducted a fascinating study in 1972. The study took place at Jones Beach in New York and was set up to observe the social behavior of strangers. A member of his research team left his radio on his beach blanket unattended while a few minutes later, another member stole the radio. Only one out of five people intervened if the victim had made no previous exchanges with bystanders. However, when the owner of the radio directly *asked* his neighbors to keep an eye on his belongings while he stepped away, people intervened to stop or question the thief 95 percent of the time. The experiment was repeated at automat cafeterias in New York City, where a suitcase was left by a participant in the study and taken by a "thief" participant while the owner walked away for a few minutes. The results were virtually the same. Strangers were far more likely to intervene on another's behalf when they'd been asked by the owner of the item to watch over their belongings. The results of this study support the idea that conflict often prevents bystanders from intervening, but asking ahead for someone's help, even though you've never met them, creates a commitment whereby even a bystander becomes responsive to the needs of a complete stranger.

Think about this study in terms of your own life. We all have troubles, dramas, and needs we'd like to have met. But it's likely, because of the way humans are wired, that they are not going to jump in unsolicited, to help solve your problems or give you the assistance you could really use. How many times in your life have you heard "it's none of your business"? It could be we generally feel like it would be presumptuous to come to someone's aid uninvited and it would be perceived as meddling. So we stand by and give people their space. It's important to remember when people aren't coming to your rescue, offering to assist, or to help you in some way that it's likely because you've never invited them to do so by simply asking.

This doesn't mean it's okay to rush out with an air of entitlement or pushiness, demanding that someone fill our lack, need, or even greed. It means you approach someone with an open, humble, and sincere heart, confident that what you're asking for could possibly make you better, someone else better, or the world a better place in some way, large or small. Ask with confidence—not arrogance— knowing that somewhere out there, at some time, your request is already granted. It simply hasn't caught up to you yet! It is our own

responsibility to make our lives work out in the best way we can—
not someone else's job. Asking is simply a tool that allows human
beings to interact in a way that we can help fill each other's needs
or requests for the good of all without taking something away from
someone.

Asking Opportunities

No matter who you are, what you do, or at what stage of life you are,
recognizing the opportunity to ask will continually advance you to
the next stepping-stone toward your dreams of a better life or better
way of living. When we request, inquire of, and question one another
and allow those answers to come, it brings us to a new understanding
or gives us the feedback to improve a relationship, a project, or a life
goal. Movement in a positive direction toward your dreams, your
goals, and a better quality of life is just a question away. There are
endless scenarios that present wonderful asking opportunities.

- A mother who asks her child how the child feels about their
  relationship
- Business colleagues who ask how they can better support one
  another
- A friend who asks for true insight into a difficult problem
- A corporate executive who asks for feedback to solve problems
  and become a better leader
- A husband and wife who ask each other to see and affirm the
  good in one another
- A teacher who asks a student's opinion regarding the key to
  improving the classroom performance
- A neighbor who asks another neighbor to watch over their
  home
- Network affiliates who ask for referrals for more business

- The doctor who asks the rehabilitation victim his opinion of the most important part of the care relationship
- The high school coach who asks his players if there are personal issues outside sports that affect his performance
- The politician who gets face-to-face with constituents to ask what truly matters to them
- The colleague who asks a friend or colleague to help launch a business idea

Rita Davenport is an award-winning keynote speaker, humorist, and author. Rita is an internationally recognized expert in the principles of success, time management methods, goal setting techniques, creative thinking, and building self-esteem and confidence.

Her careers range from social work and teaching to broadcasting and writing. She produced and hosted her own award-winning television show in Phoenix, Arizona for fifteen years and was viewed in over 32 million homes on her cable television show *Success Strategies*.

She has appeared on over 200 radio and television shows, including ABC's *Good Morning America*, Regis Philbin's show and *The Sally Jesse Raphael Show*. She has shared the speakers' platform with such notables as Erma Bombeck, Art Linkletter, Og Mandino, Dr. Joyce Brothers, Tom Hopkins, Zig Ziglar, Les Brown and Mark Victor Hansen.

How I Missed Out on a Three-Billion-Dollar Business: Rita Davenport's Story

Asking is the most important life skill if you want to be successful. I think we all have heard the saying *you have not because you ask not*. One of the speeches I give to my network marketing audiences is: *Get Your Ask in*

Gear. Most people have such a fear of rejection they won't ask. And if you don't ask, the answer is always no because you have never asked. I think it's the most powerful component of success.

I have a lot of stories where I let myself down because when I did ask, and someone said no...I didn't keep asking. I once took no as the final answer that defined a huge missed opportunity for me. In spite of the tremendous success I've had as a television personality, network marketer, author, and speaker, I still have some regrets of not continuing to ask or find other people to ask when I knew I had something really good to offer. One of the greatest examples I have of letting myself down is, years ago when I did a cooking show on TV 5, KPHO, in Phoenix, Arizona, called *Cooking with Rita*. I knew how popular it was, and I knew that it was something that could really be a huge hit. So, I approached the Meredith Corporation, the company that owned Channel 5, and pitched the whole idea of doing a food network: "I think a food network would be powerful. People eat three times a day. They don't even have sex that much unless they're weird. Will you consider doing this? It will be a great success; I just know it." They just laughed. Their answer was no. I stopped asking.

My cooking show was really fun because I had local personalities, movie stars, and celebrity guests all the time. I had famous cookbook authors, including Julia Child, Jacques Pépin, and Wolfgang Puck. All kinds of interesting, different people came on the show as my guests. There was a live studio audience for each show, and the reception was amazing! Our ratings were fantastic. We had the top-rated local show.

At the time, a great guy named Jack Clifford was general manager at Channel 3, the ABC affiliate in my city. My friends at Channel 3 used to tell me that Jack watched my cooking show every day, even though I was on a different station. "We really thought Jack had a crush on you because we weren't allowed to disturb him when he was watching *Cooking with Rita*," they said. "He would shut the door and *study* your show."

So, as it turns out, Jack Clifford, the man who launched the ground-breaking channel called the Food Network, got the idea from my show, and he admitted it to me when we were both honored at the Arizona Broadcasting Hall of Fame celebration. He and I connected years after he had become a gigantic success with my idea. I told him I was proud of him and once had the same idea to do a food network.

"Yeah, Rita, I stole your idea."

I teased him, "Jack, you know the book *Seed Money in Action* by Jon Speller? He says you're supposed to give something to your source of inspiration. Especially when the inspiration turns into a huge success. You know, I was making peanuts on local television at the time…maybe thirty-five thousand a year. Did you ever think about giving me a little something for the idea?"

"You're right," Jack said. "I should have given you something for the idea. I sold the Food Network for two hundred million dollars, and today it is valued at three billion dollars."

So that was my three-billion-dollar idea that I let slip through my fingertips. Just because somebody at Meredith Corporation said no to me when I asked the first time. Years later, when I ran into one of the Meredith executives at a fundraising event, I told him the story. He smiled and agreed, "Boy, that was our three-billion-dollar mistake, wasn't it?" He said it was just staggering to know they could have had it because they owned other assets like the magazine *Better Homes and Gardens*, and the food network would have been a perfect fit. I shouldn't have accepted the first no. I should have kept asking.

If someone says no, it's usually because they don't *know* enough about your idea. We should not ever let that cause us to stop asking for our dream. We need to keep asking until we find the person or people who see our vision or dream and want to be a part of it. It's amazing, if you watch children, how you can say no to them, and they keep on asking if it's something they really want. They just keep asking and keep bugging until they wear down the resistance of the parents for that candy bar or whatever it might be until they get it. I think children dare to keep asking because they're probably not as damaged from the previous *no*s that they've heard to give up on something. I just think that it's the most powerful thing to see in a child!

So when somebody said no to me in my former network marketing business, I used my sense of humor for support. I'd start laughing and say, "Okay, you're right. I've got to find somebody else who really needs this." I have played all kinds of mental games when someone said no to me. One of the funniest ones that I tell people in my speeches is that, when someone says no to joining your business or buying your product, you can say *to yourself*, "I'm so glad to hear that because you would drag down the reputation of my entire company if you joined my business. So thank you!" In the beginning of my network marketing career, I'd say to myself when someone said no, "Heck, this was only a courtesy call. I was just being nice and sympathetic to you. Was really hoping you would say no. Now, I can mark your name off my list quickly." I liked turning something that could potentially pull me down into something funny. This always worked for me. I teach sales clients to turn the word *no* around: it actually means *on* to the next person.

The point I'm getting to is that the *no*s were motivation to me. We all know every successful person has been subjected to prejudice or felt inferior. When somebody would reject my idea or my presentation or what I was going to do, that would fire me up even more. There's one thing I had that not everybody has. I never thought I was all that talented, intelligent, or good looking, but I always had a strong work ethic. I was never lazy, and I never stopped until I achieved my dreams.

The reason people are so afraid to ask is that they're afraid of rejection. Rejection is just part of the game. It's in direct proportion to your success. You are going to have some rejection for sure when you ask, so you just always say, *"Next!"*

When my son was in the third grade, I was driving him to a skating party. On the way there, he told me he was going to ask a little girl named Nicole to skate with him. I got really nervous because you know how mamas are about their little boys. I was afraid he was going to get rejected and that it would make him weird for the rest of his life! Those little third-grade girls who wear earrings, eye shadow, and high heels at school could really hurt my little boy's confidence! I was a scared mama thinking of how he might get destroyed by rejection if he asked this little girl to skate and she said no.

I worried the entire time he was at the skating party.

When I picked him up afterwards, I said, "Scott, how did it go?"

"Oh, it went good," he said.

"What? Did you ask Nicole to skate with you?"

"Oh yeah, I did."

"What did she say, Scotty?"

"Oh, Mom, she said yes."

"Well, what if she had said no?"

Looking at me, he kind of bent his head over and flipped his hair up with his little hand and said, "Well, Mama, there are seventeen other girls in my class."

Inside, I said to myself, *"Yeah, he gets it!"* If that one little girl had said no to him, there were seventeen other girls he could've asked to skate. He wasn't planning his entire destiny on whether that one said yes or no. It was a proud mom moment since I teach people that when you get a *no* you move *on* to the next person. I'll say when I'm teaching, "There are three hundred sixty million people in this country alone who have never heard of your product, so keep asking to get to the one who says yes."

No is just part of the game; you have to play to win. It just factors in. When you get a no, it's just kind of a test. It also tests your sense of humor. If you don't learn to laugh when you get rejection, then you won't even know how to appreciate it when you get a yes.

"If it's to be, it's up to me." You have to tell yourself that over and over again. Whenever I back away from rejection because it creates fear in me, I remind myself that the word *fear* is actually:

False
Evidence
Appearing
Real

When somebody disappoints me by rejecting whatever offer I might be presenting, I just ask, "Do I really want to let one person shut me down from fulfilling my destiny?" We're sent here with a purpose and all the necessary skills and talents to fulfill that purpose, and our assignment is to develop our gifts and then to give them away. If somebody doesn't spot your greatness, it is because they have no greatness that they are aware of, and you can't depend on someone else's awareness to dictate your life and your destiny. You spot it, you got it.

I think that people are flattered when you ask them a question. Whether it's to sell a product to them or just because you're interested in them. Just like I'm flattered to be asked to be interviewed for this important book. One of the best things you can do to make somebody feel good about themselves is to ask for their input or their opinion.

Many years ago, I interviewed the actor Milton Berle. Afterward, he said to me, "You are the best person who has ever interviewed me."

"Really?" I said. "I'm so flattered! You've been so famous and interviewed by so many celebrity broadcasters. Why do you say that?"

"Because you listen. A lot of times somebody will ask me a question and they won't listen to my answer, but you listen, and then you let me reflect on what I just said before you go to your next question."

I teach people to be nicer than necessary. Part of that is to give them a compliment and to ask questions about them. This shows people you're curious and you care. Truly, everybody wants to talk about themselves. It makes them feel flattered and respected when you want to know more about them. I've always thought that one of the most powerful ways to connect with people and to be successful in life or in work is to ask questions. It has always worked for me!

Ask the right person the right question:
"Does your dog bite?"
"No."
Man pets dog, dog bites him.
"I thought you said your dog didn't bite!"
"It doesn't. That is not my dog."
—Peter Sellers

Why Suffer in Silence?

You need help from your friends or loved ones, but instead of asking, you suffer silently. How many times in your life have you played the lone ranger? You've come into some difficulty, a troubling situation, or a problem you haven't been successful at solving on your own. Yet you avoid doing the thing that could most powerfully start to solve your dilemma. You just can't seem to bring yourself to ask anyone for help or guidance. Through the years, these are some of the reasons people have shared with us for not ending their suffering and just **asking** for help from their friends or loved ones.

- Disgraceful: "I hoped I'd never have to admit it."
- Ignorance/forgetfulness: "I thought you already knew."
- Embarrassing: "I really don't want to talk about it."
- Underestimating or disconnecting from the importance: "It seemed trivial."
- Too upsetting: "I hoped I'd find an answer or solution by myself and not upset anyone."
- Assuming the other person figured it out on their own: "I thought it was obvious."
- Assuming the other person is uncaring or usually in a bad mood and can't be bothered: "They probably won't listen or care."

Many of us face this same resistance to asking. In most cases, the reasons we give ourselves to resist asking for help aren't necessarily true or rational. Often, when we're dealing with a challenging situation, all we need to do is to open a conversation with someone and ask what their thoughts are about the thing with which we're struggling. Asking someone to listen and help you process some of your thoughts around the issue can help you release some of the burden you're carrying alone. You'll not only experience a huge amount of relief, but it can tremendously refresh the way you've been looking at the problem, so you can more easily find a clear path to the solution. With the right amount of preparedness, we can all become better askers and, as we do, see the daily positive shifts that come as we journey across the **ask** bridge to our ultimate destiny!

Bill Lobel

We are blessed to meet some of the best people in the world. Bill Lobel is one of them. Bill is bigger than life. Brighter than bright. Exceedingly well read. Hangs with world leaders. Travels with the rich and famous. Yet in our experience, he is a kind, thoughtful, and compassionate true friend and an amazing listener. Bill is a high-level bankruptcy lawyer in Newport Beach, California. When several people we know, respect, and care deeply got into financial trouble, he was always willing to meet them and help them work out their problem, solve it, or come to a new perspective about it.

Bill has a keen knack for discovering special and unusual experiences, and he takes great joy in providing them to his cherished friends. Together we have enjoyed profoundly interesting conversations over tasty oceanside brunches or one-of-a-kind seven-course meals with exotic tastings. Bill's greatest pleasure is to find these unusual experiences and treat his friends to them. One such experience was an amazing evening where one of the top sommeliers/wine critics in the world served a private dinner and wine tasting in his home. Bill arrived at our house in a limo to make sure we wouldn't be driving back from Los Angeles to Newport Beach on our own. We arrived at the small private event where the sommelier had five-hundred-dollar bottles of wine wrapped up in brown paper. The twenty attendees were to test and rate them against the one hundred-point scale of the number-one wine critic in the world, Robert M. Parker, to see which came the closest. Surprisingly, my (Mark) taste buds rated over twenty wines almost identically to Parker. My ratings were closer than anyone's. In jest, the host suggested I become a taster of wines. As I nursed my suffering through a thick-headed hangover the next morning, I was glad that "official wine taster" never surfaced on my opportunity plate.

As we've seen and experienced our friend Bill's generosity time and again, what strikes both of us even more profoundly is the gentleness this rare man expresses. In his law practice, as he deals with some of the most self-centered, difficult people who exist, he deploys the strength of a lion with the heart of a lamb.

Asking to Get to Reality and Truth: Bill Lobel's Story

As a seasoned business bankruptcy attorney, I have asked, and been asked, a lot of questions. After fifty years of active bankruptcy practice, I have come to understand the repetitive patterns in bankruptcy proceedings on both sides, perhaps better than anyone. I have a series of questions with each and every case that must be asked and thoroughly answered so that I can serve my clients properly. Basically, I represent debtors in bankruptcy court and in out-of-court restructuring. For the most part, in each new case, I already know the judges and the bankers and other lenders with whom I will be meeting again. In court and in settlements, my word is my bond, and it is an important part of the process that what I say is always truthful.

As a high-priced lawyer in the bankruptcy world, I get the immediate attention of the giants in business who are having colossal problems. As a result, I can support my love of fine dining, luxury exotic cruises, deep-sea fishing, and limo rides. But I take my work for my clients very seriously. If I'm on a cruise, I still work four to six hours a day. I am usually successful in court and at talking my clients into settling out of court.

I generally take bankruptcy cases over the fifty-million-dollar mark for people with super-big problems and am involved in a case at the moment in which the individual client has a debt of over two billion dollars. My well-heeled clients are certainly not destitute. They have assets and liabilities in the eight- or nine-figure zone. The problem is that they usually owe more than they can possibly pay. They are often high-flying real estate developers, entrepreneurs, sport promoters, or franchise owners, or they own auto dealerships or other businesses. Their creditors have typically run out of patience and want to be paid back immediately. In these types of cases, the debtor stands to get crushed.

When these industry titans come to me, I do all I can to keep their expectations from getting out of hand. They all know what they own but don't really know who they are about to become through this fact-revealing, soul-baring, and humiliating bankruptcy process ahead. They are used to controlling everything around them with their thinking and their money. By and large, they are males and are narcissists. Unfortunately, they often treat women as objects.

So now begins my pattern of asking the questions. I start by asking questions to gain a total understanding of their financial situation and how they got in trouble. More often than not, I have to ask the same question two or three times to get them to respond fully. They profess they don't know; it is almost always a surprise to them. Most are incurable optimists who have always been able to work themselves out of every jam, until this one. It's the big one they have no way of figuring out. They literally do not realize the magnitude of their problems and always insist it is not their fault. I start by explaining the psychology of what is about to happen, as their lives and lifestyle will be totally disrupted for the next two years, at a minimum. Because they have no grip on the reality of their situation, they often cannot comprehend it.

Most super-star business leaders have a hundred million or more in personal net worth and assume they are safe. What they typically haven't paid attention to is the fact that they personally signed and guaranteed much more debt than the amount of their assets—so say goodbye to the three homes, cars, yachts, ranches, and corporate jet. I tell them that their toys are going to go away. I say grief is going to hit you hard. I humbly ask both the husband and wife to read and take ownership of Dr. Elisabeth Kübler-Ross's four stages of grief, outlined in her bestselling book, *On Death and Dying*. I explain to them that it will be hard for them to accept the truth that chapter 7 or 11 is happening to them. As they sit there in denial, I assure them with all sincerity that I can really help them. I say, "I will tell you the truth: it will be painful and disruptive throughout the process. If you want to be lied to, go hire a litigator and you will lose more and suffer greatly." Most of these people going bankrupt distrust the legal system, a system that they believe is unpredictable, and they don't know whether they will win or lose. They want to get immediately beyond this system and back to business as normal.

On to asking the next question. This is a very important question and goes like this, "Can you please tell me only what you want me to know? I will not and cannot lie for you in court. If you have hidden assets off-shore and tell me, I will be ethically bound to tell the judge, banker, or your creditors. If you don't or won't tell the whole truth, don't hire me. If I learn that you are lying or otherwise not being totally honest, I am obligated to withdraw from this case."

Because they don't know their full business numbers, I ask the next critical question: "Who knows your financial details intimately?" Ultimately, I get to the comptroller, CPA, or in-house accountant—who does know the true financial situation and generally tells me everything. Then comes my next question. "Can I speak to your wife or significant other?" Pretty much without fail, the wife or significant other really has a different perspective on the story and is frequently very enlightening. After that, I ask all the company secretaries, upper corporate staff, and sometimes the vendors everything they know about the situation. I learn more and get the full story and complete picture. I get all the facts. Once I've assembled those facts, I take it a step further. I go out of my way to play devil's advocate and ask myself, "What's my client not telling me? How can I understand this case better?"

My goal is to attempt to settle out of court, so I meet with their lenders, who in some cases earn less per year then my client's discretionary monthly spending. I ask them to give me time to settle on a basis that will be financially better for each lender than they will receive in chapter 11. It's an extended negotiation. Some banks prefer a work-out like that, where the debts can be paid through my client's and my efforts to work to liquidate or pay an agreed-upon amount out of future profits. Many lenders have been involved with me previously in similar situations and know that a negotiated restructuring is a better option than a chapter 11. Other lenders prefer to resolve the issues in court. I say something like: "The debtor owes over five hundred million. That will never be fully paid. My client can come back and succeed as a builder or whatever. But only with your patience, help, and cooperation will you both win. It is truly the better alternative."

Since my clients are almost all narcissists, when I am meeting with the client and his wife or significant other, I tell her what is about to happen and what to expect: "He will love you, but as a warrior used to winning, he will be hurtful in unwarranted ways. He is worried. He is the most vulnerable he has ever been. He will be all screwed up. You can't blame a rattlesnake for a snake bite or him for continually lashing out at you due his narcissism. He unfortunately will mirror the bad things going on his life on everyone close to him, and you are the closest." Wives often get divorced during this time, not because of the loss of money or downsizing of their lives, but because they can't live with a narcissist undergoing hard times. The narcissist will not and cannot look objectively at himself. He simply won't change his lifelong behaviors. So, often the wife has to leave to save herself.

If the marriage starts to unwind, I tell him, "You are extremely vulnerable now. You must double question every decision you make, because there are many who will try to take advantage of you. There are women out there who prey on people in your situation." Unthinkingly, men, especially narcissists, fall for it because they need to feel good about themselves again.

Every client asks how I get paid if they go chapter 7 or 11. I tell them, "It may cost you over a million dollars." The bankruptcy code gives lawyers priority in getting paid. Bankruptcy laws were written by lawyers and confirmed by politicians. If the lawyers weren't protected by the priority payment in the bankruptcy code, getting paid in a bankruptcy case could be difficult.

It is a very interesting and unusual group that I deal with as clients. They measure their lives and histories only by the dollars they have or owe, and not by their own self-growth or development. They have always wanted a bigger boat, bigger ranch, or faster plane, secretly being driven by the knowledge that someone always has something that is bigger, better, or faster. They paid their bills on time, but as their king-doms grew and then failed, oftentimes so did their morality. I tell them honestly their morality is at risk, and that is what they really need to pay attention to now. I know they are so lost in this area and will hit random low points they have no idea how to deal with, so I tell them they can call me around the clock, and I will answer. I always assure them, "I will tell you the truth about what and whom to trust and believe. Remember, you are more vulnerable than you have ever been."

As a fascinating footnote, they feel they created and controlled their world and want to be adequately remembered for doing so. Because most of my clients are seniors, they seem to care deeply about the eulogies that will be spoken over them after it is over. In so many ways they've messed up by seeing their world through the narcissis-tic lenses through which they've viewed their lives. Because of that, they have a profound lack of awareness of the havoc their attitudes have wreaked. In spite of that, they all want people saying exclusively positive things about them when they're gone. The best question I can ask them at that point is "How can you learn the moral lessons that could help you be better remembered in the latter innings of your life?" Getting them to answer that question authentically is probably the best way I can serve them.

Prepare to Be a Good Asker

It's important to prepare to be a good asker. Getting into the **right mindset** and understanding the **power of the tools** and how to navigate through the process are important to manifesting the answers that will continue to guide you along destiny's path.

There are four elements to put into practice to help fortify your results:

1. **Belief:** Believe and trust that the answer is there somewhere— waiting for you. Expect it!
2. **Action:** Keep taking steps in the direction of your dreams even if you haven't received all the answers. Your actions will continue to prompt more questions and open up your curiosity so that your requests and inquiries become bigger and more relevant.
3. **Visualization:** Use the power of your imagination to create positive images and feelings around the answers you seek. Allow yourself to create mental pictures of having issues resolved, relationships healed, wishes completed, and dreams fulfilled.
4. **Prayer:** Never forget the existence and wisdom of a higher power in your practice. The Creator of you, the Universe, and everything else is certainly your greatest and most benevolent ally when it comes to the fulfillment of your destiny!

Now take out your journal and let's work through this exercise together. Write down the categories and answer the questions after:

Define your desires: What is it that you really want? Do want more cooperation? More understanding? More intimacy? More friendship? More riches? More adventure? More love?

Connect to your core beliefs: What is driving your current state? Do you think you're not worthy? Do you think your happiness is your or someone else's responsibility? Do you believe you deserve to have your greatest desires fulfilled?

Understanding someone else's core beliefs: In any relationship, it's important to know where someone else is coming from. How can you better understand the core beliefs of the people who matter to you? Asking is the best vehicle to use to get to new understandings with the people who are important to you in your personal or work life.

Honor your values: "What am I not willing to compromise— ever?" Define it so you can ask for understanding and honoring of your values when you're in relationships and those values are challenged.

Heal misunderstandings: While it can seem like a powerful advantage to hold up your hurt or disappointment as a bargaining chip, it usually leads to deeper turmoil. Ask yourself:

"What does it cost me to hang on to hurt?"
"What would I gain by releasing it and starting with a clean slate?"
"What steps need to happen for me to release this?"

Discover the Truth: Everyone experiences their world from their own particular state of consciousness. What we hold up as truth may be more the result of our own subjective set of conclusions based on our own experiences. This is where asking really pays dividends in relationships. Ask the other person what they think happened. What the experience or reality is to them.

Define the Steps Forward: "Where do I really want to go from here? What do I hope to get out of this experience? What do I see as the best resolution or conclusion? Where do I see myself a year from now? Five years from now?"

We recommend turning to your Ask journal frequently to review your questions and answers. You'll probably begin to see that you're evolving as you go. That you're overcoming some of the hurdles that used to hold you back. Make sure you keep a victory section to acknowledge and remind yourself that, step by step, you are moving into your dreams and toward your destiny!

Lyn Marquis is a career master fundraiser. Her fundraising résumé includes working with Arizona State University as director of the President's Club, where she focused on raising funds for important university initiatives. Lyn learned at an early age from her mom and dad how to effectively ask and answer questions. Mom taught her that asking is how we get to know somebody.

Building Foundations through a Foundation of Asking Questions: Lyn Marquis's Story

People feel that we value them by asking them questions, especially if we are great listeners. It shows that we truly care and are interested deeply in what they have to say and share. Mom taught me that asking will get you countless friends and open the world to you, as well as all you want to be, do, and have.

Dad taught me to ask myself: "Is this the right choice I am making? What are the advantages or disadvantages going to be?" If Dad foresaw a negative ending to my probable choice, he would load his answers to the hilt with disadvantages. It could be emotionally translated to include a real disaster or even the end of my life. Dad's insights and serious parental asking were vivid and totally memorable, and via many unforgettable experiences, asking was inculcated deeply into my mind, memory, and experience, thanks to Dad.

Because my parents were such effective askers, they taught me to effectively ask questions. The act and practice of asking became so natural it led me into philanthropy. In philanthropy I am constantly asking for introductions, help, volunteerism, gifts in kind, meetings, to be on a board of directors, or financial donations. Money often makes the biggest difference to charities and educational institutions. Donators only donate after someone sees the value to them, feels respected, and feels that you care and can be trusted. They want to be remembered from their previous gifting and donations or want to be recognized in some meaningful way, such as having their name on a building to leave a more permanent legacy.

While working zealously very early in my career, my mentor asked me what I wanted. I said to finish my college degree. His next question was, "What are you waiting for? Quit wishing and start hoping. Hope is a verb to strive for something you didn't think was attainable. For you, that's attainable. Remember to strive to become the person of influence, example, and leadership that everyone sees you as already. We are here to support and encourage you." That gave me confidence. Because of his pivotal question, I earned my bachelor's degree from Warner Pacific College and am tremendously thankful. That question and lesson stayed with me, and two years later, after moving to Phoenix, I continued my education, earning a master's degree from University of Phoenix.

ASK!

One of my most memorable philanthropic experiences was one in which I had a dream to create a great summer camp for kids. I began asking for donations. One of my first meetings was with a lady who had a family trust and was exceedingly well off. I was nervous inside because of her reputation and status. We had never met, yet I secured a face-to-face appointment with her. After chatting and sharing my vision with her, I had to ask her for money. I was so nervous that I just could not hide it, so I just admitted it. "That's okay," she said. "How much do you want?"

"Five thousand dollars f-for one kid," I stuttered.

"Absolutely," she answered, "but I want to underwrite the net budget for the entire group of campers. What would it be for everyone?"

I couldn't believe it! I hadn't thought of that, so I asked, "Can I have a calculator and figure it out?" I figured it out right in front of her and told her the amount.

"You will get it," she said and thanked me, and our few minutes were over. I was still happily surprised and a bit shocked! It worked! My fears vanished.

Shortly after I returned to the office, my phone was ringing with a call from the family trust representative. "I represent the family trust of [the woman]," the man officially said, "and she instructed me to send you a check. Tell me how much and to whom to write it out." I was dazed. I just got scholarships for the whole program from one donor for a six-week summer camp. The check was cut immediately. This was such an unexpected and delightful surprise—one that reminded me that it's okay to be nervous when you're about to ask for something important. The important thing is that you continue to move forward with the request.

Later in my life I went to ASU for a job. The lady interviewing me said, "You are in the wrong office." She stood up and walked me across and the hall to the office of the Director of Leadership at the ASU Foundation, and she kindly introduced me to the director, "This lady has perfected her people skills. She likes to work with people and belongs in this engagement department to help donors move up the giving scale." That started a wonderful two-year career in philanthropic engagement at ASU. I got to work with super-givers who loved ASU and wanted to improve it. Whatever was of value to them was what they contributed to, generously and ever increasingly—whether it was building classrooms, scholarships, research programs or centers, athletic programs, or the foundation.

As one who is constantly raising funds, I am frequently entering rooms and situations where I don't know a single person in the room. Because of this, it was important that I learned to start by asking non-threatening questions. A threatening question to someone who doesn't know you is: "What business are you in?" Potentially, it's off-putting as a starter question. Some people are protective about information regarding how they make money or make their living. I have a litany of questions that are gracious and conversation starters, like: "Hey, what brings you here?" "What keeps you busy?" "Are you from here?" "Do you know the host/speaker/leader?" People will pull back if you get too invasive with your questions or if you come on too strong. The nonthreatening questions I use allow me to create a more natural rapport with people. That is an important factor in successfully getting someone to grant your request to support a cause or initiative with their money or time.

Whenever I am faced with a major decision where I'm trying to figure out the right questions or the answers to something, I think about an important philosophy my dad taught me. He wisely said:

"Do you know what a ship that runs into fog does?"

"Nope," I replied.

"It drops anchor. After you have looked at all the pros and cons, if you still have no clear direction, drop anchor, and wait. The decision will become clear once the fog clears."

That advice is something I remember at times when I feel I don't have enough clarity to move forward. This allows me the time and space to understand the situation, the people, and the questions and answers to make a more thoughtful decision that will lead to a successful or positive outcome.

Have the Respect to Ask

How many problems in life could be avoided if we stopped assuming we know what people want and instead take the time to **ask** them? We're all walking around in our own subjective experience. In other words, because we think and feel something, we assume that everyone else thinks and feels the same way. In personal, business, and even political relationships, one of the easiest ways to create a major breakdown in communication is to assume you know how someone will respond before you ask them. Whether it's a question of what activities your kid wants to be a part of, the top priorities of your boss, or what your constituents want from their elected officials, asking what they want before you take the liberty of foisting your preferences on them is a very wise idea. You can avoid simple unnecessary confrontations and even all-out catastrophes by showing people the respect they deserve, and asking them ahead of time—before you enroll them in something they don't want any part of. One perfect example of the disaster that failing to ask can create happened right in our own backyard.

Preserving Sonoran Desert Wonder

We love to wake up early on a weekend morning and head to the spectacularly beautiful and pristine McDowell Mountain Preserve to hike in the serene, peaceful Sonoran Desert in Scottsdale, Arizona, a natural state park whose maintenance and longevity have been provided for by a tax initiative voted on by Scottsdale taxpayers themselves many years ago because of their love for this area. The tax fund our faithful Scottsdale citizens had accumulated amounted to about sixty-eight million dollars, which was earmarked only to "improve and maintain" the McDowell Mountain Preserve.

Politicians cannot resist the urge to spend others' money, no matter what it is saved and preserved for. Certain city council members wanted to make a seemingly dubious deal for developers using this special fund of money that had been reserved exclusively for the preserve. The city council men and women never asked the people what they wanted. The politicians resisted asking because their agenda was to take that previously taxed and stored McDowell Mountain Preserve money and use it to build a hotel, resort, and museum, which we already had in abundance in our tourist destination city. The politicians were promised special perks by developers to make this development happen, which tainted their perspective in regard to the best choice for the city. The battle had become quite ugly by the time we were asked to get involved by a volunteer worker trying to keep the preserve and its dedicated fund safe.

We had just come down from a beautiful hike through the glorious giant saguaro cactus and abundant desert blossoms. The friendly woman approached us near the information building, explaining what the developers and certain city council members were trying to do—that we were in danger of losing this beautiful preserve that families across the valley enjoyed for recreation to another master-planned commercial project that would replace the magical desert flora and wildlife with concrete and buildings. The city could have easily resolved the dispute by putting the question to the voters and asking them what they wanted for their city. Did voters want to keep the preserve money protected for only its original intention? Or did they want to give that money to developers to build a commercial sore-thumb using public money for their private, profit-driven plans? Instead, certain members became quickly aligned, by greed, with the developers and did everything they could to make it difficult for citizens wanting to keep the money for that which it was intended. They had the power to put it on the ballot, asking which plan people wanted. Instead, the council members voted among themselves on a requirement for citizens to have to organize a grassroots effort and get thirty thousand names on a petition just to get it to a vote on the next ballot. In city council meetings, they were rather snide and quite pompous against those people who opposed the development. They were certain the requirements were too difficult. They were confident that we would quit.

The citizens of Scottsdale did not quit. They asked us to join the fight to save our preserve. We didn't need another job to do, but we knew it was absolutely the right thing to do. We knew we had some ideas to contribute that would make a difference. The city was already using taxpayer money to fight us. They had paid off the top signature-gathering companies so that our side would not be able to hire them. We coalesced, got more thoughtful and resourceful. We held a couple of meetings at people's homes and decided to take new bold action. Our first decision was to raise money fast because getting the adequate number of signatures to get on the ballot would take thousands of dollars to pay for signature gatherers. We decided to hold an evening wine and cheese meeting at an outdoor pavilion in one of the nearby neighborhoods. Two hundred people attended, who wanted to keep the preserve. We had to raise an additional forty thousand dollars fast, so we could handle the legal fees, signature gathering, and other expenses to deal with the political pandering and nonsense. Crystal and I both spoke at that meeting, talking about the rights of the taxpayers whose money was in question. We also talked about the role of the city council members and mayor as our civil servants. Were they serving the people with this decision or serving their own personal interests? People became ignited around the cause, and we got some pretty good contributions that night. Then Crystal, knowing that we needed to reach our goal of forty thousand dollars to fight this battle, asked a bolder question of the audience: "Who would be willing to give one thousand dollars each to attend a beautiful wine-tasting dinner at our home?" We were amazed that forty-seven people said yes. They gave the money. We raised forty-seven thousand much-needed dollars. Several weeks later, we all bonded over a magnificent dinner with superb conversation at our home. With those funds, we paid the signature gatherers, gathering more than thirty thousand signatures. Our team showed up at the next city hall meeting and presented the signatures.

One of the young women who had been a huge champion of the preserve, since her mother was one of the original founders who created it, stepped up to the microphone to address the council members. "We were really intimidated in the beginning, when you refused to put this to a vote to the people to ask them what they wanted, and instead forced the seemingly impossible task of gathering thirty thousand signatures upon us. But now we want to thank you. Because our volunteers have been on the streets for weeks, we have personally spoken to at least fifty thousand people, and we've been able to educate them as to who is protecting their interests within the city council and who is not. Not only have we gathered all of our signatures, we've informed the voters, and with the election coming in a few months, they're armed with information." The formerly cocky, arrogant city council members who had previously dismissed our efforts suddenly became very serious and turned a very pale shade of green.

We won the vote on proposition 420 by 71 percent to keep our beloved McDowell Mountain Preserve money sacred and protected! The two council members who were blatantly pro-development got voted out of office. In the future, maybe they'll think twice about foisting their personal agenda on someone without having the respect to **ask** the right people what it is *they* want!

The Woman Who Builds International Bridges of Understanding

Meredith Walker is the chief economist for EarthX, an international environmental organization. She is a member of the Board of Councilors for the EastWest Institute, an international network of influential stakeholders committed to building trust and preventing conflict around the world. She was a Federal Reserve economist in Dallas and New York and conducts innovative research on security and sustainability. Meredith serves as chair of the America's Future Series Advisory Council, served on the Board of Directors for the Dallas Holocaust and Human Rights Museum, and is a member of Business Executives for National Security. A sixth-generation Texan, she resides in her hometown of Plano with her four children, six rescue dogs, and two guinea pigs.

We had the wonderful experience of meeting Meredith when we were asked to speak at Earthx2019. Over several of our first conversations, we realized the breadth and depth of knowledge, understanding, and real-world experience of this incredible woman seemed truly limitless. As you read about the incredible life she's lived and her journey of accomplishment through the never-ending pursuit of asking for more, you might think you'd find someone removed and inaccessible. Yet, Meredith has the warmth and approachability of "the girl next door." Today we are blessed to call her friend, as we share the philosophy and commitment of conserving and sustaining this beautiful world in which we live.

Meredith Walker's Story

Question-asking was definitely encouraged in me as a young person. I think I was probably always asking questions. My mother still talks about driving with me in the car, and how I would continually ask her questions. I was reading before age four, so I think I was born with a desire to find out about everything.

My grandfather, whom I called Papaw, was an attorney here in Dallas. He worked on some important initiatives and cases, including helping to get the Texas Scottish Rite Hospital for Children built. Besides asking a lot of questions in my home, I remember the first formal interview I did in the fourth grade with Papaw—asking him about his profession, why he chose to be a lawyer, and things like that. Things I admired or thought were special about him. I remember that was very important to me at the time. As a child we would go visit my grandparents, and my dad would go off to one room and talk with my grandfather and I would play or read in the other room. We would often go out to dinner as a family. But I didn't often get a chance to speak with him in depth one-on-one. When we sat at the table that day at his home, just the two of us with him taking the time to answer my questions and speaking into my tape recorder, it made me feel important. It was very inspirational to me, so at that time I decided I wanted to be a lawyer! I knew that before he was an attorney, he had wanted to be an actor, so I thought: *Oh, maybe I will be an actress because if I was an actress too, it would work out well for me like it did for my grandfather.* That was a very sweet time with him that I cherished, and I know it shaped me. To this day, I still have the tape of that important interview.

Then a little later at age eleven I got to interview my great-uncle, Major General Charles R. Bond Jr., for my history fair project. He was an amazing man who served with the AVG—the First American Volunteer Group of the Chinese Air Force in China during World War II (1941–1942). Through my questions and his answers during this interview, I discovered so many remarkable things about my great-uncle. I learned that a couple of the raids he led really changed the course of the war and kept the Japanese from taking over the western capital. The AVG, nicknamed the Flying Tigers, was composed of pilots from the United States Army Air Corps, Navy, and Marine Corps, recruited under President Franklin Roosevelt's authority before Pearl Harbor and commanded by Claire Lee Chennault. It was an unusual mission as they were flying under China's flag under the directed command of the United States. They were called mercenaries by some at the time, but it really was a government-sanctioned mission and finally in the early nineties the government officially recognized that and in 1996 awarded the Flying Tigers pilots, including my uncle Charlie, the Distinguished Flying Cross.

Uncle Charlie lived in mainland China while this dangerous operation was underway. He was shot down twice, once over a village called Baoshan on the border with Vietnam. The villagers who saved him were hiding in a cemetery behind the tombstones. When he was shot down, he was badly burned and didn't have on his jacket so they couldn't see who he was, but they saved his life, and he returned to flying. Because of this he had a lifelong fondness for the Chinese people.

For that interview and then my subsequent history project, Uncle Charlie lent me his parachute rip cord from that harrowing event, which had been burned into his hand. That rip cord became a metaphor for me. Like Uncle Charlie, I say to people when they're having a tough time, "hang in there" and imagine holding the rip cord that saved his life. It's a great visual to get you to say, "Okay, I can do this." That special experience with my great-uncle, being able to question him with my youthful enthusiasm, was when my interest in China and in the military and international relations began.

Formally learning to ask questions of people whose courage I so admired really changed and helped shape my life as young girl. To be a part of these powerful and impactful stories connected by my family ties really opened up the world to me, helping me understand there was so much beyond what I saw in my everyday world.

Through these experiences of those who came before me, I received a legacy of courage and achievement that had global impact, which continues for me to this day. Just recently I met with the Chinese consul general from Houston and was able to speak with him in Mandarin. We discussed the Flying Tigers legacy. What a wonderful experience that was!

Later when I got into high school, I did go into acting like my grandfather. I ended up doing plays, musicals, and such—and from that, I went into speech and debate, which has its own theatrics. Fortunately, my high school speech coach was great. She made me do debate. I didn't want to debate. I was very happy competing in poetry reading, but she saw something in me and said, "You must do this." She also encouraged me to participate in student congress, and I competed at Nationals, thanks to her belief in me.

Ultimately though, rather than going into law, I went into economics. At fifteen years old I was part of the Texas governor's school and was invited to University of Texas at Austin for a month. I took a course in international economics and also in Asian studies. Eventually, I ended up being awarded a scholarship to University of Texas at Austin for my undergraduate work and studied economics, Asian studies, and French. I was also part of the honors program that was basically liberal arts. We studied everything fascinating! I graduated with a BA from the University of Texas at Austin Plan II liberal arts honors program in economics, with minors in Asian studies and French. During that time, I did internships at the Pentagon and State Department Bureau of East Asian and Pacific Affairs, Office of the Assistant Secretary.

I went on to the University of Illinois for graduate school, studying economics there. I completed my MS in economics there, with a Chinese language and area studies fellowship. I decided to stay in Illinois in the Urbana-Champaign area for another year after grad school, working for a US-Chinese consulting company. As part of my job, I traveled to China first in 1995 and traveled several regions of the country, setting up joint venture companies in China and helping Chinese companies come to the US. That was a really outstanding experience. It was a very small company with only ten people involved, but we were working with some of the largest companies in America—and enterprises in China that could support the large companies.

Eventually I moved back to Dallas and was very fortunate to get a position with the Federal Reserve Bank of Dallas as a research economist. I was an assistant to the chief economist and then ultimately to the president. I worked there three years. During that time my work with China continued. I spent a month in China traveling the country looking for new types of companies and talking to government officials on economic development. My experience was terrific, and the people were very kind to me. One time I even had a Communist Party official bring a Bible for me that was published in Mandarin! My work was under the purview of the Dallas Fed, and we published a report that was given to Congress by Senator Phil Gramm.

I loved the work I had been doing, but an exciting opportunity was offered to me when I was asked to join the Federal Reserve Bank of New York. I had always wanted to live in New York, so my answer was *yes*! I accepted the job and moved from Dallas to New York City. Shortly after that, I started my family. All four of my children were born in New York.

Since asking questions had been so instrumental in guiding me throughout my life, I knew it was important to foster that same curiosity in my own children. With my kids, I always encourage them to ask questions about anything and probe for the answers: "Why do you think this?" "Why do you think that?" And they ask me such brilliant, insightful questions I would never think of myself. But the questions we end the day with are: "Who did I help?" and "Who helped me?" Whatever the days may bring—whether they are exciting days, slow days, you have a health issue, or the occasional crisis we all encounter from time to time—those are the two questions that always bring some measure of peace and comfort. To ask and wonder every day who they can help, whose life they can make better, and whose help they should be grateful for fills every day with meaning and purpose.

There was a point after I had my children when I noticed that in my business and work, things were changing for me, and I really started asking deeper questions of myself. "What is it that I can do that I really feel is my purpose—my life purpose?" Some people do follow one profession for a lifetime. I found that I needed to dig deeper and ask more profound questions of myself at that point of my life. I began asking those types of questions of myself with a great depth of wonder. "Professionally, what impact can I make in the world that truly matters?" Through my questioning, I knew for me the answer was building international bridges. Working at the level of nations to bring people together.

Eventually I ended up going through a painful divorce and was awarded sole custody of my children, as well as the right to move my children home to Dallas where we could be with my devoted parents. When I returned, my Dallas Fed colleagues were very supportive, even though I had been away ten years, and invited me to events and made strategic introductions for me.

Due to my family's military service and having been in New York on 9/11, I resolved to support military and veterans, from World War II through the War on Terror, and to preserve the values we hold dear for future generations. I met government and business leaders who involved me with Business Executives for National Security and the East-West Institute and was invited to join the Board of Councilors to support international conflict resolution.

One day I received an email that told of the passing of Col. Edward J. Sims, who had spent the final years of his life working on the Congressional Medal of Honor for James Megellas, the most decorated officer of the 82nd Airborne. The email asked, "Who will take up this cause?" I remember thinking, this is important, but what can I do? A few weeks later, the email came again. I knew some reporters and members of Congress who would help me, and so I answered.

Now I am blessed to count James "Maggie" Megellas, age 102, his precious wife Carole, and their family my dear friends. We traveled to Washington, DC, for receptions on Capitol Hill and at the French Embassy and have presented the America's Future Series Megellas Award annually to distinguished veterans. This year, we sang "Silent Night" together at their family Christmas party with country artist Danny Griego, and then Maggie told us about singing it in the mountains of Italy on Christmas Eve 1943 while his platoon was being shelled.

Maggie described what it was like when he arrived at the Wöbbelin concentration camp in Ludwigslust, Germany. As he wrote in his book *All the Way to Berlin,* "It was not until our men witnessed this that we fully realized what we had been fighting for. The destruction of the monstrosity the Nazis had created was the cause greater than ourselves, that we had often alluded to but never fully understood. It was a defining moment in our lives: who we were, what we believed in, and what we stood for."

Maggie says he is still living at 102 because he has not completed his mission yet. He agrees with me that we each have our own mission to fulfill. I now serve as Chief Economist for EarthX and bring people together to find solutions for the sustainability of our earth. Our earth is one home, our home. We all live on the same planet; we share the same air, and the same water. In my professional life, I'm focused on discovering what kinds of international bridges we can build around those issues. I love that, because it is the one thing we have most in common.

I also support the Dallas Holocaust and Human Rights Museum and am inspired every day by the will to live of our amazing survivors, such as Max Glauben, who was named 2019 Texan of the Year. The Holocaust, genocides, and other atrocities occur because people do not stand up for the rights of others. Max and others encourage us to be Upstanders.

At the church where I worshiped when growing up, we were always encouraged to ask questions about our faith. "Why do we believe this?" "Why do people suffer that?" We were encouraged to read the Bible for ourselves, ask God for guidance and then expect the right answers. As the Bible says, *ask and you shall receive.*

I know in my heart that when I started asking those questions, God delivered an answer that ties right into my purpose and destiny. I wouldn't be here without that process.

For me God always comes through. I'm laughing now because usually those questions come out along with many, many tears! But through years of inquiry and amazing experiences, I'm in the perfect place for me, doing what I need to do to make an impact on the world that truly matters.

111

Ask Gold Nuggets

- Asking creates an immediate bond—you can connect to others through asking.
- Human beings are wired to help—but you have to ask first!
- There are asking opportunities in every relationship.
- If someone tells you no once—don't stop asking. Don't give up on your dream until you get it.
- Questions are the only way to get to the reality and truth of a situation.
- "Is this the right choice I'm making? What are the advantages/disadvantages going to be?"
- Respect others enough to ask before you assume you know the answer.
- Probe life deeply to build bridges of understanding and opportunity.

Nurture Intimate Relationships—by Asking

Our intimate, romantic relationships provide the emotional foundation upon which we rely for stability and security in our lives. Because of that, they are perhaps the most important area to constantly practice and hone our asking skills. If we can't clearly communicate our needs to our beloved, it eventually leaves us feeling disappointed and lonely. Ultimately, this leads to resentment and distance between two people who originally intended to become ever closer. Somehow, the concept of asking in other areas of life seems more acceptable. But when it comes to asking for something from the person with whom we have an intimate relationship, we expect them to be psychic. We tell ourselves things like:

"He should know that by now."

"She should see how that bothers me."

"I've told him before what types of gifts I want. I shouldn't have to keep telling him."

"She should understand how hard I work and acknowledge me for it."

"He should know that makes me uncomfortable."

As a rule, if we don't ask, we're not going get what we want. Asking can make us feel more vulnerable and less in control, but a willingness to ask is crucial to your relationship success and satisfaction. A negative response to your question may have nothing to do with you. The person you're asking might be in a bad mood. People do the best they can from their own state of consciousness.

Opening the "I Deserve More" Door

As you journey across that bridge to your ultimate destiny, remember that your learning and breakthroughs will continue for a lifetime. One of the most important parts of this journey, in fact the very purpose of this entire journey, is to learn to live in joy! No one gets more mired in dutiful purpose than we do, and sometimes we need to kick ourselves or give each other a nudge to realize it's time to take a break and enjoy the small things right now! As we each gain perspective, embrace our own bravery, and challenge ourselves to new heights, we also need to remember to be kind to ourselves, and be willing to ask inwardly to experience more joyful moments. One of the best ways to do that is to regularly ask yourself, "*What small, happy gifts could I give to myself weekly?*" It's not only okay to take care of yourself, it's critical to your ability to accept that you deserve all good things. Knowing that will strengthen your resiliency and sense of deservedness in the asking journey. Here are some of our favorite possibilities to get you started on your own list of asking for and celebrating the little pleasures of life!

- Fresh flowers in a beautiful vase to brighten my room
- Stargazing at night
- Playing my favorite music list that makes me want to dance or sing
- Time giggling with children
- Painting or coloring with beautiful colors
- Fresh, juicy cut fruit on a plate
- Sunrises and sunsets
- Hugs and kisses
- Being with animals
- A picnic after a beautiful hike
- Ceramic making with best friends
- Sunlight warming my body
- A walk by the ocean, river, or lake
- Planting an herb garden or a tree
- A glass of wine with friends
- More laughter
- A quiet walk through the trees

Answering your own need for these small but meaningful gifts to yourself will instantly pick up your mood and change your energy! When you ask for and answer some of your own simplest needs, you open that door called "I Deserve More." Once that door is opened through a request and reward to yourself for small things, you'll find that it remains more open for bigger and bolder requests to be filled!

Harvard Study on Asking Questions

Harvard Business School published the results of a study it did in 2017 in the *Journal of Personality and Social Psychology*. The study is titled "It Doesn't Hurt to Ask: Question-Asking Increases Liking." What the researchers discovered is that asking questions makes you more likable. They found that people who asked more questions were better liked by their conversation partners and were perceived to be more responsive and caring. They even extended the study to observe speed daters who were in conversations getting to know each other. They found that daters who asked more questions during their dates were more likely to get a second date! Interestingly, they also discovered that despite the evidence of persistent benefits to asking questions, most people don't realize ahead of time that question-asking increases the degree to which someone will end up liking them. They worry that their queries might come across as offensive or that they may seem ill-informed to their partner. In other words, people *need to be taught* to deploy the art and science of asking. It doesn't often come naturally to people, or we don't naturally understand the benefits. Even if it seems unpleasant at first, we need to get over our fears. Based on Harvard's research findings, being a good asker offers significant benefits for our business and personal relationships. "It spurs learning and the exchange of ideas, it fuels innovation and performance improvement, it builds rapport and trust among team members," the researchers write. "And it can mitigate business risk by uncovering unforeseen pitfalls and hazards."

When it comes to building more happy, successful relationships, and even dating with more success, we'll do better if we hone our asking skills to the fullest!

Understanding the Correct Process of Asking

Use Power, Not Force, When You Ask Someone

> *A traveler walked alone down a country road on a cloudy day, wearing an old cloak. The Sun and the North Wind decided to have a contest to see who could remove it. "This will be easy," the North Wind said. He sent a powerful blast of cold air toward the traveler, who only pulled his cloak tighter. The North Wind tried again and again, blowing so hard that birds were pushed from their paths and leaves scattered from the trees. The shivering traveler hunched against the wind and held on to his cloak. "Let me try," said the Sun, as he moved from behind the clouds. As he gently poured his warmth on the traveler, the traveler opened his coat and within minutes took it off.*
>
> —AESOP'S FABLES

This wonderful fable describes what often happens in our relationships concerning the process of asking. The North Wind tries to force the man's coat off; the Sun simply shines its light to effect a gentle result. We love Dr. David Hawkins's book *Power vs. Force* because it enlightens the reader to the understanding of the higher quality of actions of *power*—as opposed to the manipulative or even subversive actions of *force*.

In our relationships, we all want to be heard and understood. Unfortunately, often we try to accomplish this by forcing our will on someone either passively or aggressively. If we don't like what's happening or what's being said, we lash out with coldness, hostility, or demeaning or aggressive rhetoric, which leaves us feeling unhappier and more disconnected in our relationship. These emotionally charged exchanges take us *further* away from those with whom we desire to be closer.

When you find yourself in one of those exchanges with your loved one and it doesn't seem to be going anywhere, this is the time to agree to sit down together and ask some **self-intervention questions** to help calm each other and understand what you're truly feeling. The best way is for each person to write their own responses and then share them. It's amazing how a brewing storm can be easily calmed by utilizing this process.

Self-Intervention Questions

- "What thoughts am I having, right now, about this experience?"
- "What emotions am I feeling, right now, about this situation and why?"
- "What beliefs are behind these emotions?"
- "What are the automatic negative thoughts that are popping up and why?"
- "What did I actually see or hear, in regard to this occurrence?"
- "Am I responding to what I actually saw or heard, or to something inside me?"
- "Are my perceptions accurate, or are they just my way of seeing things through my previous conditioning or biases?"
- "Is the belief that is bringing up turmoil right now loaded with old emotional baggage that doesn't serve my highest good?"
- "Are the negative emotions I'm experiencing due to old thought programming that I can release now?"
- "Am I willing to put down emotional baggage for good and leave it behind instead of bringing it with me wherever I go?"

Stopping to check in with yourself and asking your partner to do the same is a great way to stop careening down a destructive verbal path with each other that will only make matters worse. Being vulnerable with each other by answering these questions together has a way of taking you from ego-based arguments to authentic human understanding. That is the place where real solutions and resolutions can happen!

Lead by Example

Often, we want someone in our lives to make a change, improve on something, or participate in something they're currently not doing. We've tried asking, but it seems like our requests are falling on deaf ears. An important art-of-asking technique we've learned is to start by doing exactly what you're asking someone else to do. My husband and I (Crystal) were on a luxury cruise recently. After dinner at the French restaurant one evening, we wandered into the lounge to enjoy the pianist-singer who was entertaining that night. This guy was very talented, fun to listen to, and really working hard to engage the audience. He kept looking around at the audience, asking us to sing with him. You could see people squirming and smiling at the same time. Like they wanted to break into song, but they were too shy and not willing to put themselves out there. I kept thinking, *Come on, guys, just sing with this guy—it means a lot to him.* I suddenly decided the only way to get anyone to do what the poor guy was asking was to go ahead and sing. I started singing—full out. I don't have a terrible voice, but I'm not Celine Dion. But so what? I realized everyone there wanted to express more than they allowed themselves. Mark joined me, and as we both sat there singing loudly with our host, it was amazing to see how, one by one, others joined in. Soon enough we were all singing and swaying together, and everyone seemed to be completely enjoying themselves!

If you've asked your reluctant teen to sweep the floor and you're not getting any action out of them, grab two brooms—one for her, one for you, and ask her to work along with you to get this done fast. If you ask your coworkers to get the files organized and you hear some moaning or excuses, start organizing and ask them to help. If you've asked for a referral from someone, offer at the same time to refer them to someone who would be beneficial for them to know. It's more difficult for someone to refuse your request when you're already in action doing the thing that needs to be done; plus you'll begin to engender bonds of solidarity by being "in it together."

There are scores of books written on leading by example. That's because it's a really effective tool to utilize in influencing personal relations, business transactions, sales, desire for improved health and fitness, or any area in which we'd like to influence an outcome we desire. People are definitely influenced by one another's actions. Sometimes it's not enough just to ask; you have to lead with action. In the realm of learning to be an effective asker, leading by example sends the message to the person from whom you're asking help that you are capable and you walk your talk. That you are asking from a desire to improve a situation, your life, or your business, not because you're weak and needy.

Always Say Thank You

Great leaders and influencers will tell you that people need to know their action mattered. If you've asked something of someone and they've granted that request, the most important thing you can do is to take the time to *clearly* communicate to them how much you appreciated their help and the specific difference it made for you in your life—even if it was a small thing. People need affirmation, and when they get it they want more. When you take the time to affirm the positive difference someone's help made for you personally, you will form a bond of loyalty with that person and they will be much more likely to grant your request, or even rush to your aid, next time you need them. **Appreciation** and **gratitude** are two of the most powerful virtues you can share as you navigate the bridge of asking to your true destiny!

Discover What You Really Want Before You Ask

THE FOX AND THE GRAPES

A FOX, just at the time of the vintage, stole into a vineyard where the ripe sunny Grapes were trellised up on high in most tempting show. He made many a spring and a jump after the luscious prize; but, failing in all his attempts, he muttered as he retreated, "Well! What does it matter! The Grapes are sour!"

—FABLE 33 HALM; THOMAS JAMES'S TRANSLATION

In my coaching practice, I (Crystal) can't tell you the number of times I've done an extensive intake interview with a client where they go on and on about how hard they've worked to stay in a job they can't stand, or how they keep coming back for more unpleasant experiences in a personal relationship they claim they can't tolerate. When we begin to break it down by asking the most important questions, they realize that the "reward" they're seeking through all this effort isn't actually something they truly want. How often have you put tremendous amounts of effort, pain, and punishment into something, only to realize your reward will not be a sweet juicy prize but—like the fox discovered—more like sour grapes.

Ask—*"What is my reward if I continue in this situation? Is that reward worthy of my efforts?"*

Kent and Sheryl's Story

Kent and Sheryl had been coming to me for life coaching as a couple and individually for several months. They were struggling tremendously in their relationship. They had been surprised by an unplanned pregnancy several months into their relationship, which resulted in the birth of a baby boy, whom they both seemed to love very much but couldn't find a way to effectively co-parent together. They had moved into a rental together without knowing if they even loved each other. They were getting pressure from their families that made them feel there was no choice but to get married and face up to their responsibilities. When they were together in a coaching session, their communication was mostly accusatory; when they were in individual sessions, they each would complain about the other's shortcomings and problems, the things they hated about their relationship and living together, and how they wished the other would just change. They each complained about how the other wasn't doing enough to help pay the bills, the other was sloppy and disorganized around the house, the other had a negative attitude, and on and on. They were so stuck feeding into a negative pattern they had created together that they couldn't reach the part of themselves that needed to be accessed for changes to begin.

After trying several techniques and challenges to get them out of their negative cycle with each other, I decided to take a different approach. At each of their individual sessions that week, I recommended that they move into different homes for at least three months. I didn't give either of them advance warning that this was going to be my suggestion. They were both shocked and even suspicious that the other one had asked me to bring this up to have an excuse to separate from the other. After a few phone calls back and forth, they both warmed to the idea and started to see the wisdom in it, knowing that at the end of the three months, all options were on the table, including moving back in with each other. Kent arranged to get another temporary place with ample space that allowed him to have his son on certain days and arranged for his mother to help out with the baby on those days while he was working. They were given assignments to work on themselves for those three months, and at the end, we would revisit their feelings about their home life, their relationship potential, and what the future might look like for them.

Not surprising to me, they both chose to continue their separation permanently at the end of that period. They had to break out of their codependent pattern to be able to ask and answer the questions that would get them to the truth. Once they were in their own space and their codependent destructive pattern was broken, they were able to answer the questions with clarity. "Is this person compatible with me?" "Are we together for any other reason than we had an unplanned pregnancy and now a baby boy?" "Is this really the person I could be happy with for the rest of my life?" The answers were pretty much *no, no*, and *no*.

Sheryl, who had been absolutely sure in the beginning that they must move in and live together for the benefit of their child, realized that she was much happier not living with Kent. There were so many things making them incompatible that she wasn't in touch with when they were enmeshed in this negative dynamic that had become a pattern they couldn't break out of.

Kent also realized that as much as he respected Sheryl, and his religious upbringing was telling him that he must marry Sheryl and stay married, he was thankful to see clearly that their personality differences and lack of passion and commonality would have created a miserable life for both of them. They decided to go forward with their own lives and work cooperatively to co-parent their child, and as a result, they've both found a greater level of happiness and respectively more harmonious relationships.

It takes an inquiring mind and heart to effectively ask the right questions. So often, we become mired in our circumstances or misery that our minds start to go in circles, replaying the same troubling habits. If you find yourself in that space, try to find a way to take a break or a "time-out" from your situation or circumstances. Breaking out of the nonconstructive or destructive pattern, even temporarily, will help you still your mind. It is from that more balanced and quiet state of mind you can begin to embrace and foster a more inquiring mind.

- Asking expands awareness.
- Asking reveals wisdom.
- Asking opens up new and different possibilities.

Asking for Your True Love

Finding that person with whom we want to share our lives is one of the most important things we'll do in this lifetime. God made human beings to need each other. We were divinely designed to pair up—each bringing a different set of energy, emotions, and ideas to the relationship. Sadly, people are gathering together less and less, which makes the spontaneous possibility of that happening more difficult. As we all process life behind the screens of our computers, many feel a bit sad and alone because of the isolation our ever-more-digitized world has caused. We're troubled when people we talk to who would love a beautiful relationship with someone have resigned themselves to the belief that it probably won't happen. All questions, because of the law of attraction, get answers. Questions keep you vitally engaged, stimulate more curiosity, and prompt infinite reasons for feeling alive and joyful. So when you long for true love, become very curious about everything around you! Not only will you begin to learn more about people and connect with them at a deeper level, you'll become a more interesting person by being more interested in others. Try not to prejudge people or places where you think love might be found. When you express a deeper interest in someone through your inquiry, a bond could likely be formed, and you never know where it will lead. Someone may find you interesting enough to want to introduce you to their sister or cousin. Inquiring about yourself and others ultimately makes you easier to love because you're more connected to everyone's experience. It helps you learn about people and opens up your awareness of how people feel, what's important to them, and what they want for themselves. We're encouraging everyone who wants to find great love, and has not yet, to rekindle their curiosity about life and about everyone they meet and start to employ the art of asking to find that beloved one who also wants to find them!

Finding that perfect *one* often happens as the culmination of a lot of little things. So, if you really want to manifest that perfect person and not just dream about her or him, the questions and answers to small but important things may make all the difference. It's a great way to start shifting your potential for love to the positive zone!

Looking for Love in All the Right Ways and Places

Are you asking for help?

Finding your sweetie pie might be as easy as calling a friend. Many life-long couples still meet by friends introducing them to each other. There's no one who knows you better than your good friends, so ask for their support in finding your true love. Most friends are happy to help, and since you like them, they like you, and you share commonality, chances are you'll have more in common with other people they know, whom you may not have met. It's also nice to have them along at the first meeting, whether it's dinner or a party at their house. They can help keep the conversation going, smooth over awkward moments, and brag about you in a way you can't do for yourself.

Have you joined a new group lately?

There are all kinds of groups that meet up to participate in things the members all love, like bicycling, book clubs, hiking, art, cooking, or traveling to exotic places. Research those and challenge yourself to participate. Practice conversations at home and prepare yourself to be open and comfortable striking up a conversation with anyone who looks interesting.

Are you free to be yourself?

One of the most attractive qualities in a person is authenticity. Think of the people you know who are always surrounded by people who are interested in them and what they have to say. Those are the people who can relax and just be themselves. Being yourself is the most attractive way to be because you're the only one in the world who can be you. Confidence is both physically and mentally attractive. Have confidence in yourself to express the real you and your own unique journey.

Are you a hunter or a magnet?

Make sure you don't become consumed with hunting down the right match. Remember, people naturally run away from hunters because they feel like they might be caught! Being a magnet is a much better strategy. Practice the tips we've talked about and then just put yourself out there and be you. Stay in wonder about what might come from it. Don't force anything. As an interesting individual who celebrates life, you'll become the magnet who draws people to you naturally.

Is your body speaking its own language?

Body language speaks volumes to people. Are you sitting there with arms crossed, slouching and stiff? That can subconsciously be a signal to people to stay away. Relax. Put your shoulders back and avoid slouching.

Are you judging the book by its cover?

Does it seem like no one you encounter is a likely match, so you pass on the opportunity to say hello or connect? Open up to the possibility that you may not be seeing the person for what or who they are. Remember the adage: *You can't judge a book by its cover.* While the person may not fit the preconceived stereotype of your dream person, consider the prospect that as you get to know them, they might have the traits and qualities that would blossom into feelings of beautiful amour.

Be Ready to Forge a Bond When Opportunity Arises

When you do have an opportunity to talk with someone who might someday become the perfect partner for you, it's important to be ready for that opportunity. We know by now that asking is important to success. But let's hit on a couple of really great tips that apply to those moments when you're connecting with someone for the first time and trying to put your best foot forward. There are some really great research-based question-asking techniques that were published in *Harvard Business Review*. Researchers found when these techniques were used, they built rapport and trust between people.

It's alluring to be curious.

We all have patterns we've used from way back when it comes to building a relationship with someone new. But when you're a bit nervous or excited because you want to make a good impression, you might be tempted to launch into a long explanation about you and your life: everything you've done and want to do. Most of us have been stuck on a date or the middle of an encounter where the guy or gal begins to babble nonstop about themselves. By the time your time together ends, you can hardly wait to get out of there. Often in an attempt to lay it all on the line, people will likely miss a chance to have a truly bonding conversation. It's fine to say a few things about yourself but better to be more curious about the person you're trying to connect with. The point, after all, is to discover what is in another person's mind.

Follow-up questions are almost always smart.

We've learned that we're supposed to ask questions to get to know people, but how we ask those questions is just as important if we're expecting to have a successful exchange. If you're not deliberate about your conversational habits, your follow-up questions might be all wrong. Stringing together completely unrelated questions that switch topics each time can lead to a disjointed communication and limit the depth of your conversations. These "full-switch" questions are not the best way to go deeper with someone.

Rather than having the conversation go like this:

"Where did you grow up?"
Listen to the answer.
"What was your favorite food?"
Listen to the answer.

127

The following would be much more engaging:

"Where did you grow up?"
Listen to the answer.
"Oh, Twin Falls, my cousin lives there with her husband. I visited her once. I was amazed at how pretty the Riverwalk is. Did you go to the river a lot?"
Listen.
"Every weekend in the summer. Wow! Was it just you, or do you have siblings?"
Listen.
"Oh, who were you closer to, your brother or sister? What was your birth order?"
Listen.
"Oh, yeah, I'm the third-born too...."

Negative framing can lead to a positive outcome.

This technique is a bit counterintuitive, but it works. If you're already in a relationship or forming a new one, it will really help keep your relationship on a respectful, honest level. In all relationships, life unfolds, and stuff happens. Because people aren't perfect, using **negative framing** in a question creates a frame for the person to be truthful without feeling like your wrath is going to fall upon them when they give their answer. For example, you say, "You're not going to be on time tonight, are you?" Your assumption allows them to be truthful and not feel like they're going to shock and upset you with their answer if it's not what you want to hear.

With every question, remember that tone always matters. If your tone is menacing or angry, it's likely your partner will shy away from a candid response. No one wants to feel attacked or accused.

Get past the superficial.

Once you've gotten into a few minutes of conversation, don't be afraid to explore a little bit with your partner. You can do that through your conversation by pushing past the superficial dialogue. See what happens if you can get into questions that are more powerful. A certain magic begins to happen between two people when you can feel comfortable asking and answering those types of questions. Questions like "If you could change anything in your life, what would it be?" cause people to open up, think deeper, and share more of themselves. The listener feels heard and respected when you can ask and follow up on these deeper types of questions. You'll both come away feeling more connected and that your time together was truly meaningful.

Questions can lead to intimacy.

A study led by psychologist Arthur Aron discovered that mutual vulnerability fosters closeness between people. The key pattern they discovered that was associated with the development of a close personal relationship was sustained, escalating, reciprocal, personal self-disclosure. The method they used to foster a sense of increased intimacy between people involved having participants ask each other a set of questions that became increasingly probing, such as these examples:

- "Would you like to be famous? In what way?"
- "Before making a telephone call, do you ever rehearse what you are going to say? Why?"
- "What would constitute a 'perfect' day for you?"
- "When did you last sing to yourself? To someone else?"
- "If you were able to live to the age of ninety and retain either the mind or body of a thirty-year-old for the last sixty years of your life, which would you want?"

- "Is there something that you've dreamed of doing for a long time? Why haven't you done it?"
- "What is the greatest accomplishment of your life?"
- "What do you value most in a friendship?"

It's difficult for most people to be vulnerable as they're getting to know someone, but becoming so is such a necessary part of participating in rich intimate relationships. Questions like these are a wonderful way to build that bridge!

How to Intentionally Find True Love: Audra and Aren's Story

We were sitting with two lovebirds at a fun restaurant in Houston. Our nephew Aren and his fiancée, Audra, whom we were meeting for the first time, clearly had some loving vibes between them. Aren has always been a super achiever. He graduated at the top of his class from the University of Colorado's business school and immediately was recruited by Shell Oil as a financial analyst. Audra, herself a superstar, graduated from Harvard Law School and started earlier that year at a major Houston law firm. As we chatted playfully with them, getting to know Audra and the journey of their relationship, we became curious and interested. This one was obviously different. Why? We knew Aren very well, but never had we witnessed the level of engagement and connection he seemed to have with this bright young woman. They seemed to be a perfect match. We started pondering, was there something in the way they met and pursued their relationship that facilitated a pathway to finding more of a true-love connection? As it turns out, there were some differences, as you'll see through the sharing of their story of falling in love.

AREN: I think a lot of people believe that love happens randomly and should be spontaneous when you least expect it. While mentally and emotionally that was appealing, to me finding a partner was important, and I wanted to be purposeful about it. That's why I pursued online dating. It was my way to be open and vulnerable to the world for dating. I think it's great that the stigma of online dating is fading, and it's now widely encouraged. I wanted to make the Universe know I was open and willing to find love and from there the Universe would do its part, and it brought me Audra! Audra and I both happily share that we met online with friends and family.

AUDRA: The largest difference about meeting Aren was that I met him online. When I moved back to Houston, I was ready to "put down roots" and meet someone I could see myself with long term. Around this time, I also started working at a large law firm and was putting in long hours. It wasn't conducive to meeting new people, so I followed the lead of many of my friends and joined Match.com. I met Aren relatively quickly, and from the very first date, we hit it off. One of the great things about Match.com is that it asks its users to answer a series of questions to get a baseline idea of compatibility, so in this way, questions were a big part of getting to know each other from the very start! Since going on our first date, I think one of the best parts of our relationship is that we never run out of things to talk about. After almost two years of dating, we still have to keep an eye on the clock in the evening so that we don't stay up all night talking. It just flows very naturally with us each taking turns sharing stories and ideas or asking each other questions about our day. Communication has been a big part of not only getting to know each other but also just staying connected in our busy lives.

AREN: Unlike Audra, I'd been dating online, so that was not new, but our first date instantly struck me as magnificent and new. Never before had I been so impressed by another's perspectives, spirituality, intellect, and beauty all in one. Finding one of those things is possible, two is hard, all of them had been impossible until I met Audra. So many of our first conversations I remember like they were yesterday, down to the little details. Questions flowed so easily and even with a little sass from her on occasion, for fun.

From the beginning I noticed she was a master question-asker! I remember halfway through our first date, I was thinking how I'd been loving talking to her, but that, in fact, I hadn't yet learned as much about her as she had learned about me! She was so good at asking me questions and happy to listen the time flew by, but I became more intentional about getting to know her, too, that night. Ever since, it's a theme that's played out well; we love to ponder the big questions of life and the simple questions of how our days were. We're still asking each other questions and getting to know each other.

AUDRA: I think one of the things that I admire about Aren is he experiences life with an open heart. I try to as well. I think we'd both agree that our connection is very deep and unique. It's amazing to have someone who has enough in common with you that you feel like the other person understands you—that's been amazing to feel with Aren.

AREN: Having become more committed to Audra than anyone in the past, it's only natural that we dive into topics and questions I've never needed to cover before. But that's the beauty of our alignment, that when an otherwise "big" or "stressful" question comes up, once we talk about it, we're almost always aligned or at least respect each other's thoughts, so that makes asking questions to better understand each other a lot easier.

AUDRA: In my relationship with Aren, I never felt I had to question where he stood. He was amazingly open, and things were just very easy with him. There wasn't much guessing whether he would text or call, when we were going to see each other next, or whether he was open to a serious commitment.

AREN: On our first date, I asked Audra, "What does religion and spirituality mean to you?" With online dating you can find someone who is spiritual or religious via a filter, but it doesn't answer how they see the world and what it means to them. I wanted someone who was both religious and spiritual, open-minded, and spiritually curious, and I found all that with Audra!

AUDRA: Some of the questions that made me realize Aren was someone who was truly compatible with me were, "What are you passionate about?" "What were your dreams as a kid...how about in college?" "Where do you see yourself in the future?"

AREN: The things I love and respect the most about Audra are her empathy, creativity, and passion. She is more empathetic than anyone I've ever met and can read my own emotions in many cases faster than I can! We can be together, and she will ask, "Where did you go?" and I'll find I was lost in thought. She is, all around, a great partner. She has an elegance to how she solves problems and finds creative solutions, and she has a drive and passion to see it done with ease and efficiency!

AUDRA: There are so many things that I love and respect about Aren. I love that I know I can always count on him. For example, a few months into our relationship, my work schedule became especially hectic. Aren was so sweet to take my dry cleaning in with his, put WD-40 on my squeaky door hinge, and make me dinner. He continues to be amazingly helpful with the day-to-day tasks and does little extra things for me regularly, like bringing me coffee in bed before he leaves for work! I know that Aren is on my team. I also love that he always supports me. Whether I wanted to switch practice areas of law, take a new art class, or go on a weekend trip to see friends or family, Aren wants me to be happy and encourages me. Finally, I've always respected how close he is to his family. Family is very important to me—I talk to my parents almost every day, and Aren gets that. We've already become pretty integrated into each other's families. I asked his sister to be my maid of honor, and he asked my brother to be his best man. It's also really nice that our families can spend holidays together.

AREN: I think it's incredibly important to stay curious about your partner's thoughts and feelings; it's how we grow our love deeper and continue to learn about the other. We're both curious people by nature, exploring and wanting to learn more, and that definitely goes for each other.

AUDRA: I believe that staying connected definitely requires having a strong sense of curiosity about each other. Building our lives together has only fostered more curiosity between Aren and me.

AREN: I'm naturally prone to share with family and loved ones and don't usually need a lot of questions to become chatty, but I've learned that Audra appreciates when I ask her more questions to show her I care. I love when Audra asks me questions about things that I'm passionate about or excited to talk about, even if it's about something very technical related to one of my interests or about my job. I want her to feel respected and cared for by making sure I'm asking how she feels or what she thinks.

AUDRA: I think that making a point to regularly ask one another what the other is thinking or feeling shows respect and caring that creates important trust and bonding. I don't always naturally talk about myself and share. Sometimes, I just try to keep my worries or thoughts to myself so that I'm not burdening others or so that I give others the opportunity to express themselves. In a way, it's my way of sharing love. Although I know deep down that Aren cares about me and about how I'm doing, sometimes I need to be asked in order to open up. When Aren asks me questions about how I am, what's going on at work, what I'm thinking about painting next, or just what I want for dinner, I do naturally feel loved.

AREN: As we move forward in our lives together, we want to stay in alignment with each other. For me, some of the most important questions we can ask each other are: "Are we growing together, strong and confidently?" "What else can I do to support you?" "How else can I show up in the world for you?"

In my mind, there was *no* question more meaningful or important to ask Audra than the one I asked her just a month ago. I asked this beautiful lady, "Will you spend the rest of your life with me?" Her answer was even more important. Of course, she said, "yes!"

We're counting down the days to our intimate Italian wedding and celebration back home. We have had a lot of fun planning everything and can't wait to spend the rest of our lives together. We foresee a lifetime of travel, laughter, and late nights talking. With our friends and family, we are confident that our lives will be full and joyous, and one day we hope to have children of our own.

If you live to be 100, I hope to live to be 100 minus one day,
so I never have to live without you.
—WINNIE THE POOH

Asking to Find Love and Your Best Relationship

Ask Yourself...

- "What kind of person is my ideal mate?"
- "What are her/his family goals?"
- "How does she/he enjoy spending her/his time?"
- "Do we like doing the same things?"

- "What are her/his spiritual/religious beliefs?"
- "What is her/his idea of a great life? A great future?"
- "Does she/he share my values and dreams?"
- "Are we ultra-compatible?"

Ask Others...

- "May I introduce myself?"
- "Can we talk for a minute?"
- "Could I invite you out for coffee?"
- "Can I sit with you?"
- "Can I help you with your project?"
- "Can we spend time together?"
- "What do you like to do for fun?"
- "What's the most important priority in your life?"
- "How can I make your day better?"

Fill in your own list in your Ask journal. Let everything you're learning in this reading journey start to help you to live in a new age of boldness and abundance. You are here to expand your horizons. Existing resources become yours almost immediately the minute you decide to start asking.

Choosing a Passionate Relationship

What deposit are you making into your Love Bank Account? To make your relationship light up, be exhilarating, and shine? What can you do daily to become the happiest person and happiest couple ever?

To live happily ever after is a choice and not a movie or fairy tale dream. You can do it by asking yourself first how to maximize your passionate romance and forever improve yourself.

The well-known cliché is: *The road to self-improvement is always under construction.* Yet, research shows that only 3 percent of us take the journey. It is worth it. It takes consistency, dedication, and unrelenting desire.

> *In all affairs, it's a healthy thing now and then*
> *to hang a question mark on the things*
> *you have long taken for granted.*

—BERTRAND RUSSELL

The other day, one of our good friends shared a wonderful idea about how to keep love vital and alive in a marriage. When rekindling and recommitting to their love after a near-divorce twenty years ago, his wife started a loving habit that delights him to this day. She is forever writing mini love notes and placing them in unusual places where he can find them. He finds these surprise notes in his underwear, socks, briefcase, desk, computer, pants pocket, steering wheel, jewelry case, travel folder, glove compartment of his car, shoes, or on his mirror or at the top of his ink pen. They all begin with *I love you because…*followed by a *very specific* behavior or quality she loves about him. Taking the time to notice and acknowledge those things makes him glow with joy and utter thankfulness. He says when he gets one of these notes, it makes him realize how lucky he is regardless of what kind of difficulty he might be experiencing that day. Affirming one another in different ways, like her special notes, is just one of the many things that has made the second twenty years of their marriage an entirely different experience than the first twenty years. He keeps every note as a precious collection.

In relationships, we get comfortable and set in our ways. But to keep things alive and passionate, we need to keep checking in with ourselves, using a big dose of honesty, and question our relationship dynamic. If you fear your relationship has gotten caught in a serious doldrum, don't be afraid to start questioning what is going on:

- "Are we being romantic with each other every day?"
- "Am I criticizing more than I'm affirming my spouse?"
- "Do I remember to open the door for her?"
- "Are we too tired or burned out for intimacy?"
- "How long has it been since I've told him he looks handsome?"
- "Have we gotten into a comfortable rut?"
- "How can I make her/him feel special?"
- "Are we remembering to *date* each other like we did in the beginning?"

When the answers to these questions reveal a relationship that's lost some of its verve, it's time to intervene with some good old-fashioned romance.

Romance is the never-ending unfoldment of love, joy, and togetherness. There is no age limit on being romantic and creating treasurable and unforgettable memories. Too many of us get so busy and involved with our lives and livelihoods that we neglect our basic romantic natures. Research shows that there is a high correlation between couples having fun together and staying happily in love. More fun means a happier and more lasting relationship. Make being more romantic a delightful challenge to create positive memories. Each day it is wonderful to remember to kiss, hug, touch each other fondly, and say I love you. Even doing a twenty-second shoulder rub or squeezing each other's hands while you're talking about something rekindles important bonds. Be considerate by asking your spouse what they would like to do on your next holiday together. Make a point to do thoughtful things like bringing your spouse coffee or tea in the morning, showing concern that they're eating right, getting their annual physical checkups for health, or that they have the right outfit, so they look great at an upcoming event. Make life together more fun by getting special event tickets to sports, theatre, dance, or musical concerts, or calling friends and scheduling a wig party for her birthday, or a scramble golf tournament for his birthday. It's important to check in with each other regularly and **ask**:

"**How can we be more romantic?**" Here's a list to get started.

1. Write a gushy love letter like in a Nicholas Sparks book.
2. Establish goals together.
3. Kidnap and sneak her away to a special surprise rendezvous.
4. Enjoy a sunset picnic.
5. Eat dinner on the roof, if possible.
6. Re-create your first romantic date.
7. Watch a starry sky together during the next meteor shower with a bottle of great wine.
8. Surprise your beloved with a candlelight dinner.
9. Visit a park and just *be* with each other, delightfully discussing all your best times together.
10. Take a sail or rent a paddleboat.
11. Dance in the rain and make some hot cocoa while you're drying off.
12. Watch the fireplace blaze at home, or in a hotel, restaurant, or cabin.
13. Go to a spa or resort.
14. See a morning movie.
15. Ride in a horse-drawn carriage down Fifth Avenue in New York City.

16. Create your family photo story together, in an electronic or physical album.
17. Make an exotic dinner together from scratch.

As a couple, we're challenging you to ask and answer your own questions to kindle more excitement and romance in your lives. Life becomes so much sweeter when you do!

Ask Gold Nuggets:

- Asking in intimate relationships increases likability.
- Use power, not force, when asking someone.
- Lead by example when you want someone to comply with your request.
- Discover what you really want before you ask.
- Questions lead to intimacy.
- Be intentional to find your true love using curiosity and exploring questions.
- What deposits are you making into your Love Bank Account?

---

3. Ask to Achieve Ideal Health, Vitality, and Fitness

What is a human? *A self-balancing, 28-jointed adaptor-based biped; an electro-chemical reduction plant, integral with segregated stowages of special energy extracts in storage batteries, for subsequent actuation of thousands of hydraulic and pneumatic pumps, with motors attached; 62,000 miles of capillaries; millions of warning signals, railroad and conveyor systems; crushers and cranes (of which the arms are magnificent 23-jointed affairs with self-surfacing and lubricating systems, and a universally distributed telephone system needing no service for 70 years if well managed); the whole, extraor-dinary complex mechanism guided with exquisite precision from a turret in which are located telescopic and microscopic self-registering and recording range finders, a Spectro-scope, etcetera, the turret control being closely allied with an air conditioning intake-and-exhaust, and a main fuel intake.*

—DR. R. BUCKMINSTER FULLER'S
Nine Chains to the Moon, written in 1938

Master Your Health with the Right Questions

As you perused the passage above, you could have easily thought you were reading about some highly refined energy and processing plant. Inventor, futurist, and author Buckminster Fuller's description of your body as a magnificently functioning machine makes you stop and pay attention to the elegant complexity and extraordinary value of this human body through which you live, play, work, and love.

Think about a time when you felt great about your health and fitness. Your sense of serenity probably soared along with it. You showed up differently in your relationships. You were kinder and more gracious; you brought more optimism to the relational dynamic. Even in your work life, when you've felt good about your health and fitness, you probably had more energy, confidence, and enthusiasm, and could push yourself a bit further toward excellence. But the most beautiful qualities of the soul are dampened when we are fighting low energy or poor fitness and health.

This is why it is vitally important to be connected to yourself at every level of your being.

The asking journey gives you the opportunity to start connecting all the parts of you. When you start to acknowledge the connection between your mind, body, and spirit, then your life will get a whole lot better! Your zest for life, your fun-loving spirit, your smile that lights up your face, your compassion for others, your contribution each day to the people around you—all these are enhanced and multiplied when you know you are honoring your body and yourself in your behaviors and choices.

The only way you can truly respect yourself and become the greatest expression of *you* is when you are living in a state of awareness and connection to all the gifts that are yours in life, particularly your own body.

Where Is the Love?

As I began to work with people to achieve better health and fitness, I was utterly amazed at what I found. Many of my clients, particularly the women, had tried dozens of diets throughout their lives, some of them quite extreme and punishing. When we started asking the questions that led to clearer realizations, the most surprising discoveries were three things:

- They were convinced they were doomed to be overweight and didn't believe, when they lost weight, they could keep it off.
- When they became slimmer for a while, they felt like imposters in their own skin.
- They didn't like their bodies. In fact, some of them hated their bodies!

Whoa! Stop there! Time to ask some *really* important questions:

- How can you ever be successful at something in which, deep in your heart, you have no confidence?
- If you feel you don't deserve to look and feel your amazing best, how long will you honor your health and fitness goals?

- Your body is a living organism. If you hate it, how will your cells respond?

Your beliefs about yourself come from a lifetime of experiences and feedback you've taken in from the world, plus the scenarios you imagine in your own mind. Each one of us walks around with a little bit of every experience inside us, and those events and our impressions of them become the filters by which we process the rest of our lives. Those beliefs and filters create entrenched programs that run automatically at the subconscious level, whether you know it or not. To continue across that bridge to our best, most fulfilling destiny, we need to be willing to peel ourselves open, bit by bit, by asking the right questions.

Be Honest with Yourself

Are you ready to get real about health and fitness? Then we want to ask you some tough questions. Answer them with raw honesty. Honesty with yourself is foundational for every positive change. It is human nature to try to fool ourselves or ignore the truth, especially when we know deep down that things need to change. We want you to remember this truth: the more you are willing to embrace change, the greater your chances for success in every area of life. Health, weight, and fitness are no exception.

Exploring Health and Fitness Questions

- Have you given up on staying healthy, fit, and looking great?
- Are you taking the best care of your body?
- Are you truly happy with the shape you're in?
- Are you ignoring the truth about your physical energy and vitality?

- Are you ignoring the potential health consequences of neglecting your body's needs?
- Do you take care daily to do the best you can for yourself?
- Are there other areas of your life that feel out of control?
- Which area of your life is causing you the most stress right now?
- Which current situations cause you the most emotional instability?

You can never start to move in the right direction if you don't know where you are now. The answers to this honesty exercise will help you begin to clearly and honestly assess where you stand with current health and wellness. When you truly consider how you feel about your self-confidence, health, strength, vitality, and well-being, do you have what you want from life or are your questions hanging out there begging to be answered? Use this exercise as a starting point on the path to something so much better. After you have answered the questions, reread your answers a second and third time. When you read the answers the third time, imagine them as the end of a mental and emotional place from which you are ready to move forward.

Starting today, make a decision to live this day with purpose and intention to honor your amazing body with each choice you make.

Positive Intentional Questions
- "Am I willing to apologize to myself for the times when I've given up on myself?"
- "Am I ready to be fully honest and about the areas I've neglected myself?"
- "Am I being truthful and authentic to myself about the consequences of ignoring my health and fitness?"

- "Will I honestly acknowledge the times I feel out of control in my life and take quiet time to reflect on why?"
- "Am I ready to recognize and admit the things that cause me the most inner stress?"
- "Will I pay attention to feelings of emotional instability I experience and then write down the circumstances and events that trigger those feelings?"
- "Can I be authentic and truthful with myself, allowing me to move forward in a clear direction with my health and fitness?"

You may not be there yet, but eventually you'll reach the point where every answer to the questions above is a resounding *yes*!

Ask What Is Getting in the Way of Your Best Health

Sometimes life delivers events to us that prompt us to ask the questions that can lead us to the right answers to receive true health and healing. Everything you ever think, do, become, or create will happen through your body. We love the living examples of people who have asked powerful, life-altering questions that have changed their destiny from one of poor health to one of robust health, strength, and balance. Asking the right questions can interrupt patterns we've formed that are destructive to our health and can revector us to vitality and wellness.

My Most Important Question: Mayor Brad Cole

As the former mayor of Carbondale, Illinois, I had a lot to worry about and stress over. I used to have terrible headaches and be stressed out, upset, and easily agitated. All this made me feel depressed and often made it very hard to work. I basically never felt really great because of it. After being tired of feeling that way all the time, one day, in a moment of desperation, I asked myself in a very sincere way, "What can I do to change all this?" The answer came spontaneously: *get mind balance*. I instantly knew exactly what the answer meant. Mind balance is staying centered and calm in the midst of the storm forces, problems, and noise of the world. When I received this answer, it caused a profound change in me. I immediately reset my mind-center with calm, quiet, peaceful feelings. Within minutes I felt completely different. I felt balanced and calm in my mind, and suddenly I felt none of the pains I'd felt for so long. This mind-balancing technique that came to me as a clear answer to my question allowed me to continue with that job and have successes I wouldn't otherwise have had. Now, I am happy to resolve everything by being calm in the midst of turmoil and strife.

One of the best examples of problems I solved more effectively from this new state of mind as a mayor was the inland hurricane that occurred in our city on May 8, 2009. It was graduation day at Southern Illinois University, with a community student population of thirty-five thousand students. Inland hurricanes are virtually unheard of in that part of the country, but one hit us that day. It unexpectedly struck with a ferocious velocity, wiping out four thousand trees in a few minutes' time and stopping everything in its tracks. I gathered together my team and asked them, "How long will it take to clean up this mess?" I was told three months. I looked at them earnestly and said, "I'm asking you to do the impossible and get it done in three weeks." Three weeks later, there was not a leaf on the ground. I learned long ago to ask a better question to get a better result. The big issue is to not think about what won't work when you ask. Rather, I ask myself and others, "How do I/we think about a new or different solution to have impact now, even in a small way?" I conquered bad health by asking in that way. The answer that came to me that day completely revectored the way I processed life and made me far more resilient and balanced in my health and wellness.

There Is a Lot Riding on a Healthy, Fit You

Let's consider the following aspects of life that depend on your healthy, well-cared-for body:

- How you experience your spousal or primary love relationship
- How you experience friendships
- How you bring life and nurture life—children, grandchildren, nieces, nephews, siblings, parents
- How you express your creativity—arts, dance, music, architecture
- How you express your intelligence—science, language, mathematics
- How you make your contribution to the world via a career, a business, or philanthropy
- How you experience God and your relationship with God

The Whole You

When it comes to utilizing the power of asking to achieve your greatest health, vitality, and fitness, it's important to think of yourself as a whole person. True health usually isn't achieved with the latest health craze; it is about understanding yourself, loving yourself, and learning to support yourself with healthier habits. I (Crystal) was raised by a mother who was way ahead of her time when it came to her pursuit of a naturally healthy life for her children. She questioned everything about how to be and stay healthy, and as a result, we grew huge organic gardens and did juice cleanses long before they became chic, and our primary physician was a naturopathic doctor. As a result of my mother's relentless pursuit of health and her unwillingness to accept what the doctor told her without further investigation, she raised nine ultra-healthy kids who grew into healthy adults.

ASK!

My Mother's Grand Mal Seizure

One night when my mother was pregnant with me (Crystal), my father woke up to an eerie moaning sound that scared him. He reached over to touch my mother, and her body was as stiff as a board, and he realized the sound was coming from her. He flew out of bed and turned on the lights and realized she was having a grand mal seizure. He called an ambulance, and she was rushed to the hospital to undergo testing. The seizure had stopped by the time she arrived there, but the doctors were baffled by what had happened. They decided a couple of days later to send her to the nearest neurologist, who had an office in a town thirty miles from my small Idaho town. Strangely, while in the neurologist's waiting room, she met another pregnant woman who had also had a grand mal seizure a few days before. Her doctors had not given her any answers, so she was also referred to this same neurologist. After my mom returned home from that doctor, she called my grandmother crying and upset. "The doctor basically told me he had no idea what was wrong with me or why the seizure happened, but to take this prescription for two years and then come back to see him."

My grandmother was outraged! "Don't you *dare* put those pills in your body with that baby in your womb, when they don't even know what's wrong with you!"

"What am I going to do to solve this mystery and keep my baby and my own health safe?" my mother asked.

My grandmother started looking for the answer. She lived in the small town of Rexburg, Idaho, thirty miles north of our town. She started asking everyone if they knew of an alternative doctor who might be able to help my mother without harming her unborn child. Miraculously, Grandma got her answer. Someone she met told her a new naturopathic/chiropractic doctor had moved to the town of St. Anthony, which was another twenty-five miles north of Rexburg. This person told her this doctor had been healing people who weren't healed by traditional doctors. Grandma told my mother she needed to take the hour drive north the next day because she had an appointment for her with Dr. Long. Once there, Dr. Long gave my mom a chiropractic adjustment, did some holistic testing, and gave her some herbs and vitamins to take home with her. Mom continued to see him until I was born, thankfully strong and healthy with no complications or issues.

Fast-forward to my eighth year. I was taking ballet lessons each week with a wonderful teacher, whom I enjoyed very much. One day I came home from class and said to my mother, "Mom, I saw Miss Gossman's son get off a smaller bus today, and when he walked in, she said something to him, but he can't talk. Someone said he's my age. He looks as tall as me, but how can he be my age and not be able to talk?"

Mom sat me down and told me for the first time, the story of the grand mal seizure she'd had when I was in her womb. She finished by saying, "Miss Gossman was the woman who was at the same doctor that day. I'm afraid she took those pills, and they might have done brain damage to her poor child."

Dr. Long ended up becoming basically our main family doctor. We saw a traditional doctor on rare occasions, and my mom raised nine extremely healthy kids. I'm so thankful to this day that my mother and grandmother had the courage to question what they were told. That they didn't just accept something that made them very uncomfortable. That they kept asking and asking until they found the right answer that gave us a new direction with our health care, which has proven to be a great blessing through the years.

How Much Is Your Body Worth?

I want to share some information that caused me to bask in wonder when I first heard it years ago, as it still does today. Earl Nightingale's *Lead the Field* audio series talks about the value of the human body, if you were to quantify it monetarily or scientifically. Nightingale says:

> *We are God's highest form of creation, yet most of us have no idea how much we are worth. If the electronic energy in the atoms of our bodies could be utilized, each of us could supply all of the electrical needs for an industrialized country for close to a week. Scientists discovered that the atoms of the human body contain potential energy of eleven million kilowatt-hours per pound of electrical energy, which would make an average man or woman worth about $85 billion. The electrons in your body are not just particles of matter; they're waves of living energy that spread out in patterns of light. And as they move, they sing. With the right hearing device, you would hear a great symphonic concert as these waves play and flow, merging with the waves of other matter. These electrons in your body not only sing, but they also shine. If you stood in front of an infrared television camera in a dark room, the screen would show you from top to bottom as a glistening, radiating form. If you tried to reproduce your mind mechanically, it would cost billions of dollars, but you would still not be able to do it. And not only are you amazing and infinitely valuable, but you are unique. You're unlike any human being that's ever lived on earth, or ever will live on earth.*

Do you get it? There is nothing more valuable than your body, which God so uniquely and beautifully created!

So how do you treat your most valuable possession? Let me tell you what I've found in years of working with people about their health and well-being. We tend to treat our cars better, our houses better, and other people better than we treat our own bodies.

Why? There is no good answer. But here are some of the reasons I've uncovered as I've asked people this very question:

- We have the misguided idea that taking care of ourselves is selfish.
- We undervalue ourselves and begin to think others must be more important.
- We think we are shortchanging those we love if we don't give away every bit of ourselves to them.
- We fool ourselves into thinking that after we've done everything for everyone else first, then eventually we'll get to ourselves.

My friend, this is faulty thinking! Say out loud: "This needs to change now. I need to start treating my body better *today!*"

What is always speaking silently is the body.

—NORMAN BROWN, PSYCHOLOGIST AND AUTHOR

Why Don't I Deserve Better? Penny's Story

My (Crystal) client Penny was the ultimate mother. She was smart, kind, loving, and patient with her children. She also worked a part-time job as a legal assistant. She was on top of everything. Nothing in her world slipped. Penny went out of her way to feed her kids very nutritious meals, and she loved decorating their rooms, sewing custom character pillows, and making them feel as though they lived in a special fantasyland. She tutored them each evening, so they always got top grades in their classes, and they were never late to a musical lesson or soccer practice.

Not only was Penny the ultimate mother, but she was also an outstanding wife. She talked about her husband's work as if it was more important than hers, even though people at her job swore they couldn't live without her great skills and efficiency. Penny came to me to be coached in organizational efficiency, essentially asking, "How can I do a better job for everyone in my life?"

The tragedy? Penny couldn't see how neglectful she was being to herself, and how it was affecting her health. While the kids ate healthy meals, Penny would catch up on calls and emails, then go flying out the door with peanut butter crackers or a bagel for her breakfast or dinner. Whenever she found a free moment to feed her starving self, she would resort to diving into the doughnuts at work or grabbing fast food on a five-to-ten-minute lunch "hour." As far as physical activity? Forget it. Even during soccer practice or ballet lessons, instead of taking a walk, Penny caught up on work-related reading. Not surprisingly, Penny rarely felt good. She just kept driving herself harder.

When Penny came back for our second appointment, I asked her if she knew what the most important help was that I could give her. She seemed a bit uncertain, then said, "I'm hoping you could help coach me to more success in my life." I asked her if she knew how important she was to the people she loved, and what would happen to them if she wasn't around because she wasn't willing to take care of herself.

Penny looked stunned for a moment and didn't say a word. Then the floodgates opened. As she hung her head and tears gushed, her answer came. "I don't know how much longer I can go on doing everything and being everything to everyone." She admitted, "I feel like I don't exist sometimes." She shared that the more disgusted she felt with her own body, the more she ignored it. "I feel like I live a thousand miles away from my own body. I'm afraid even to acknowledge my needs because I've ignored them for so long."

Penny was overweight, in terrible physical condition (in spite of having a husband who played tennis and stayed in great shape) and had lost all the luster and shine in her face. She had been a pretty woman, but at some point, she stopped asking for anything for herself.

That was Penny's turning point. When she got honest with herself and answered those tough questions, she knew what the answer was. She needed to change her priorities. She needed to put herself first more often. She needed to let the people she loved step up and take more responsibility. She needed to learn to trust that her world, and the people she loved, wouldn't fall apart if she took some time for herself. Fortunately, those realizations made a profound difference in her life.

She started honoring herself with time alone, exercise, and some self-nurturing, and from that, began to feel like a brand-new woman. After a few months her changes began to pay off. She began to feel like a person again, instead of feeling like she was merely everyone's accessory. She told me her husband and kids seemed to respect her more. She finally realized that came with respecting and honoring herself. That no one in your life can respect you until you do.

I've talked to many people, especially women, who have a little bit of Penny in them. They stop questioning what it is they need, and ultimately, their health and well-being become their lowest priorities. It's a realization that can make you feel desperately sad. Why? Because deep down, you know you deserve better.

Ask yourself: "How much of my life will I let slip by before I realize that this is the only life and body I've been given?" Isn't it time to honor that?

God made your body with a perfect accounting system. No matter how much we delude ourselves into thinking poor eating choices, a lack of healthy active movement, and just ignoring our health needs will somehow reconcile themselves in the end, our body's cells and systems can't be fooled. If you think of your body and health like a bank account—with poor eating and sedentary habits being debits, and wholesome foods, vital exercise, and good sleep being deposits or credits—then you understand that you can't keep writing checks and taking withdrawals without replenishing your account with new cash deposits. Just like you could end up financially bankrupt by running your financial life that way, you could end up bankrupting your own health.

> *You can't eat six apples Saturday night and get the health benefit.*
> *It's an apple a day that keeps the doctor away.*
> —JIM ROHN

Do It for the Ones You Love

Sometimes it's hard at first to get comfortable to ask for time for ourselves or ask our family to put our needs first. Many parents are used to giving themselves away to their family, career, and relationships, and there's just no room left to take care of themselves. A great asking technique involves bringing loved ones into the picture, and it goes like this:

Gather some photographs of yourself with your parents, children, friends, and other important relationships. Also get one photo of just you with your favorite spiritual picture or scripture verse next to it. Then tape these pictures to a piece of paper and write next to each one:

- "Why is my best health and fitness important to my husband/wife?" (list all the reasons)
- "Why is my best health and fitness important to my children?" (list all the reasons)

- "Why is my best health and fitness important to my job?" (list all the reasons)
- "Why is my greatest health and fitness important to God and me?"

If you're one who struggles with self-care time, spend five minutes of quiet time each morning going through those photos and questions. It's a powerful daily reminder that your health is an issue for everyone you love and who loves you, not just yours.

Retrain Your Palate, Listen to Your Body

Some of the biggest health issues today are caused by overeating. Things have changed a lot from the days we had to toil in the fields or spend hours trekking through the woods to hunt and gather our food each day. It's wonderful that modern-day humans are being fed more conveniently and far fewer people are starving, but now we've created another problem. That ever-convenient fare is pretty much in front of us wherever we go and causing obesity and sickness. Society has taken a big shift from eating because we're hungry to eating ever-larger amounts of food just because it's there. The best way to intervene in this temptation to overload your body is to start with a question.

When you feel the urge to eat, *ask* yourself: "Am I truly in need of energy, or am I just feeling a habitual signal to eat because of stress or sensory stimulation like the smell or sight of something cooking?" Also, listen to your body to find out when it's full. There is a spot in the lower esophagus that begins to close off when you have fed your body enough. People with weight issues have learned over time to ignore that signal completely and instead keep relying on their sensory signals like smell and taste. They keep eating what their bodies are trying to tell them they don't need. It's important with your health to ask questions that lead to answers that prompt a keener sense of awareness about your current health habits and stimulate a new commitment. These questions below are crafted to elicit answers that will help you commit to make better health choices each and every day. We suggest that you write them out and put them on a mirror or somewhere you can easily see them as you're getting ready for your day.

- "Am I willing to feed myself the highest-quality nutrition so that I am satisfied?"
- "Am I eating food for my greatest health value and nutrition, not to soothe my stress or emotions?"
- "Am I listening to my body's natural signals and discerning true hunger from other types of stimuli?"
- "Do I make it my business to be consciously aware of the nutrient values in foods and provide my body with only the best?"
- "Will I forgo white, low-nutrition sugars and starches that do not enhance the health of my strong, healthy, gorgeous body?"
- "Am I eating vegetables, nuts, and high-quality proteins that keep my blood sugar at steady, healthy levels?"
- "Am I eating the greens that give me vitamins, minerals, micronutrients, and fiber that make my cells healthy and my body feel great?"
- "Do I deliberately eat high-quality proteins throughout the day to keep my blood sugar stable and my energy and stamina strong and steady?"

What's Your Best Move?

You can find hundreds of reasons to include healthy activity and movement in your life. According to the Mayo Clinic, exercise helps elevate mood, fight disease, improve your sex life, promote better sleep, boost your daily energy level, and, of course, manage your weight. Wow! I want all that, don't you? Still not convinced? Exercise burns the calories you consume, increases brain function, strengthens your muscles, and supports your joints.

So, what's the dilemma? Computers, cell phones, and many other technological advances have consolidated business operations and transformed how we do our work in today's world. We're able to hold conference calls with participants from around the world, negotiate terms, docu-sign on important deals, and form and share a full marketing strategy all from one small computer at a desk in our homes. I often marvel at the way Mark and I can compress activities that used to take weeks virtually into hours. The problem? We hardly move anything but our hands and our mouth when accomplishing these tasks. Since our modern environment doesn't demand that we move much, we need to demand adequate movement for ourselves that supports our vital bodily functions and health. The only way we have to use the food calories we put in is to participate in enough movement to burn them as energy. So how do we take care of our bodies' need for healthy movement when we don't even have to walk from the car into the office and out again?

A fair number of people I've worked with aren't successfully integrating healthy activity, exercise, and movement into their day. There are typically two main reasons they have for that.

- They don't have time to fit it into their day.
- They get bored with a workout routine and quit after a while.

Life is certainly busy and, at times, crazy for each of us. So, my advice to them is to take a look at the life they live and ask how they can fit movement in to what they're already doing!

Here are some of our favorite ideas:

- **Can you sneak in workplace movement?** There should never be a barrier between you and movement. If you are stuck at the computer most of the day, take seven to ten minutes out of sixty to stand up, toe touch, twist, bend, and do arm rotations or leg lifts. If you get stuck sitting for too long, start to clench and relax your legs, glutes, abs, and arm muscles as often as possible. And don't forget to stretch out those cramped muscles. Each small chunk matters and adds up to a leaner you!

- **Could you divide lunchtime into lunch 'n' walk time?** Most people take an hour for lunch, but if you think about it, is it really necessary to do another hour of sitting after you've been sitting all day? Doesn't make a lot of sense, does it? Instead, break your lunchtime in half. If it's an hour, have a salad with protein and a couple of whole grain seeded crackers for a half hour, then take a nice half hour walk around the neighborhood. Some people like to reverse it. Walking first and eating second. Either way, plan it and follow through with your plan. Even if you only take a half-hour lunch, fifteen minutes of fresh air and brisk walking will refresh your mind, get your metabolism pumped, and clear your head for the rest of your workday.

- **Can you stand up for yourself?** Who says we need to take information sitting down? At our office, we encourage people to stand and pace as they're processing their thoughts or listening. We find people get more productive when they intersperse sitting with standing or pacing.

- **Why not walk and talk sessions?** Meetings don't have to take place inside. Instead of facing each other across the desk, ask the person you're meeting with if they'll walk with you. My husband and I have found that employees, colleagues, and clients relax more and are often more authentic when we take them outside the office for a stroll around our office campus during a meeting. The break refreshes and invigorates everyone, especially if you've had an intensive discussion for an hour or so. After ten minutes of fresh air and strolling, they're ready to dive in and get back to work. A brisk ten-to-fifteen-minute walk in the middle of a long afternoon can perk you up so you're far more energized and productive for the final hours of your workday.

- **Why are you sitting there, Mom?** Why should kids be the only ones who are getting the healthy benefits of exercise outdoors? If you find yourself spending a fair amount of time at soccer practice or even taking kids to the park to play, resist the urge to just sit there and read a book or chat with other parents. It's a perfect time for *you* to get in some healthy movement while they're preoccupied. Take a fast power walk around the ballpark while you enjoy nature. Lift your knee to the opposite elbow while "crunching" in a bit as you watch them scramble up the monkey bars. Do forty reps of this for two or three sets and I promise you you'll be breathing hard like the little ones! There's just no reason to spend great outdoor opportunities like this doing more sitting! Get up and *move it!*

- **Could commute time be more fun as move time?** If you live far from work and have to drive or take a bus, consider parking farther away and walking the last ten or fifteen minutes, or getting off at the bus stop before yours. If you take a crowded train, choose to stand instead of fighting for a seat. If you're close enough, take a little extra time and walk to work. Activity choices that only add up to ten or fifteen minutes in your day *might* end up adding ten or fifteen years to your life!

- **Enjoy TV? Do it while you walk!** You don't need to be a couch potato even if you can't miss your favorite television programs. Try moving while you watch. I keep small dumbbells tucked right under the sofa within easy reach. Do deep pliés, holding the weights along your thighs as you move up and down. You can also hold the weights over your shoulder and do switch-leg, walking squats in place. Add in some push-ups, crunches, and leg lifts. If that treadmill has been collecting dust in the garage, clean it up and bring it in. You can get a solid hour of walking in, relieve your stress of the day, and not even miss your number-one show! Remember, research shows that the longer you *sit* and watch television, the greater your waist circumference and your risk of dying from heart disease.

- **Isn't it time to rekindle your love life?** Couples often get too busy for each other as life's demands begin to get in the way of love. Reconnecting your relationship with your spouse and burning calories is definitely a win-win. Having sex burns about 150–250 calories per half hour. Sexual activity also has a number of great health benefits and studies show that more frequent sex creates greater longevity. The great thing is it's very enjoyable, it's free, and it creates a deeper bond between husband and wife! Let your love machine become the ultimate exercise machine!

- **Why not be a kid again?** Playing with your kids can not only create some of the best bonding times together, it is also an easy way to clock in some serious fat-burning, muscle-building time. Grab your kid and a basketball and shoot some hoops for a half hour before dinner. Pick up that old tennis racket and walk or jog to your local tennis courts. Who cares if you're not an A player? Hitting the ball and running across the court will let you laugh, learn, and sweat together. Be creative. This is time *very* well spent!

Repeat this affirmation throughout the day:

> *"I am living my life with the intention*
> *of taking the very best care of myself.*
> *I deserve it."*

From Fat and Sick to Healthy, Lean, and Happy: Dr. Nick Delgado's Story

Dr. Nick Delgado is an amazing man and longtime friend of mine (Mark). We met while parking our respective Rolls-Royces next to each other outside the Hyatt Regency Hotel in Irvine, California, before entering to talk at a Tony Robbins meeting. We had never met. We smiled and almost simultaneously said: "Nice wheels!" We shook hands, introduced ourselves, and started a never-ending conversation about health, wealth, and happiness. We have been great friends ever since. Coincidentally, he occupied the office building diagonally across from mine in Costa Mesa, California. Because of our work proximity, Crystal and I visited with Nick frequently. A few years ago, knowing he was an award-winning physical culturist, I asked if we could train together. Nick invited me to join him three nights a week at 5:00 at The 12 Costa Mesa Boot Camp. We partnered up and were rigorously trained by a tough Navy SEAL sergeant trainer from Camp Pendleton. It was exhilarating, exhausting, and refreshing for us to be the oldest in class, with mostly twenty- to thirty-somethings. We managed to keep up and finish each class exhausted and very sweaty—but always with a smile and a high five! Nick believes that if you live long enough, you can pretty much live forever because scientific breakthroughs in health and longevity are happening so rapidly! If you listen to his encouraging and motivating antiaging talks, you become a true believer in the value of disciplining yourself to a healthier lifestyle.

Nick grew up eating what he assumed was a healthy American four-square meal, what we were taught and considered the four basic food groups consisting of dairy, meats, chicken, and fish and far lesser amounts of fruits, vegetables, and breads. As a young kid he began to put on excess weight and get horrible hormonal skin outbreaks (acne) from eating that way. Starting in elementary school, kids were making fun of him because he was extremely husky. By age twelve they mocked and called him names like "Fatso" or "Omar the Tent-maker"; he was relatively short, five foot eight, and was forty pounds over the weight limit for Pop Warner football. He was repeatedly told by his coach at weigh-ins that he had to cut weight. He starved himself by trying to live on one egg a day and a small bowl of cottage cheese. He also ran five miles after football practice and barely made weigh-in every week at 115 pounds. Constantly feeling hunger pangs, he felt weak, tired, distracted, and traumatized starving himself thin far below his ideal weight, and cried himself to sleep nightly. He said he felt hungry so often that it gave him an inkling of what it must feel like to be starving in a third-world country after he visited countries like Africa and India. Because of the trauma he felt from his own self-imposed starvation, Nick developed a strong empathy for people who are truly hungry and on street corners begging for food. Now, he makes it a point to carry extra food in his car with him to give to homeless people.

As a college football prospect, Nick was asked to gain weight, which he did, to over 220 pounds. At the age of twenty-two, on Thanksgiving Day, he was playing in a football game as a linebacker against the Pasadena Police Department team. He made several good tackles; however, by halftime, he felt dizzy and helplessly fell to the ground. The entire right side of his body was paralyzed. He had what was later diagnosed as a transient ischemic attack. That is, a stroke, where the blood supply is blocked from the brain. When he was finally able to stand up again in the next few days, he knew he was in trouble. All the medical doctor's recommendations and blood pressure medications did not work—in fact, they made it worse, and he felt and looked terrible.

Fortunately, Nick happened to be watching TV one night, and he saw Nathan Pritikin, author of the bestseller *Live Longer Now*, being interviewed about how he had solved the problem of cardiovascular disease for thousands and even made it disappear. (This original *60 Minutes* interview is featured on Nick's website still today.) When he finished the program, he finally asked himself the most important question of his life: "Am I going to continue to do what I've always done and be fat, miserable, and sick, or am I going to do something different that has proven success?" The answer was clear for him. It was then that he decided to take his health into his own hands. As recommended by the Pritikin philosophy, he cut out all meats, cheese, fatty oils, and eggs while he increased the fiber with plant-based, starch-resistant foods and continued his daily exercise regimen. Dramatically, he began to look and feel like a completely different person. He went from being very sick to feeling better than he had in his entire life!

A short time after, Nick found out that Nathan Pritikin would be appearing at an event in Pasadena, California. He went to the talk. There were six hundred people in attendance, and like Nick, each one was carrying Pritikin's book. Nick was mesmerized by the six-hour talk Pritikin gave, so much so that he stood in line after his talk to chat with him. He was last in line, and it was late at night. Nick told Pritikin that he had saved his life. He showed him his "before" and "after" pictures. Nick was only twenty-three years old by then and finally felt like he was a new man with an exciting future. Pritikin was so impressed with Nick that he asked him to come and work with him at his Pritikin Longevity Center, where a live-in program was offered and conferences were held with the greatest experts in nutrition and health.

Nick was humbled and honored, and immediately took up the challenge by accepting Pritikin's offer. It became Nick's postgraduate work starting in 1978. He was an enthusiastic learner and employee for two years. Nick mastered what is now called Lifestyle Medicine after extensive studies in health science at Loma Linda University and became director of the entire outpatient program as he maintained his focus on life extension. He hired and trained several health educators and doctors to teach courses to the community with weekly courses offered to transform lives. Eventually, Nick created the Delgado Protocol, using proper diet and his own formulations of natural supplements to support antiaging. Over the years, he has improved upon the taste and simplicity to prepare quick meals or order out at restaurants to make it easy for his followers to enjoy the program.

Graduates like Phyllis Ginsberg rave about the impact Nick's program has had in their lives: "I was nineteen years old when I started the Pritikin Program, taught by Nick Delgado and his team of health educators, including his mother, Bea Delgado. After I graduated from USC, my husband, Michael, and I took your Optimal Health Course in Garden Grove, California. Six weekly classes—I still have the books! I've lived a life of prevention on purpose after lowering my high cholesterol and triglycerides to normal in six weeks! That's probably why I look young for my age. I just turned fifty-eight this month. He saved my life since I was motivated to change because my mom died at the young age of thirty-seven from breast cancer, with a cholesterol over 400 and triglycerides over 1,000. Now, nearly forty years have passed after meeting Nick Delgado, and my lipid levels, glucose, and chemistry levels are all still ideal. I have followed up with Dr. Nick Delgado to have him take me to the next level of optimum hormone levels, cellular health, and well-being."

Dr. Delgado has spoken at over sixty medical conferences and is one of the most followed antiaging experts in the world. An author of over ten books, his newest releases include *Acne Be Gone for Good*, *Mastering Love, Sex & Intimacy*, and the cookbook *Simply Healthy*. After our interview, he flew to Kuala Lumpur, Malaysia, to assist a large group of Asian doctors, from ten countries, to integrate Rejuvenating Medicine by using the four things it takes to create a truly healthy body, mind, and spirit. Teachings that include the need to detoxify, nutrify, fortify, and utilize the power of our minds.

Nick's beliefs go deep, as a hard scientist, on what each of us needs to do with our 420 different cell types, our need for stem cells, genetics modified by a healthy environment, rejuvenation treatments, bioidentical hormone therapy, anti-inflammation testing, and studying and learning from life-performance experts and elite coaches. He encourages everyone to commit to lifelong questioning and learning to take the best care of themselves. He implores people to value the wisdom of books, audios, videos, and conversations with experts who can help them achieve a healthier lifestyle reinforced by positive directives.

He personally only eats a plant-based unprocessed diet. Annually, he tests his strength against the finest young Olympic and pro athletes and wins. He has set countless records and achievements in the world of strength and endurance. He has curled fifty pounds over 1,038 times in one hour and pressed dumbbells from the waist overhead, lifting 2,000 times for one hour, setting the world record of 50,645 pounds; he next plans to exceed the record for healthy aging. As a full-time life extensionist, he sees age as a number, but not the deciding factor in our health and wellness. "All cell life is basically the same—originally," he says. "Imagine this, we now know that sponges live fifteen thousand years in the ocean, and trees can live five thousand years, and lobsters five hundred years. We humans are just breaking through a hundred years."

It's remarkable to think that all this started out with a young man in failing health who asked and answered a life-pivoting question. Dr. Nick Delgado's iTunes podcasts and YouTube videos have been listened to and viewed by millions. His students are experiencing and enjoying break-through health by overcoming obesity, heart disease, diabetes, fatigue, and hormonal acne, and raising their odds for a longer, healthier life. Nick also has a passion for helping those with kids on the spectrum with autism, autoimmune diseases, and depressed immune systems, making them more susceptible to cancer. We can all be better in spite of our genetics or the mistakes we made in the past. Nick cheerfully says, "I plan to be totally healthy, fit, enthusiastically alive, and make love on my one-hundred-twenty-fourth birthday—making, yes, another record." Find out more at: http://NickDelgado.com.

> *Assume the feeling of your wish fulfilled*
> *and observe the route that your attention follows.*
> —NEVILLE GODDARD, *The Power of Awareness*

When You're in Desperate Health, Don't Stop Asking: J.B. Davis's Story

My husband, Walt, was dying in front of my eyes. He had suffered with kidney disease for many years, and it was getting worse. Insurance would not pay for a transplant. We had moved through the options of the possibility of other family members donating a kidney, but because of multiple reasons and complications, none of those options was panning out. Walt was having to get constant treatments and dialysis just to stay alive. In spite of his health difficulties, his boss kept insisting he travel back and forth to New York. Finally, in May 2001, he flew back from another trip to New York to make it in time for our daughter Nina's birthday. He walked in, and I was frightened. He looked horrible. The next morning, as I watched him lie there in bed, his face a strange gray color, and I knew I was losing my husband. I knew there was a good chance my two young children would grow up without their father. We had already vetted every option with family or close friends to get Walt the kidney that would save his life. My kidney wasn't an option because my blood was type A positive and his was B negative.

I left the house that day to run necessary errands but feeling so desperate as I drove away to take care of my duties. I kept talking to God, saying, "This *can't* happen! My kids can't lose their father! I can't lose my husband! What should we do?"

Suddenly the question came to me: "Why not test me?" It seems now like a crazy question because we already knew my blood type was a wrong match, but when the question came to me, it somehow gave me this determined feeling that my blood should be tested. Without an appointment, I drove to Oregon Health and Science University, where Walt's care was being administered. I immediately asked to speak to Regina, our transplant coordinator, whom I had grown close to throughout this ordeal. She came out and greeted me, and I asked, "Regina, will you please test me?"

She could have refused me, or thought the stress was making me nuts, since we all knew what my blood type was. But she didn't. She said, "Okay, let's do this!" Thirteen vials of blood later, we stood by waiting for the results. I wasn't going to leave until I had my answer. Regina came back with a surprised look on her face.

"What? What is it?" I asked. Her answer was amazing. She said that for some crazy reason, it turns out I have this really unusual factor in my A-type blood, that is some kind of A positive squared. "It's almost unheard of," she told me, "but you have it. It makes it possible for you to donate your kidney to your husband even though his blood type is B."

I didn't bat an eye. I knew God had entrusted me with this responsibility. I knew that moment I was donating my kidney to my husband. I knew that my kids would be fine. I knew that everything would be fine. That was seventeen years ago. Even though Walt has had some health challenges along the way, related to antirejection drugs and other medications he must be on, my little kidneys are still going strong. One inside me and one inside my husband.

Some of us will be faced with health problems we never expected nor deserved. It's so important when that happens not to give in to the fear and not to give up. Ask the questions and continue probing for answers from yourself, others, and God.

Your Body's Reaction to Your Circumstances

An emotion is an amplification of your thought patterns. If you're feeling good, you can be certain that your thoughts are taking you in a positive direction. If you're feeling "bad," they are probably negative recordings playing in your mind that may be more subconscious than conscious, directed thoughts. Asking is a powerful way to find clarity and awareness of buried emotions we're carrying that could be hurting us and our physical health.

A Man Who Found Forgiveness to Heal His Body

When we bought a home in Arizona, whenever we were in town, we began attending a chapel service at The Little Chapel. Many miraculous healings of illness and maladies have taken place in people who have attended the "healing service" at The Little Chapel. Interestingly, at each service, the pastor will tell everyone, "I have no ability to heal anyone. If I did, I would go to all the hospitals and clean them out. What I do here is to hold a special space for people to be healed through God's healing power. I ask God continually to help me facilitate an environment where His healing love and light can be felt. God and the faith of the healed do the healing, not me."

We have attended those church services and have witnessed for ourselves some of the miraculous events and testimonials that have taken place there. Once such testimonial came last December at the beautiful Christmas service. A man, who was a resident of Newport Beach, California, and had traveled from there, was in attendance and was asked to give a testimony of the healing he had experienced. He said he had come to the chapel originally after he had been fighting stage-four colon cancer for some time. His story, which included the day he received this devastating diagnosis and how his wife fell to the floor sobbing uncontrollably at the diagnosis, was heart-wrenching. After many months of treatment, his doctors had told him that there was nothing more they could do for him, that they couldn't give him any more radiation or chemotherapy, and that none of it seemed to be working. The cancer was still growing. The seven big polyps were still there in his colon.

As a last, desperate resort, someone had invited him to this healing service, and he had decided to come. We listened carefully as the man told us how he had no idea what to expect from this healing service, but he basically had been given a zero chance of survival by his doctors. He said as he began to listen to the pastor give her sermon, he locked into something she spoke about. She told the audience to try to focus on one thing and it will help them in their healing today. As he listened, she said something about asking for forgiveness. About the importance of asking God, others, and yourself for forgiveness for the things you've done that you're not proud of. Things that were wrong or hurt other people. Ways you've hurt yourself and your own life. He decided that was what he needed to focus on. Forgiveness. As the healing service continued, the man said he started asking with all his heart to be forgiven. So many memories of terrible things he had done came flooding to his mind, and he kept pouring out his heart to God, asking if there was any way he could be forgiven, asking to help others forgive him, asking for a softer heart to forgive everyone and anyone who had hurt or betrayed him in any way.

When the pastor finishes each service, she reminds everyone to make sure they check with their doctors, even if they feel like they've been healed. The man did just that when he returned to California. When he went back to his doctors a few weeks later, they were baffled. There were no polyps whatsoever on his colon. They had written him off and stopped all treatment; it had been hopeless. How is it they now couldn't find a trace of cancer? He was cancer-free. Many months later, he has remained cancer-free. He said during his testimony, "I know I was guided to ask for forgiveness because asking for and accepting forgiveness was the key to my healing."

Asking for forgiveness and asking to forgive are two of the most important things we'll ever ask for in this lifetime. We're all human. We all mess up. We do hurtful, insensitive things. We do inconsiderate things. We sometimes do very bad, hateful, and deceitful things. When we do such things, or those things are done to us, they trigger the most negative and desperate emotions inside us, such as guilt, shame, blame, hostility, resentment, and anger. When we hold these emotions in our heart, they become like a toxic dump seeping into our minds and bodies. Holding on to such toxicity over time can have devastating effects on our mental, emotional, and physical health. Asking for forgiveness, or asking to forgive someone who hurt you, is the signal to open the lid on that pain and devastation and release the toxic contents.

Sadly, the forgiveness ask can be the most difficult for people. They hold on until, like the man in this story, their body can't tolerate the effects any longer. The two of us try to regularly practice forgiveness toward each other and others, even when we feel grumpy, sad, or hurt, and it's hard. When you're feeling that way, the tempting thing to do is to double down on your position to make sure the other person knows how bad you're feeling and how much they've hurt you. As tempting as that is, all it does is to prolong your own agony and pollute your own mind and body. We use all the tools we can—including scripture, verse, inspirational cards, and especially prayer and meditation—to guide ourselves to a better place so that we can humbly ask for forgiveness and forgive those who've hurt us. There is no better way to lighten your life and the load you're carrying than that!

One of the most important tools in achieving better health is to forge a closer relationship with your own body and to ask the questions daily that support your healthiest choices. Doing so will help you recognize bad habits and integrate simple habits so staying healthy becomes fun and interesting.

If you continue to develop a curiosity about your health options throughout your lifetime, you'll continually cause a positive shift in your mental attitude when it comes to taking better care of yourself. Your health deserves attention so that you can live the highest quality life and feel your best! The answers are there for you, so ask!

Ask Gold Nuggets

- What is getting in the way of your best health?
- Getting mind balance can change your state of health and well-being instantly.
- Ask for other health solutions when you don't feel confident with one that is being recommended.
- Why don't you deserve better? It's time to honor yourself.
- What's your best way to move for better health?
- When in desperate health, don't stop asking for the answers.
- Could asking for and granting forgiveness improve your health?

4. Ask to Accelerate Business and Earnings

If you don't go after what you want, you'll never have it.
If you don't ask, the answer's always no.
If you don't step forward, you're always in the same place.

—Nora Roberts

Benefits to Asking in Business

There are innumerable benefits to learning the art and science of asking when it comes to your business or career. Asking has accelerated success for us and for so many people we work with, know, and love. Some of those benefits include:

- More effective teamwork with colleagues and coworkers
- Smoother negotiations when putting deals or proposals together
- Better rapport with clients
- More options for customers, financing, services, and/or products
- More successful sales and closings
- Greater marketing success
- Better relationships through networking
- The ability to create valuable masterminds
- Finding talented and powerful people to work with or work for

The more you polish your asking skills, the more confidence you'll begin to feel as you pursue your career dreams.

If you don't ask, you don't get.

—GANDHI

Both of us have been involved in entrepreneurial businesses most of our adult lives. Being an entrepreneur is a great training ground for figuring out how to have successful human relationships. That's because finances and money represent so many things that are essential to human happiness, such as a sense of freedom, power, and options in life. When traveling to various locations around the world, we love to strike up conversations with people. Usually one of the first topics that comes up in the form of a question is: "What do you do?" The way in which we spend our time to achieve success and monetary freedom seems to be a large part of the identity we give ourselves as human beings. We've found that many people are eager to share the story of how they're building their business or career because they're looking for feedback, validation, or advice. Isn't that what asking is? Inviting someone to hear about the steps you've taken to get where you are and to frame for them where you want to go from here is a wonderful way to engage other minds in the creative process of finding better solutions or sourcing better ideas. Having a great product or service isn't enough to achieve exceptional levels of success. We've found that *asking* is probably *the most important tool* to achieve real and lasting success in business.

One Question Can Pivot Your Entire Career

The Question I Asked Myself That Changed My Future

My (Mark) best and worst year was 1974. I went bankrupt virtually overnight, and it was the most excruciating experience I had ever endured. In my twenty-six years of life I hadn't felt such mental and emotional turmoil because I felt like the bankruptcy was a failing grade on my business skills and perhaps my future. My self-esteem suffered like it never before had. I was barely surviving—paying a meager rent by sharing a small house in Hicksville, Long Island, New York, with three roommates. I was trying to understand where I'd gone wrong and how to change it. When I'd lie in bed before going to sleep each night, I'd ask myself again and again, "What have I done in my life that I've loved the most?" After struggling for about six months of doing odd jobs, the answer finally came to me. From the time I was a college student, I had voraciously consumed positive, motivational materials and thirsted for conversations with people who had overcome the odds to create success. What I truly wanted was to connect with people and inspire them to be their best. I knew that, even as I was desperately struggling to be my best. My answer told me the best way to do that was to become a professional motivational and inspirational speaker and author.

One morning I asked my roommates, "Do you know anyone who *isn't* a celebrity, a white-haired senior, or doctor or lawyer out speaking and getting paid for their speeches?"

Surprisingly, my roommate, John, said, "Yes, there is a superstar motivator talking this morning, cheering up all the downtrodden realtors in Haiphong, Long Island, New York." I got the address from him and immediately raced out to hear this wonderful speaker and trainer, Chip Collins, who delighted the standing-room-only crowd of realtors who had come to see him. I watched Chip enthuse and excite these people to believe in themselves, despite the horrific economy. He taught them how to rise up to profitability and performance with his dynamic and easy-to-employ formulas. As I watched the session unfold, I knew that helping people improve themselves and their performance was definitely going to be included in my destiny.

I asked Chip if he would go to lunch with me. Through lunch I asked him to share some of his techniques and insights so that I could enter this speaking/motivational world. Chip shared his techniques with the proviso that I stick to the life insurance business and leave real estate to him. He gave me the four steps and suggested that I begin at once, whether I was ready or not.

I was truly ready. The next day, I called on ten life insurance general agents and managers and booked a talk with one. That one gave me a directory of leads to everyone in his Metropolitan Life Insurance Company—at the time number one in the industry. Within two months, I was doing four talks a day. I did over a thousand talks a year for my first three years in the business. My very successful speaker friend and mentor Cavett Robert said, "Life either grinds you down or polishes you up." I came through the bankruptcy "polished up" because I *asked the question* that would truly pivot my life in a direction that ultimately has made me tremendously successful and prosperous in ways I could never have imagined. That pivot to a speaking career inspired my signature storytelling talks, which led to the creation of one book, *Chicken Soup for the Soul*, that multiplied over four decades, into what has amounted to over five hundred million (yes, that's a half billion) books sold with my name on them worldwide, with more sales daily. So the right question, at the right time, to yourself and others can pivot your life from distress and failures to abundance, prosperity, and inevitable success.

At my rock bottom, I asked myself what I really wanted to do and then asked my friends for an answer that would help me get there. Asking delivered a new plan for my life. I kept asking along the way as I followed that plan to unimaginable success!

When you are at rock bottom and feel lost, confused, or like you've failed—ask yourself what you really want and ask others to help you get there. Asking can deliver a new plan for you, and if you follow it like I did, it may lead you down a new path to a new career for which you are destined.

Throw your dreams into space like a kite,
and you do not know what it will bring back,
a new life, a new friend, a new love, a new country.

—ANAÏS NIN

Deborah Rosado Shaw is a self-made wonder who epitomizes the American dream, proving success isn't determined by your circumstances, but by your commitment to your own excellence. She is the author of the book, *Dream Big! A Roadmap for Facing Life's Challenges and Creating the Life You Deserve*. Deb's extraordinary journey has been featured in textbook case studies and multiple media outlets, including ABC, *Forbes*, Telemundo, *The Oprah Winfrey Show*, and

USA Today. She has been recognized with numerous awards, including the 2017 Fortune "50 Most Powerful Latinas in Corporate America," *Latino Leaders Magazine*'s "101 Most Influential Latinos," the National Foundation of Women Legislators Entrepreneur of the Year Award, and the Women's Leadership Exchange Trailblazer Award. She was declared a "leading and powerful voice" by iconic PepsiCo Chairman Indra Nooyi and described as "inspiring" by Oprah Winfrey. President George W. Bush penned his appreciation, and President Bill Clinton commended her for being "a testament to America's free enterprise system." We are delighted to know this wonderful woman and so happy to share a piece of her amazing story here.

When You're Uncertain and Overwhelmed—Ask! Deborah Rosado Shaw's Story

Deborah was a young mom of three little boys facing the likelihood of divorce and becoming a single parent. Early one morning, with the kids off to school, she stopped at a giant Target on her way to work. While seemingly there on a routine shopping trip for diapers, laundry detergent, and lunch snacks, Deborah knew that something about this morning felt different. Struggling to figure out the next steps in her life and the lives of her precious boys, she walked the aisles praying quietly for strength, courage, and guidance.

Cherishing these few quiet moments to herself—with no kids in tow and no work demands to manage—she allowed herself the treat of wandering through the book section. As she turned around the corner, glancing through the many titles and subjects, one particular book seemed to leap off the shelf and to her attention. The title mesmerized her, but she shook it off and walked away, hurrying to get her shopping done before heading off to a full day of work. Deb continued to pray, asking for guidance about leaving an abusive marriage and how she would continue to grow her little business and have enough to care for her family.

As she pushed her cart up and down the aisles, Deborah couldn't get this book out of her mind—it seemed to have a magnetic pull, drawing her back. She gave in to this force and returned to the book aisle. Once there, it just so happened this particular section was being restocked. As the young man worked to refill the shelves, the same title fell to the floor. She carefully picked it up and went to place it back. But once the book was in her hands, she couldn't let it go. It was as if she were receiving a whisper from God, that this book was for her. The book that fell to her feet was *The Aladdin Factor*, which I (Mark) coauthored with Jack Canfield.

When she arrived home that night after a long day at work, it was pouring rain. As she trudged up the steps in the cloudy darkness, with diapers and groceries, she slipped and fell, ripping her knees open. She got inside, wiped off the blood with hydrogen peroxide, and bandaged herself up.

Later, when the kids were in bed, she pulled out the book and read it cover to cover, absorbing its insights, wisdom, and suggestions. The book suggests repeatedly that asking yourself the right question will generate the right profitable, wealth-generating result. It was the right message, at the right time, for a woman hungry to succeed and ensure that her little family would never experience the poverty she had known growing up. The place Deborah had called home as a young girl was the poster child for urban blight. A neglected neighborhood where lacking city services left garbage piled high, a place where her family sometimes suffered cold nights with no heat or hot water, and where gangs ruled the street corners and drug deals happened in plain sight. A life where her "pretty clothes" came out of the rummage bins in church. She was determined that would never become her children's experience.

As she fell asleep that night, she kept repeating the words she'd read: "What are you waiting for? Go for it."

Inspired by the book, she gave herself permission to dream really big. Her resolve and belief growing fiercer each day. She made copies of a page from *The Aladdin Factor* and hung them on her bathroom mirror, on the refrigerator, and on the dashboard of her car. It read:

Remember, there is no perfect time for anything. There is only now. We encourage you with all of our hearts to begin your journey to a greater level of fulfillment and productivity now. Don't wait until everything is just right. It will never be perfect. There will always be challenges, obstacles and less than perfect conditions. So what? Get started now. With each step you take, you will grow stronger and stronger, more and more skilled, more and more self-confident and more and more successful. Everything you want is out there waiting for you to ask. Everything you want also wants you. But you have to take action.

She followed the advice. She started talking positively and correctly to herself, saying: "I can do this. It is within my personal reach now. I can achieve greater levels of fulfillment, achievement, and joy. I can start right where I am, right now." Always curious and observant, Deborah had an insatiable desire to rise higher. Having spent several years in the fashion industry selling specialty tote bags and umbrellas, she knew the business cold and had great relationships at every level. Focused and always paying attention, she kept seeking that next great idea that would help her little business take a giant sales leap forward.

One day, shortly after the book had fallen into her life (literally), Deborah visited a museum and became inspired by the fancy, beautiful umbrellas sold in the gift shop there. She asked herself, "Why are these only sold at museums and expensive shops? We could make beautiful umbrellas that would be affordable to everyone!" She got to work and created and manufactured her designer umbrellas featuring images by Van Gogh, Renoir, and other classic pieces of art on the fabric. She said, "I knew I was following inspiration that was coming to me because I had asked, I believed, and I followed through with action. With a series of carefully crafted bold moves, I was able to sell my first single million-dollar order to Walmart with many more to follow. My next idea was one *everyone* told me was impossible. I followed my inspiration anyway. With three little boys, Disney was an ever-present force in our home: stuffed toys, books, movies. One day it dawned on me that there were no Disney kids' outdoor umbrella sets. I sketched some ideas and did the research about what it would take to get a licensing agreement. Finally, after months of plotting and asking, our little company was granted the Disney license, and we would go on to sell millions of dollars of kids' products too! Even the people around me couldn't believe I was able to make that happen!"

Because Deb's desire to ask for and believe in her dreams was so powerful, a unique and original idea was given to her, and she would go on to sell the product to thousands of retail outlets—not only Walmart, but Costco, Toys "R" Us, and many others. She asked and she received. And she asked some more and received even more, not only for herself and her own family, but for countless others. Over time, Deb built and then sold her company, which had grown to become one of the top fifty Latina-owned companies in the country. Deb would go on to share her success strategies with tens of thousands of aspiring moms just like her. She has written a book, appeared on *The Oprah Winfrey Show*, and keynoted all around the world. In a career that has spanned being an award-winning entrepreneur and Fortune 50 senior executive, today

Deborah is a respected and trusted advisor and transformational leadership coach to some of the leading companies and organizations in the world about culture, diversity, and engagement.

> *Man who waits for roast duck to fly into his mouth*
> *must wait a very, very long time.*
> —CHINESE PROVERB

Mark and I (Crystal) live a beautiful life for which we give thanks every single day. On our road to success, we've been blessed to achieve wonderful things and to experience extraordinary people, travel, and events that have made our lives significantly richer and more fulfilled. Some who look at what we've accomplished, individually and as a couple, might assume that it's all been rainbows and butterflies along the way. That couldn't be further from the truth. While we've been fortunate in so many ways and enjoyed cherished family and friends, who add so much love and meaning to our lives, there have been many times when we have been scared, lost, and unsure what our next move should be. The truth is, no one who is alive escapes those experiences. Those are the times we toughen up, learn the most, reach to a new level, or find a better version of ourselves.

One such time was after Mark and Jack Canfield had fought for three years to get someone to support the vision of their *Chicken Soup for the Soul* book. It seemed like everywhere they went, they were met with rejection and dismissals. No one could see what they were seeing. They were under financial pressure after putting a lot of effort, money, and time into its making, and their respective spouses' patience was running thin. The confidence of everyone around them was waning. The easiest thing would have been to throw in the towel and admit everyone else was right: this wasn't going to work. If Mark could be summed up in a word, it's *persistence*. He was not going to stop until his vision for this book was fulfilled. Luckily, he wasn't afraid to ask for help.

Don't Be Afraid to Ask for Support for Your Vision: Charley Green's Story

The year was 1992 when Mark Victor Hansen came to Unity Church of Overland Park in Kansas and delivered the Sunday message to our congregation. With a confident presence on the platform, he held in his hand, up high for everyone to see, a manuscript of a book he and his partner, Jack Canfield, had written. "We have been turned down by twenty-eight publishers who told us this book wasn't good enough to make it in the market," Mark said. "However, Jack and I believe so deeply in this book and its message, we know the right and perfect publisher will show up; now, we need your help. I want all of you to hold in your hearts, in your minds, and in your prayers, you see *Chicken Soup for the Soul* in every bookstore, airport, library, and school in our country." Everyone in the audience stood, applauded, and affirmed his request and vision. Today, over five hundred million copies of the *Chicken Soup for the Soul* series of books have been sold worldwide.

Following this meeting, Mark asked everyone to fill out an order form for the book, which was not yet available. He asked them to put their credit card number on the form and promised the book would be sent to them as soon as it was printed. Talk about a bold and fearless ask! That day Mark took home 560 preorders for his book. He and Jack continued going to audiences and asking for orders for books not yet printed. It was largely because of their persistent asking that *Chicken Soup for the Soul* became the world-renowned phenomenon that has changed so many lives for the better. If they hadn't been willing to ask, none of this miracle would have, or could have, happened.

Every New Opportunity Should Start with Questions

In his 1936 classic *How to Win Friends and Influence People*, Dale Carnegie advised, "Be a good listener. Ask questions the other person will enjoy answering." Today, Carnegie's advice—written more than eighty years ago—is more relevant than ever. Attentive listening is typically more challenging for most people than speaking. Being a good listener requires patience, focus, and a dedicated desire to have real communication with others. If we're apathetic in our listening skills, or we expect to be bored by someone's answers, we likely will miss the opportunity to create a successful personal or business relationship. Often, people listen only long enough to figure out how they're going to respond. It's so important to be alive and awake in each and every conversation. It is the only way you can truly understand the person's point of view. When you have an occasion to start a potentially valuable relationship or to forge a stronger one, avoid the temptation to be overly confident that you probably already know the person's answers. It's likely you don't, and by listening actively, you'll create deeper connections that lead to far greater successes in all your personal and business relationships.

> *Every man, every woman who has to take up the service*
> *of the government, must ask themselves two questions:*
> *"Do I love my people in order to serve them better?*
> *Am I humble and do I listen to everybody,*
> *to diverse opinions in order to choose the best path?"*
> *If you don't ask those questions*
> *your governance will not be good.*
>
> —POPE FRANCIS

Lead with Questions

R. Rex Parris has been the mayor of Lancaster, California, for twelve years. He loves serving in his hometown, and the citizens have voted him in four times in a row. He is a man of vast accomplishments.

In addition to being mayor, Rex is a top litigator who almost always wins big against the bad guys—in at least three major jury trials per year. Rex makes things happen investing in ideas, products, and services that will make our world better. He is an activist for change—modeling what works and enthusiastically cheering people on to immediately stop the disaster and destruction of climate extinction, in every wise way possible, or he predicts drastic heating up of our beloved Earth—and yes, he is a tree-hugging, hard-working Republican. Rex doesn't embrace any ideology thoughtlessly. He carefully and thoughtfully considers all issues on their own merit and puts them through a rigorous system of asking questions to get to the truth. Rex is a conservative politician who is also a relentless crusader to save the planet, and he has become the face of alternative energy. The EPA recently designated him the Green Power Leader of the country. (See his videos on YouTube.)

Are We Running Fast Enough? Mayor Rex Parris's Story

When it comes right down to it, leadership is knowing how to ask and whom to ask, and then having the persuasive ability to keep asking until you get the agreement of thought that you want. I ask this question to everyone about each project endeavor: "If we meet 100 percent of success, what does that look like?" True accomplishments in my life happened because I developed the ability to ask and have the courage to ask. Leadership depends on having the ability to ask.

I learned the social skill of asking about fifteen years ago, when I went to Gerry Spence's Trial Lawyers College. It changed my life, business, and future, and inspired me to take on leadership challenges and become mayor of Lancaster. We were taught to start with a small ask and gradually make it bigger and bigger. That is how persuasion happens. Asking questions lays down the stepping-stones to persuade someone to come to the same understanding at which you've arrived. Persuasion is the act of successfully conceiving of and then generating impactful, meaningful, and lasting results that matter.

We are a proud city. We challenge our city employees to take the first shot at courageously running projects that no one has had the risk-tolerance to try. When we decided we wanted our city to have IBM Watson artificial intelligence help us spot trends and risks before they manifest into a problem, a young woman on the staff raised her hand and said, "I can make it work." Because of her, we have Watson. We became the first 5G city and the first truly and completely "Smart City." With 5G, robotic cars become a safe reality because cars can communicate with each other and share information surrounding them. A 5G network offers twenty-seven times the bandwidth of 4G. We decided to provide free Wi-Fi to every kid to do their homework because we didn't want that important tool for research and homework to be available only to affluent kids.

We are reigniting democracy with questions and open-forum discussions. I know our success depends on solving the questions and concerns of the citizens and together coming up with the best solutions. We are rethinking health care for everyone—projecting medical issues in advance. We reduced our murder rate from twenty-four a year to zero in two years. Our burglary rate is down 40 percent, with city-wide CCTV on every street light. We will be able to predict crimes before they happen by downloading the video into IBM Watson analytics. Employment is up, and gang members are gone or in hiding.

We approach our problems as a city, with mutual concern and caring. Not long ago, we were about to lose our biggest car dealership, so I asked the city to lend the dealer five hundred thousand dollars. We did. He survived and thrived and is now the largest dealership of his kind in America. I believe in our people, and because of that, they give back more of themselves.

I'm proud to say we are the first net-zero city in the world, which means we put more electricity from the sun back on the grid than we use. All new home construction must have solar installed on the rooftops and store the electricity in self-contained batteries. We started by insisting all municipal buildings in our high-desert city have solar energy. When I found out it took six to eight weeks to get solar retrofits permitted, I instructed: "Reduce it to twenty minutes and do it over the counter." The planning department said okay. We now issue the permits online. We are the model for what tomorrow's green, clean, sustainable, smart city can do, but we do it today. People from around the world visit to study our operations, and they leave unable to stop talking about what can be done with the right thinking and questions.

When we visited China, on my own nickel, we asked the battery-making company BYD to consider basing its manufacturing operations of electrical buses and batteries to our relatively small and little-known city of Lancaster, California. Incredibly, BYD agreed and brought ever-expanding employment and business to Lancaster. BYD chose Lancaster instead of Los Angeles, San Francisco, or another large city because, as it turned out, I was the only mayor to visit the manufacturer and ask for its business. To date, over three hundred EV Buses have been made in Lancaster, and those buses travel over a million miles per year in America—pollution free.

I asked our staff, "How do we get all new homes to be net-zero?" This question was a challenge to solve. We went to KB Home (Kaufman and Broad), and I asked, "What are the obstacles to achieving this?"

"How long will it take to get building permits?"

Looking at my watch, I asked, "How long do you want it to take?"

An affordable net-zero home had never been built before. I got BYD's president, Stella Li, to agree to create cost-effective batteries for homes, and KB Homes to reinvent how they build energy-efficient homes, and with the City of Lancaster pushing and pulling them, they changed the world in under five months. They are now selling homes we call Net Zero 2.0. Initially, the homes cost forty thousand dollars more; however, the economics work because the owner never pays an electric bill. It amortizes out, and banks cheerfully lend the money. We've perfected a business model for affordable housing that is pollution-free. We want everyone to consider implementing it.

We got so tired of corrupt energy companies and the captive agencies that regulate them that I asked two women who knew nothing about buying and selling power to create Lancaster's own utility. The ladies did it in a record two years. Lancaster is now buying and selling the power for Lancaster and for ten other cities. We set rates and can beat the major utilities' price significantly. We are called the Clean Power Alliance and are on our way to replacing California's biggest utilities. We do it more efficiently, at six cents a kilowatt, whereas previously they were charging nineteen cents a kilowatt to our citizens. It's the heart of a revolution to end the monopolistic power of the utilities.

We question the status quo each and every day so that I am confident we are serving our city in the best way possible. Together we've achieved breakthroughs in government operations, jobs, lifestyle, and a clean, healthy environment for all. We will continue each day to make improvements to our own city and hopefully be a model to the world for how a city can create the highest quality of living and do our part to keep our Earth clean, healthy, and sustainable. We are in a race to save our species from extinction, and my question every day is: "Are we running fast enough?"

> *It is easier to judge the mind of a man*
> *by his questions rather than his answers.*
> —Pierre-Marc-Gaston de Lévis, duc de Lévis

The Right Questions Beat Out a Multi-Billion-Dollar Behemoth: Preston Weekes's Story

Several years ago I joined a clean energy development company as the COO. One of the most important protocols I established as an officer of the company was how we would approach clients and develop our sales pitches. My philosophy was not about selling the client. It was about discovering the client's needs first. The way we did that was through asking the right questions. The company began to grow rapidly. We were getting referrals to develop bigger and bigger solar projects, and it was exciting to see our dreams to contribute to a cleaner world take shape.

One day a good friend, Mike, who is an international attorney, called and said he'd like to set up a meeting with our company and one of his large clients, a company that happens to be one of the biggest mining companies in the world. Our team prepared for the meeting, and on the appointed day we all met at their enormous headquarters. We had four or five of our team members at the meeting, including me. Our lawyer's friend and contact at the mining company was a woman named Mel, who greeted us at the door. She was a down-to-earth woman from Montana with a warm demeanor, who had vast international experience helping run mining operations abroad for many years, including in

South America and Africa. She was delightful and interesting to talk to and, because of her close relationship with our attorney, had insisted on having the two top people running energy for the company internationally present. We hadn't realized that we were going straight to the top to meet with *the* decision makers who decide how hundreds of millions will be spent for energy to power their mines around the world. Once we entered that conference room, we rolled up our sleeves and began to make our presentation in the manner that was in alignment with the company philosophy I had established, which goes basically like this:

· Don't go in and try to sell the client something.
· Ask what they need—then fill the need.

One by one, each of our team took the baton and discussed their operations, their priorities, how they feel about their current energy configurations, and if the company has any real program for renewables or not. Asking question after question, with warmth and interest, we began to get a very complete picture about the entire company and their philosophy about energy, how they use it, what matters to them, and what's in their future.

Only about one-quarter of the meeting was spent with us sharing our capabilities in energy production and storage, and the financial models necessary to make it all work. As we continued to ask them questions about themselves, spending relatively little time bragging about how great we are, we watched them relax and begin to open up. By the last third of the meeting, they were deeply engaged with us and sharing far more information than they had originally said they were prepared to when we started the meeting. The meeting ended an hour and a half later, only because they had to get to another corporate meeting. They were reluctant to bring our meeting to a close and extended it, making themselves almost ten minutes late for their next meeting. They wanted to keep talking because we had bonded through asking and understanding what was really important to them.

They said they were sorry to bring the meeting to an end and asked if we could schedule a second meeting to go deeper. They said that, at the next meeting, they would come prepared to share some specific mining projects they wanted us to look at to give our analysis of what a good energy solution package would be.

Later that afternoon, coincidentally, we met with a consultant we work with named Paul, who has worked many years with a huge mining-equipment behemoth. His company not only sells the mining and earth-moving equipment they also sell mechanical components to generate and regulate energy for microgrids, and we use them as one of our suppliers. We sat down for a business lunch with Paul and started chatting about the great meeting with the mining company we just finished, how well it had gone, and how they were eager to have us back for a deeper analysis of their specific mining project.

Paul seemed a bit baffled and asked, "Who did you meet with in the company? Was it one of the local people who works in their energy department?"

"No, it was the two top guys who are the international heads of energy," we replied. "These guys are great. They loved us and our company and want a second meeting soon. We think we might want you to go with us as a major equipment supplier."

"I was invited to join a meeting last week with the same mining company," Paul told us. "Four top executives who used to work for our company, but now sell our energy micro-grid systems from a new company they formed, had a meeting with those same people you met with to sell them a solar plus micro-grid system. It didn't go well at all. They weren't interested in anything we had to say, and they didn't want a second meeting with that group. I can't believe you guys got a second invitation to come back when these guys, and the former top execs from our company, fell flat on their faces. They are supposed to be top of the field!"

When our team got to the car to head back to the office, we all celebrated what we knew was our secret to success. How did we beat out four top executives who had been in this energy space with a multi-billion-dollar behemoth for many more years than we had? Because we used the *ask* philosophy so thoroughly in that meeting that we created a bond that otherwise couldn't have been created. It's a bond that happens when you ask about all the things that make someone what they are, because only then can you begin to understand what they want and how to help them!

Asking Strategy to Understand Your Client's Needs

- Ask about them first.
- Ask what their problems and concerns are.
- Ask how you can be of service to them.
- Ask what it would look like; what is the ideal scenario for them if the problem or problems were solved.
- Ask if you were able to accomplish those ideals or goals, how much pressure and stress it would take off them.
- Ask how doing so might improve function, flow, or profits of the operations.
- Ask fearlessly, so you can talk persuasively from your heart.

I have led several companies to unprecedented levels of success. In each case, this philosophy of asking about the customer's needs first, getting in touch with those needs, and then filling them has consistently been the secret to my success!

ASK!

To achieve your ultimate career/business destiny,
ask what they want—don't tell them what you want.

We have enjoyed many wonderful experiences with our great friend Peter Guber, and relished our time with this accomplished man and his wife, Tara. Peter is chairman and CEO of Mandalay Entertainment, making such well-known films as *Batman, Rain Man, Flash Dance, The Color Purple, Gorillas in the Mist, The Kids Are All Right,* and many more. Peter's films have grossed over three billion dollars worldwide and received fifty Academy Award nominations, including winning Best Picture for *Rain Man*. He is author of the *New York Times* bestseller *Tell to Win*, a co-owner of the Golden State Warriors National Basketball Association team and the Los Angeles Dodgers Major League Baseball team, and owner and executive chairman of the Los Angeles Football Club. We wondered what the questions were that set Peter on his career path. Peter's story demonstrates how the journey for most successful people starts in a humble way, with a driving curiosity that moves their dreams into their destiny.

Look for the Problem to Make a Fortune: Peter Guber's Story

As a nine-year-old boy, I vividly recall nobody in my Boston neighborhood wanted to rake the fall leaves or shovel their snow after a snowstorm. I decided I would do just that, because my parents were cautious to me with their funds. I wanted to earn the money for myself so I could enjoy the freedom to spend what I wanted. I started soliciting and taking on customers. Being quick and efficient, and sharing the joy of completion with my neighborhood customers, created a positive buzz. Soon more and more folks called to sign up. However, I was constrained by the fact that I didn't want to shovel five or six driveways daily. In other words, my opportunity exceeded my capacity. My problem was that shoveling just three driveways a day was exhausting. So I asked myself, "What is the problem that is not allowing me to do the work for the people who want it done?" Suddenly I realized the problem was my opportunity in disguise. I decided that I'd go to the kids in the neighborhood and ask them if they wanted to make some easy money. If they did, I would hire them to rake or shovel, and I'd deliver the customers and split the profit so they could earn their money. I realized going out and finding more kids to handle the labor was better than me executing the whole business. They were glad to earn money and soon enough, I had them doing all the labor side of the business. I made a lot of money, yielding a lot of economic freedom as a very young boy. It was all because I shifted my mindset on the problem to reveal my opportunity.

In my earliest years at university I realized I had the same problem. I didn't have enough money to allow me to participate in activities with my college friends, who had generous allowances from their parents. As I was complaining about drowning in debt, a pal said, "Are you waiting for someone to rescue you?"

I let that question wrap around me for a bit and realized that if I thought I was really drowning, wouldn't I swim? "So," I mused, "why not just be active in your own rescue?" I thought to myself: *Wow, that's an interesting question! Is there something that folks here don't want to do that I am already doing and could do for them, which would yield a profit for me?*

I reviewed my childhood experience, when I desperately wanted money and had to figure out a way to get it. I asked myself a high-quality question: "What do lots of students here all really need to do but hate doing?" The answer: the whole process of collecting, cleaning, and delivering their laundry. I had certainly experienced it. If I could find all the people who have that problem and combine them with a few people who wanted the opportunity to work and earn easy money—then I could collect the customers and engage my partners to do the work. If I could do that efficiently, I would have a real business. Once I was in operation, I lined up all the deals with the student customers, contracted the student couriers to split the profits, and made arrangements with the laundry companies and dry cleaners, creating my enterprise value. Then I managed the relationships between them, which was critical. I had around seventeen folks working at different times. They were really working for their own profit, but indirectly working for me. I created relationship capital with our customers, as a whole service provider that was worth a premium. I provided the template and the business outlets. The bulk-price discount I negotiated with the companies became an instant cash cow for student partners who wanted to make money. There was no competition. It was 20 percent less expensive, twice as fast, and hassle free, cheaper and better than the customers could do it for themselves, and the marginal profits were mine. It was a win-win for everyone. It was my first taste that inspiration trumps perspiration every time. The jackpot was my economic freedom.

I used this economic paradigm extensively during my student years. I perceived the struggle students had in getting cheaper airfares for long flights across the country or, more significantly, for overseas school experiences and sessions. I knew my audience—a customer base. What else could I do with that audience?

I learned that students wanted to travel everywhere and stay in inexpensive places. So I took my ability to aggregate around students' needs and desires, and I put them together in what today we call group travel packages. I was able to aggregate the travel and sell flights on twelve different airlines at deep discounts. At this time, no one was able to do that and connect students and airlines. I didn't have to do any of the final transactions. I didn't have to take the cash. The airlines and travel agencies had the entire infrastructure. I just solved the problem by providing the connection and the collection, so to speak. By doing that, I was given giant numbers of airline miles, which was another value proposition. That enabled me to travel the world, which was something that I very much wanted to do. The idea that came from my big question was to find other people's problems and desires, figure out what magnifying solution would work, and then execute it.

You can extrapolate what happened as I was providing service and value to customers: they told everybody how well I served them. That's how I built my business. In business, you have to be able to make your customers' experience so good that they tell your story going forward. They advertise you. They promote you. They sell you!

The bonus was that when Tara, my wife, and I married, we were able to go on an eight-week honeymoon around the world. We saw so many different places, including Russia, Africa, India, Japan, and Europe. I had such a business enterprise in college that we got to go in style.

So I learned at an early age that success is in the eye of the beholder, and knowing how to scale is key to creating an economic engine for that success. If you can find the answers to the problem, and if you can do it at scale, you can make it an economic change in your life and future. So that must be your intention, and then you put all your attention on that intention.

That codec gave me the freedom to do in my life what I want to do. Capital, which is the value of having money, gave me a currency for action I desired to take. For me, that was empowerment to turn my dreams into my goals.

Questions are *key* to the process because they challenge your perspective. When I was young, my questions were transactional in nature. Now I look at a question and I think *not* what is the question telling me, but what is it asking me? What problem or need or desire is it calling me to solve? I don't try to exert my authority or superiority over the question or the questioner. That focuses me to look at the problem and solve it and achieve the benefit.

Your willingness to identify your desires,
to foster your curiosity and creativity in the world of business
could help bring to you the unclaimed gifts or riches
that are yours when you begin to ask.

Questions to Accelerate Your Business and Career

Ask Yourself...

- "What work or service have I loved doing in my life?"
- "Have I gained enough knowledge at my place of work to build my own business?"
- "If I imagine great success in _____ business/career, does it make me feel happy?"
- "What are the best companies with which my skills would be a great fit?"
- "What can I innovate?"
- "Am I willing to learn fast?"
- "Who can I enroll in my vision or plan?"
- "How can I run my department more like my own business for greater success?"
- "How can I create more income or profit?"
- "Where is the market for my talents, service, product, or idea?"
- "How can I do it better than my competition?"
- "What additional benefits or enhancements would improve my offering?"
- "What is the business model that would succeed in today's market?"

- "How can I tenfold my successes?"
- "How can I extend my reach and influence?"
- "What hidden niches do I see that could be exploited positively?"
- "Whom do I need in my network?"
- "What are the groups whose members enhance my career or business?"
- "Whose influence do I need to accelerate my business?"
- "What is my five-year plan?"
- "How do I retro-engineer to make that plan happen?"

Ask Others...

- "How did you get started?"
- "What was your biggest obstacle?"
- "Is there anyone you know who would be interested in _____?"
- "Do you have any friends/colleagues who would like to go to coffee to hear about my business/product?"
- "Can I show you how to: Save time? Save money? Do something better? Have a better experience?"
- "What is your perfect outcome for this situation/plan/results?"
- "How much would it be worth if I'm able to help you achieve that outcome?"
- "What are your most important company priorities?"
- "Can I take you to coffee or lunch so that we can talk about some ideas?"
- "Is there a way we can combine our efforts for greater success?"

For most people, your business or career life is such a key part of your happiness, or the lack of it. The money you earn in your lifetime is not valuable just for the sake of having money. Its value lies in the security it provides for your future, the options it gives you each day, and the freedom it affords you. What you do for your work is an essential component of the expression of you. It's amazing that many people do so much planning and thoughtful thinking when it comes to relationships, but then allow themselves to just fall into the easiest or most obvious job that comes along. Using the asking process in your work, business, or career will lead you to a higher level of clarity, satisfaction, and success in your life. Impossible dreams become possible with questions that help you overcome your fear.

What Will Your Life Be in Ten, Twenty, or Thirty Years? Ken McElroy's Story

I live in questions, whether it is my family life, business, or charitable endeavors.

I grew up in the blue-collar community of Everett, Washington. I came from a family where no one had gone to college. I didn't have the mindset early on to do anything other than work for someone else. No one had ever asked me if I had read the right books, if I wanted a higher education, or if I planned to go on to college. Fortunately, I was a good athlete, and I earned a wrestling scholarship to Pacific Lutheran University in Tacoma, Washington. I got into the school of business, and that turned around everything. Suddenly, I was on fire with questions about communication, research, finance, advertising, and marketing. I was immersed in a world I had never experienced, and I wanted to find out everything about it. Through all my questions and the answers I got, I was getting a blueprint for my possible future.

The weird twist was that, while I was in college, my dad finally decided to start his own business. Until then, I had not known any business owners. Dad hired me to work in his heating, ventilation, and air conditioning business in Seattle. We got a contract to do HVAC systems for the fast-growing Boeing Aerospace company. For the first time in my life, I was asking endless business questions of my dad, his partners, and client mentors. At work, I was hearing what my dad and his two partners were thinking and saying daily. I kept wondering how I could use their knowledge to learn business for myself. I was inspired by the idea of business ownership, but I knew I needed to be my best to get there. I started setting goals, learning the power of the mind, and started studying and reading self-help-action books like crazy. I was a hungry and ambitious student of business, success, and wealth creation.

I really believe in the law of intention. My intentions and focus were so intense that I knew I was destined for big business. While I was still in college, one of my buddies called me and asked if I could manage an apartment building.

"What do I do?" I asked.

"Collect rents and fix things."

Thanks to having worked for my contractor father, I told him that I was great at fixing things, and, of course, I could collect rents. For that, I would get free rent and a small salary.

That began my first job: managing an apartment building. It went so well that I proceeded, while finishing school, to get my real estate license. I started working for a company that managed many properties, which really opened my eyes to real estate development. I quickly learned the value of real estate. My boss asked me to master the art of increasing rents and minimizing expenses. I was educated in refinancing, equity, and all kinds of debt. Within a year, I became a regional manager, then vice president, and then executive vice president. They would bring buildings to me, and I would quickly improve and increase the value of them. Basically, success in this business means buying something that's not performing and turning it into something that is profitably performing. I mastered it by increasing the net operating income or increasing the net profit from each of the individual properties. I stayed with that company for nine years. The way the company obtained investment money was for me to ask a group of country club buddies to formalize some kind of syndication. A syndication might have twenty, thirty, or forty people involved at a hundred thousand dollars each.

Working there, we all had pretty good salaries. I had a little bit of money in the bank, a house, and a car, and I golfed regularly and took a three-week vacation each year. But I didn't have real wealth—until an inadvertent statement revectored my life, future, and financial freedom.

I was sitting with the owner of my company eating lunch. One of my college classmates came over and innocently remarked, "Hey, Kenny, you've made it!"

The owner of the company looked at me, and said, "He hasn't even come close to making it."

That insult hurt my feelings but got me thinking and asking new questions. I had a good salary, golf vacations, and a comfortable lifestyle for my family. But I asked myself, "With 3 percent annual pay increases, am I able to get wealthy?" I knew the answer was no. I projected out ten years. I wrote down everything. "If I get only a 30 percent increase in ten years, and my cost of living goes up by 40 percent, which is easy to believe, where does that leave me?" The answer: I would be minimum negative 10 percent, and financially upside down, if I continued to do what I was doing. If I'm a high-paid employee for the rest of my life, I'm never going to live financially free.

After writing down all my thinking and questions to myself based on that insult from my boss, I realized that this map doesn't make sense for the future. I had enough educated awareness to know I wanted to experience financial freedom. Through my reading and learning, I had been inspired to be a big thinker. I asked myself, "What does my life look like in five-, ten-, even twenty-year increments?" Most people's financial literacy is honestly horrible; I could see that. I did not want my family's story to be that.

My first financial goal was to become a millionaire, because there weren't that many millionaires thirty years ago. I knew the business and the club members who knew me and would trust me with their investment dollars. I created my own business called MC Companies. My business investing in apartment building was working. I kept expanding MC Companies until today, we have over ten thousand rentals and three hundred employees in three states—Arizona, Texas, and Oregon. I love it. I ask myself and my key employees to do multiyear thinking. We have a five- and a ten-year plan for our company. We have written company goals, and everyone in the company knows what these goals are. We manage to exceed them every single month and every single quarter.

As my success grew, I was invited to become a Young Presidents' Organization (YPO) member. YPO is an invitation-only organization with over twenty-seven thousand members who are either president, chairman of the board, or chief operating officer of a company. It is the who's who of business connectivity and leadership. YPO has got me to ask more questions than any other experience of my life.

One of my YPO mentors asked me a critical life question when my kids were small: "How many summers do you have left with your kids before they go off on their own?" The question really hit home for me. I figured ten or eleven, maybe—that's it; that's all I have. They were six and seven at the time. I made a decision: I am going to stop working every single summer. I will buy a family retreat in Idaho and dedicate my summers to spending almost full time with my family there. During the summers, I started to confine my working time from 5:00 a.m. to 10:00 a.m. each day, handling all the calls and emails. It was tough at first. Yet, once I was committed, I invested the rest of my time with my family. We waterskied, rode ATVs (all-terrain vehicles for off-roading), and played all day—every day. People ask me now how I'm so close to my kids. I know it's because of the time I deliberately dedicated to them by answering that one important question.

As a family, we ask ourselves each year: "What is a major 'together' goal to accomplish this year?" This year, my two boys and I committed to, and succeeded in, summiting Mount Kilimanjaro in Africa. It took training, buying all the right gear, studying how to live and survive through five climate zones—from hot rainforests to snow-topped/freezing/windy/super-cold mountaintops—exercising, engaging in resolve and togetherness discussions, and—obviously—possessing unstoppable determination. We did it together. Climbing to twenty thousand feet requires that you be in great shape and be totally prepared because your life depends on it. Closeness with your children, especially teenagers, is a stretch, but experiences away from their friends and their lives provide great opportunities to ask and answer important questions and to bond. The most rewarding part of the Kilimanjaro adventure was nighttime, when each of my sons would come into my tent. We'd have spontaneous, deep, memorable talks. I gave them 100 percent of my attention. I listened to whatever they wanted to discuss. It was blissful.

We had an unforgettable encounter when we first got to Africa, before we climbed "Kily": we worked in an orphanage in Tanzania while we got acclimated to the mountain altitude, since we live in the flatlands of Phoenix, Arizona. The orphanage experience was eye-opening and very special to us. It became deeply etched in our hearts and minds in a way we will remember and cherish forever. We lovingly served those who could repay us with only their smiles, affection, and happiness. They expressed their love, joy, and thankfulness with hugs, asking us not to leave and to remember them forever—which we will. We know we've asked for much from life—and we're so thankful to have been given so much.

Opportunities are usually disguised as hard work,
so most people don't recognize them.
—ANN LANDERS

A Remarkable Man from a Remarkable Family

Years ago, I (Mark) heard Trammell Crow, Sr. give a talk at an open business meeting. He was a well-known real estate developer, having built many amazing buildings starting in Dallas, Texas, and then literally around the world. When I listened to him at an open business meeting, during intense questioning that felt more like an interrogation to me, he calmly and politely answered the questioner with aplomb and not a shred of anger. When he was getting barraged by a series of questions from one individual, I remember he replied, "That's not one question; that is three questions. I will answer them one at a time and tell you how the answers holistically relate." I don't think I had ever previously witnessed anyone handle such a situation with such wisdom and poise.

Later, when he asked me to come to his office to visit, I was beyond thrilled. I was enchanted with his office full of historically relevant American art treasures integrated with giant hand-carved jade pieces that he had just brought back from China. This was the early 1980s, and I was thirty years old and a business green pea. Trammell Sr. embraced me as a young friend. What surprised me was that his warmth and friendship to a rookie, and that he took a generous amount of time to privately teach me how to make sure that I owned one hundred percent of my headquarters/mothership business, which he took the time to illustrate for me. He drew my business as a major circle at the top of the page. He then drew a horizontal line and had potentially infinite circles with my future business partnerships. He encouraged me to know that they could be 50/50, 20/80, 1/99 or whatever, but he admonished strongly, "Always, always own the mothership." His kind tutelage and friendship lasted in my mind with total gratitude forever.

Years later, after Trammell Sr. had moved on from this world, I got a call one day. On the other end of the line, was a warm, enthusiastic voice with a Texas accent saying," "This is Trammell Crow Jr., Mark. I know you studied with Dr. Buckminster Fuller and you want to save the Earth like I do. I need you to be part of my EarthX event as a featured speaker."

It's not surprising I found myself for the next hour in a delightful conversation about the amazing event Trammell Crow Jr. had been building the past few years. Our shared love of the Earth and conservation of it, along with our traditional conservative values, made us fast friends. It was kind of a magical experience for me to observe how Trammell Sr.'s son had become a leader and gamechanger in his own right—setting out to achieve something no one had done before. Trammell Crow Jr. is the founder of EarthX (formerly known as Earth Day Texas), the largest annual exposition and forum showcasing initiatives, research, innovations, policies, and corporate practices serving the environment.

After several more extraordinary conversations back and forth, Crystal and I were each asked to speak at Earthx2019, with more than 175,000 people planning to attend; we agreed. Spending four days taking in some of the most amazing minds and innovations that will keep our planet going strong through the next millennia was an extraordinary experience. Our similitude of thought and purpose has created a deep friendship with Trammell. We all realize the Earth needs the stewardship of people like us and we are partnering to help provide it.

One Friday, Trammell called unexpectedly and said: "Whatever you are doing next Monday and Tuesday, change it. You are going with me to (ASU) Arizona State University's Innovation Labs, run by a genius named Dr. Bill Brandt. In two days, you will see the most exciting possible future of thirty innovations that will positively change the world, like the scientist, Dr. Klaus Lackner, who can now suck the excess carbon directly out of the atmosphere profitably and potentially end climate pollution and change." We went and befriended countless great and inspiring scientists dedicated to creating a carbon-neutral, healthy, sustainable planet. This is just one of many worlds that Trammell has introduced us to that will inspire an ever-improving tomorrow.

Our talks at EarthX were to happen a day before the Back to Space meetings in Dallas. We are on the Board of Directors of Back to Space. Their critical mission: to inspire the next generation to exponential growth in high school STEM (science, technology, engineering, and math) students—preparing the best and brightest to go back into space. The twenty-five smartest STEM students who could persuasively communicate were invited to meet all the living astronauts, who had flown on moon missions starting in 1968. Three of these distinguished men were eighty-seven years old and delightful, funny, and eager to help these youngsters fulfill their destinies. Crystal, the astronauts, and I were invited to talk to, inspire, and answer any questions these students wanted to ask us. We asked Trammell if he would join us to chat with these brilliant future astronauts.

Trammell requested no introduction, so I let him speak first. He began by asking, "What would a super-rich trust fund baby, with no obligations, want to do with his life, fortune, and vision?" These super-star students were, for the first time, speechless. Trammell said,

"That's me, I am Trammell Crow Jr., and I decided to do everything I could to save the planet and created EarthX." He went on to explain his vision and all he had accomplished so far with it. These young people all reveled in it and wanted pictures with Trammell, the astronauts, and us at the end. Then, he invited all of them, as his honored guests, to attend EarthX.

Trammell is a great and influential man, with a giant mission to which he is passionately on-purpose.

Trammell S. Crow's Story

My siblings and I had a very fortunate childhood. We lived in Dallas in a nice neighborhood. The area I grew up in, which has become a posh area today, was seen then as an affluent but unpretentious neighborhood. That's what it was like in the fifties and sixties in Dallas, Texas.

My parents were just such good people. I feel like they were pretty easy on us six kids. They led by example rather than force. They inspired us to do our best and be our best.

My dad worked very hard every day. We were all aware of his work, and I was definitely shaped by his work ethic, but family was always important to both of my parents. So, by six o'clock, he'd be home, and we'd have a family dinner every night. We had real stability growing up.

My maternal grandparents died early, before I was born, and my father's father died when I was young. My paternal grandmother would pull me in her lap in a rocking chair and read the Bible to me. It was very sweet. My mother liked to read stories of Greek mythology and world history to me. Both parents were passionate about exploring the world. They wanted us to have exposure to the world and to immerse ourselves in the experience to understand and participate in the richness of different cultures and people.

We were five boys and only the one girl, so, of course, she was kind of the favorite. When I was young, we boys didn't go to any fancy private schools. We all went to public school, so school seemed pretty easy to me. I remember wanting to go off to boarding school on the East Coast, but somehow Dad didn't like that idea. He thought I might become radicalized, so instead, I went to a conservative boarding school in Atlanta.

When I was a little kid, we didn't have the big family business empire we have now. It continued to grow as we grew, and we were all encouraged to work hard, but Dad never put any undue pressure on us. By the time we were in high school, most of us siblings had decided we wanted to go into the family business, so we tried to prepare ourselves.

During the sixties culture revolution, Eastern philosophy was in the air, and I became interested in it. It led me to meditation, which I still practice today. It taught me that love is everything, a fundamental truth still today.

My parents were pretty available, but Dad was always so focused on business. Often, he'd be there in body but not there in mind. Sometimes I remember he would say, "Ask me no questions and I'll tell you no lies." That was very frustrating so usually, I would go to my mother with simple questions I had. Kids and parent relationships were a little different in the sixties and seventies as a result of the generation gap. In church, school, home, and sports, etc., questions were encouraged to an extent, but there were taboo subjects that were too personal or politically incorrect. As a youth, I got guidance from my parents and teachers, but my most pivotal answers I derived from reading.

I was very respectful and loving of the blueprints both of my parents had given to me, but because of the generation gap, I remember, when I was about eighteen, resolving myself to the fact that my parents had essentially a different value system from mine, but that I wasn't critical of theirs. We were different, but it was okay. That understanding that I made with myself kept me from being rebellious.

I wasn't the typical Dallas boy. There was a very obvious social schism between jocks and so-called hippies, and I was more the latter. I wasn't alone in having different opinions than my folks. Few friends had parents that transcended their communications gap.

As I began my college years, I pondered the purpose of life—questioning just how many layers of the onion needed to be peeled back to fully understand it all. I realized that it's your quest that matters. Your search for the truth. Your journey.

As a younger man, I wasn't afraid of asking questions, except maybe asking girls to go on a date. The best method I learned to overcome my fear of asking such a question was to gather my courage and go for it! The most difficult situational question that I ever faced was asking my parents for advice when my love child was born. I wasn't sure how to handle the relationship and be in a relationship with the mother and the child, and it took a lot of thinking to get comfortable with the right answers. Today, my daughter is a happy, healthy young woman, and I cherish her presence in my life with all of my heart.

Life continues to deliver new opportunities and challenges, and the questions to such must always be asked and answered to move forward. Within that process, you find endings and new beginnings. For example, the best answer that I ever got to a question was my ex-wife saying "yes!" to my marriage proposal all those years ago. Conversely, the most life-changing question I ever asked was whether to agree to divorce. Through those vicissitudes of life, I think you continue to rediscover yourself and redefine yourself.

The two most important philosophical questions, in my opinion, concern morality and theology. I came to the realization that all I know is there is something larger than me. The purpose of life is to live a virtuous life, to be strong and to help others.

In my family, we were always taught that being as fortunate in life as we have been, it is not only right to give back, but it is also your *duty and responsibility* to give back and help others. I fully came to understand this principle as a youth.

My father's maxim was: *To help others, you have to make yourself strong.* My motivation to study, work hard, or excel was not to create power or fame for myself, but to use it to be the best person I could be and to give back. As tremendously successful as my parents were, I never saw any superficiality. I never saw them relishing good fortune or taking advantage of it, or others, because of it. I never saw them be ostentatious. I do my best to follow their example in that way.

The music of the sixties had a big influence on me. Listening to the music that rejected some of the normal societal traditions was very thought-provoking to me. I was wholeheartedly into Bob Dylan, the Beatles, Paul Simon, and the incredible Sting Band. It was my mainstay music and for me a great escape from the conformity I felt I had grown up with. I tell myself now—if I'd known how easy it was to make a living from music, I think I would have gone for it. But, back then, after a little bit of soul-searching and wondering if there were other careers that would be more interesting for me, I pretty quickly decided that I had a great company and that real estate was very intriguing to me. I wanted to continue with it.

What you may not know is that behind a lot of real estate developers is a frustrated architect! Design is the aspect of real estate development that I've always loved. I loved pondering and planning how to influence people's lifestyles through residential and mixed-use developments. It was very exciting! Most of my siblings also went into business, about the same time. We were all in different divisions and in different cities, so we didn't compete. We all ran our own show. Much of my business career was also spent running trade marts, both the Dallas Market Center and the International Trade Mart in Brussels, Belgium. The most vibrant, profitable wholesale centers bring together the best variety of buyers and sellers and maximize their transactions.

I have been an environmentalist since I first learned the word at age twelve. I believe marketplace solutions and conservative ideals are effective means of addressing many, but not all, environmental challenges. I began supporting environmental organizations and politicians who understood that the best environmental solutions will come, not simply from government regulation, but also from market-driven, business-led innovations. Ideas of sustainable design in real estate and electric vehicles, for example, have always intrigued me.

I'm a guy who always wants to put ideas into action. Based on my experience with trade marts, I envisioned an environmental marketplace of ideas. That's why I founded EarthX in 2011 to promote environmental education and solutions. I know that green conservative ideas can help cities and states adapt to a changing climate. Effective environmental solutions need not be at odds with economic growth; solutions can also be profitable when consumers are educated and demand eco-friendly goods and services. EarthX is now the world's largest environmental exposition, conference, and film festival. We bring together business, government, environmental organizations, and academic institutions to educate the public and inspire citizens to action. In our first year, we had 38,000 visitors and 200 exhibitors. We then expanded the event and grew into Earth Day Texas. At Earthx2019, we convened 175,000 visitors, including 10 conferences, 450 speakers, and 700 exhibitors. The participants engage in environmental conversations that would not otherwise happen because they are focused on solutions not problems.

Planning for the 2020 event started the day after 2019 ended. It promises to be bigger and more impactful than ever.

I believe one of the most important questions everyone alive should ask themselves is, *"Do I have a vested interest in sustaining our beloved planet?"* Hopefully, that answer will cause awareness that leads to action from each of us, starting with our own consumption behaviors.

The good news is that I'm certain we can change the direction, and together, create a sustainable future for all—if we will!

Ask Gold Nuggets

- One question can pivot your entire career.
- Who could mentor you to assist with your success?
- When you're overwhelmed, ask for help, answers, and direction.
- Don't be afraid to ask for support for your vision.
- Great leaders lead with questions and listen for the answers to perfect their plans.
- Don't go in and try to sell something—ask what they need, then fill the need.
- Look for the problem to make your fortune.
- What will your life be like in ten, twenty, or thirty years?
- To help others, you have to work on making yourself strong.

PART III

Explore Your Greatest Human Potential by Asking

The Four Parts of Masterful Asking

1. You Are Not a Human Being—You Are a Human Becoming

You might be thinking by now, *When will I ask all the right questions so I'm finally where I want to be in my life?* The answer is never! But don't let that discourage you. That is the most beautiful part of life. There is no final destination with life, only a journey that continues to unfold, causing us to continually evolve. You are not the same person you were twenty years ago, ten years ago, or even one year ago. You become someone new day by day, and if you warmly embrace the art of asking through this journey, we believe you'll find it to be more delightful than you could ever have imagined.

The deepest form of asking is when you ask from a spiritual perspective. The answers to these questions can be profound because they deal with the very purpose of your life, the ways to achieve everlasting joy, and even ponder the source of creation and your place in it.

Many of the world's religious texts give us clues to the importance of asking. They suggest that all questions will be answered. In the Bible it says, "Ask and you shall receive." The Hindu holy texts, the Upanishads, and the most authoritative scriptures of India encourage questioning and inquiry as a pathway to a discovery of truth. In Judaism, teaching the asking questions is a tenet of their religious practice starting with teaching the young to ask questions as an essential component of Passover. The Buddha also encouraged questioning by his disciples, and a fundamental role for questioning is still embraced in the practices of modern Buddhism. Some Tibetan Buddhist monks debate—a daily practice that involves one monk continually questioning another monk for an hour, often on esoteric points of Buddhist thought. The impressive aspect of this practice is how the monks use this method of questioning/answering to hone their skills in logic and to probe complex questions. The intense exchanges are punctuated by episodes of laughter and joy.

What is the reason for living life, other than to love it?

—Socrates

The classical Greek philosopher Socrates is credited as one of the founders of Western philosophy and the first true moral philosopher. He taught by asking questions and drawing out answers. He was known for his remarkable integrity. Socrates did not just search for the meaning of life but also challenged people to find the meaning of their own lives. He asked fundamental questions of human existence: What makes us happy? What makes us good? What is virtue? What is love? What is fear? How should we best live our lives?

The purpose of his questions was to move people toward their ultimate goals and their highest moral behaviors. We can learn much from this enlightened man about how to utilize the power of asking questions to revector our lives to a higher level of living.

Live with a New Question in Your Heart

Living in our fast-paced world, life can seem overwhelming, competitive, and even cut-throat at times. Getting through your day can make you feel like you're in battle of survival of the fittest. It's important as we become more comfortable with honing the art of asking that we not forget that happiness isn't always found by achieving status and money or accumulating more things. It's easy to start working relentlessly in a certain direction and not notice that you've gotten into a pattern that is actually taking you further away from your continued growth, progress, and true happiness. Our deepest sense of joy and peace usually comes from the feeling that we're contributing something to this experience called life.

How often do we find ourselves looking at situations in terms of "what's in it for me?" or "what can I gain out of this?" We all need to survive. We need and want to have accomplishments, material abundance, and satisfying experiences. But the pursuit of only those things usually leaves us feeling a bit empty because there is something more noble in each and every one of us. A higher calling, if you will, to be and become a better human being. There is a simple technique that will help you in that pursuit if you're willing.

Who Do I Become? Question-Switch Technique

When faced with a decision involving any personal behavior, we love to challenge people to try the question-switch technique. We use this question-switch technique ourselves, when faced with important decisions. We find that it creates a sort of revectoring that helps us to not just focus on filling our most basic primal needs but rather to also put us on a track that is in alignment with a greater purpose. With so many scenarios in life, if you replace the first question below with the second question, your answer will guide you in a more noble and satisfying direction.

Rather than asking:

> *"What am I going to get from this if I do this or act like this?"*

Ask:

> *"Who do I become if I do this or act like this?"*

Who you are becoming is far more important to your happiness and well-being than what you are getting. Each and every day, through each and every thought, word, and deed, a new version of you is being sculpted. Every time you make a behavioral decision or follow a behavioral pattern, it makes you more of *something*. It takes you further along into becoming someone. This important distinction between these two questions provides important intercession in that natural human process that normally goes along unnoticed until we consciously intervene, or one day we look at ourselves in the mirror and can't stand what we see. Are you becoming the person you want to be, or do you feel further and further away from that person you long to become? Often, it's the people who are achieving great reserves of status and beautiful material possessions in life who feel the emptiest inside. That certainly doesn't mean that you can't have a life of beautiful things and exciting experiences and still feel an internal sense of connected purpose. But usually, keeping this balance requires some deliberate awareness and thought and some tools that can be utilized when you begin to feel off-kilter in your purpose.

Substituting this one question will raise you to a higher level of operating. Instead of operating from a basic-needs perspective, which is driven by our primitive brain, this new question engages our imagination each time we make a decision, asking it to picture again and again whom we want to be or become.

Spiritual Asking

Throughout our travels around the world, we've been exposed to many people, cultures, and religions. What we've discovered for ourselves is that universally, regardless of one's race, creed, or county of origin, most people feel that there is a divine presence that is powerful and can help them if they stay tuned in to that presence. We've discovered that people are fundamentally good. That they possess similar feelings of love and devotion for their families to those we have for ours. That their friendships and community are truly important to their happiness, and that there is a higher power that calls them to become something better. We believe that one of the greatest messages that we can share is that God belongs to everyone as the Creator of all of us. That every person is worthy of greatness and the richness of life.

> *And all things, whatsoever ye shall ask in prayer,*
> *believing, ye shall receive.*
>
> —MATTHEW 21:22

Whether you think of Jesus as your savior or a Jewish rabbi who taught with great wisdom, or you don't know much about him, his promise is unequivocal and explicitly exact. We've personally experienced again and again that asking through the amazing, unquantifiable power of prayer and sacred intention is what accelerates our dreams across our Destiny Bridge into realization and completion. With prayer and sacred intention, asking power is unlimited. We consciously have the ability to create in exponential and miraculous ways by utilizing that power. It is spiritual power that is individualized in each of us. You can positively create unlimited wealth and success by asking. Likewise, all crime is the result of ignorance of this spiritual law. With this knowledge, we understand that all things are available to us if we're willing to look deeper and expand our awareness of what is possible.

Our purpose for asking in this expanded way is to change things. The very act of asking stimulates and starts psychological change. When we open ourselves to the possibility of getting new answers, it moves our mood from fear to confidence. As you begin to evolve positively through this process, you start to feel a sense of joy and thanksgiving. Asking through prayer moves your spirit toward the accomplishment of your desires. Behind every great result that takes formation in your life is the invisible formless life that started by asking for change, elucidation, progress, happiness, or success.

Any good physics teacher can explain to you that atoms are the substance that makes up every physical creation in the universe, including our bodies, and that atoms are made of protons, neutrons, and electrons. But science has gone far beyond that basic understanding of physics. What they know now is that when you break those three elements down to even smaller ones, what you have is light. In other words, everything that appears to be solid and made of matter is really nothing more than energy and light. Is that what is being shared in Genesis 1:13 when God said, "Let there be light"? When you look more deeply into the crossroads between science and spirituality, you can see how the dots all start to connect.

ASK!

A scientist named Fritz-Albert Popp, along with his team of researchers at the University of Marburg, began studying biophotons in cells in the 1970s. What scientists know now is that this "light" emitted from our cells is highly coherent energy that could possibly be responsible for the very operation of our biological systems. We believe that the light of our Creator lives within us and that science will continue to discover more evidence of the literal light connection between the physical and divine and how we can download more of that light to create daily miracles to manifest our dreams.

A Johns Hopkins University professor, Richard Conn Henry, published an article in the international science journal *Nature* called "The Mental Universe." It is a fascinating summary about the very nature of everything in existence, including theories once accepted about how our world exists in the form that it does—theories that are now being challenged by new information. Science has now proven that physical matter isn't really physical. It is made up of nonphysical light and energy that exist only in the eye of the beholder. Henry says, "The Universe is immaterial—mental and spiritual. Live and enjoy." We can't speak for you, but for us this could be the most exciting truth we know. It tells us that we can ask for, receive, and become anything we can conceive of in our hearts and minds!

Every one of us gets bogged down. Life is full of challenges, trials, and mysteries to which we are all seeking answers. When life is bogging us down and making our energy feel low and slow, sometimes we have to kick ourselves and remember to ask: *"Am I remembering the light of Creation that feeds my very existence each minute of each day?"* This is much more effective if we can take a quiet moment to ourselves and picture the light. We try to form a clear mental image of light coming from the very seat of Creation and filling us up. This is a simple but powerful exercise to reboot your mental and emotional energy at the drop of a hat when you need it most. Remember, you're made of light. So, you know those times when you feel like you're not glowing? Like your light is low, slow, or dingy? Connecting back to the Source can reenergize you and reset your attitude, outlook, and results!

One of our favorite Leonardo da Vinci paintings is *Salvator Mundi*, which depicts Christ with his left hand holding a celestial sphere containing three lights. We think that perhaps Leonardo was reminding us in that painting that we come from seeds of light. Perhaps those three light orbs represent the Holy Trinity. It is a bit awe-inspiring to contemplate what he was trying to show us in that painting.

Most of us are in touch with the reality that there is a part of us that exists beyond and outside our physical bodies. There are volumes of books talking about the experiences of people who left their body through near-death or other such experiences and realized they fully exist at a level beyond the physical with all parts of their intellect and personality, yet with a heightened awareness and freedom from normal psychological stresses. This reminds us that there is so much more to us than meets the eye. When everything you're seeing around you and in front of you is not exactly what you want, it means you're not remembering who you really are. You're not remembering what you're made of and from where you came. It means you're not asking for enough. Often, we get used to our mediocre lives and start to have mediocre expectations. When we pray or set our intentions, we ask for small things like:

- Help me get through this day.
- Let me figure out how to get the bills paid this month.

- Let me be in the same room with my teenager without getting in a fight.
- Let me endure my negative coworkers without getting upset.

It's not enough to ask to endure your miserable situation. It's not enough to ask how to squeak by financially. It's not enough to ask to cope with mediocrity or the unpleasantness you deal with every day. Do you realize that the limitations you're putting on your life only come from you? No one can limit your life unless you let them. God's abundant Universe is truly infinite and has *no* limitations. What if you decided to ask so boldly that if all your requests were fulfilled, you wouldn't even recognize your life? We all find ourselves operating in our "norms." Norms that we adopted as ours through our family's influence, cultural influences, and our community influences. We're saying it is time to get out of your norm. We want you to look at every part of your life and challenge what you've accepted as normal for too long. At the crossroads of science and spirituality you will find a new way to create a brand-new paradigm for yourself.

Question Everything

One of our dearest friends, Trudy Green spent the last few decades as an iconic rock band manager. Trudy Green Management and Howard Kaufman of HK Management were partners for over thirty years managing some of the most legendary rock bands in the world. Together they co-managed many major artists, including Aerosmith, Janet Jackson, Michael Jackson, Mick Jagger, Heart, Whitesnake, Perry Farrell, Yes, Slash, the Bee Gees, and Jefferson Airplane, to name a few. Green and Kaufman took over the management of Heart at a time when no one had a lot of belief in their ability to rebound. They did a remarkable job helping resurrect this band—bringing them back to success when their career seemed over. After signing with the management duo in 1985, Heart roared back into the spotlight with albums *Heart* and *Bad Animals*, which each sold millions of copies. To know Trudy, you would say she is one of the gentlest people you'll ever meet. When you look at her sweet face and listen to her talk about God in her lilting English accent, you might think you've encountered a love and mindfulness guru. But Trudy will be the first to tell you, "I'm tough. I'm a tiger. I didn't get where I am being a pussycat." You learn quickly that a person like Trudy, who has done extraordinary things and broken barriers the way she has, has done so by questioning the status quo, challenging the norms, and asking again and again for what she wants.

God, Prayer, and Rock 'n' Roll: Trudy Green's Story

I've lived my entire life relying on God to answer all my questions. So often, it seems like my whole journey has come from God. I didn't come from a religious family who told me about God, praying, or anything like that. I guess I came into the world like that. I just never knew anything else. I used to make up my own prayers when I was a little kid, starting at about three years old. I'd say my prayer every night, just talking to God and asking Him questions.

My parents were divorced, and I grew up without my father. I grew up with incredible grandparents, a wonderful mother, and a loving stepfather. I guess because I didn't have a father in my life when I was very young, God became my father. I thought this was just a normal thing. He has always been very deep and significant in my life. So, everything I have and everything I've done, I give credit 100 percent to God. I think for all of us this is available, but I am truly grateful for everything He has given me. I am especially grateful for my two beloved, wonderful sons,

Daniel and Ben. Both of whom are the greatest gifts and blessings in my life. I am most grateful for them, more than anything else in the world.

The truth is, I never went into my life wanting to go into the music entertainment business. I truly wanted to do something completely different, but God had a different plan. The two biggest questions I have always asked Him, and still do to this day, are *"Why am I here?"* and *"What is my purpose of being here?"* The biggest goal in my life is to fulfill my purpose for being here.

I realize everyone is here to learn how to love. That's universal. What I've learned from my journey is the goal to live with purpose, passion, and most importantly to learn how to love all people and truly love unconditionally. I got the love part. Beginning to understand what unconditional love really is started to come later in life. I honestly don't think I have truly achieved that yet, but part of my purpose for being here is to learn how to do that.

When it came to my being in a mostly male-dominated industry, I was never intimidated. I always had a purpose. People ask me all the time: "How did you manage to achieve the levels of success in such a difficult business? How did you hang in there and continue to build success when most people fail?" The crazy thing is, I never even thought about failure. When I started in the business, I was very young. I knew absolutely nothing, but I never doubted that it could be any other way. I was very insecure about some things but never in business, even though there were people all around me with so much doubt and insecurity. I never felt that in business. I guess it's because I'm strong and I'm a survivor. I never thought I *couldn't* do it, but maybe that's because through my constant search and questioning, God anchored that purpose inside me. For some reason He wanted me to be a stable anchor inside the music industry. My partner was such a big and important part of that stability. There were no other Howard Kaufmans in the music business. He was extraordinary in every way. He was brilliant, the smartest businessman I have ever known. He was truly one of the most amazing men I've ever met in my life. Beyond that, he conducted himself with the utmost integrity. I was so blessed to have this special man as a partner. Don Passman, a top lawyer in the music industry and another exceptional and brilliant man, was the one who introduced me to Howard many years ago.

When I got out of college, the only thing I wanted at that time was to be the fashion editor at *Vogue* magazine. I was completely obsessed with fashion. My mother was in the fashion business, and it was exciting. I loved all the designers, and I loved going with her to all the fashion shows in Paris. It was also the time in England when the fashion industry was a huge part of British culture. It was my true passion at the time.

However, God changed all that. He delivered a different plan to me. Out of college I told the employment agency I was working with that I just wanted to work with fashion editors of magazines. They explained to me that you have to start off in the secretarial pool, and you have to work your way up. You don't just get a job immediately working for the fashion editor. I said, "No! No! I'm going into that profession. That's all I want to do."

So, while all that was going on, I was offered my next job, which was my first job in the music industry. I started working for Apple Records, located at the prestigious Savile Row.

All my friends were saying, "Oh my gosh! You're working for the Beatles! You've got the dream job! You're so lucky! Yada, yada, yada."

"Yeah, it's great," I said, "but I'm waiting for my job to open up on a fashion magazine."

So, as time went on, I kept pushing off these jobs in the secretarial pools because I never doubted myself. I wasn't going to go into the secretarial pool. I kept saying no, no, no. I'm going to go work directly for the fashion editor. I wanted to wait for the job that I wanted. In the meantime, I had also done another job working for the head of a publicity company. I took that while I was waiting for my fashion job. Then I had this opportunity to start my own company because I never thought I couldn't, so I started my first company called Crunch Promotions. I knew nobody. I just started writing to people in the industry, saying, "I have started my own company, and I'd love to work for you." I started getting responses, and soon enough I had a thriving entertainment publicity company, which I later sold before I came to the US.

While I was running my own successful company, something unexpected happened, after this long journey of wanting fashion and getting entertainment management. A woman who was a big fashion icon at the time called me and said, "I've known you, and I want to work with you. I wonder if you would call me as soon as you can. I'm moving over to *Vanity Fair* magazine, and I want to take you with me."

Suddenly, I was on the precipice. Finally, what I thought was my dream job was being offered to me. But now, I had my own company, and I was free. I could do everything I wanted to do. I asked God, "What do I do?" I was told to stay in my own company and not take the job, so that's what I did. I would never have imagined that I would someday turn down what earlier I had thought was my dream job in the fashion industry.

Once I was living in the US, I went to work for Gibson and Stromberg, a major publicity company. In the 1980s, I was getting fed up with being a publicist and decided I wanted to be a manager. Don Passman introduced me to singer-songwriter Stephen Bishop, and he became my first client. At first, most of the men in the business didn't take me seriously because I was young and I was a woman.

I had to fight twice as hard to prove I was strong and I meant business. I saw so many people put limitations on themselves. I had this sense of purpose, and I just never put limitations on myself. I always believed that I could do whatever I set my mind to and I'd do it as well as it could possibly be done. Clearly it was God directing me because what I was doing was totally the opposite of what I originally wanted to do.

Later when I partnered with Howard Kaufman at HK Management, I got to work with the best partner in the world. Howard Kaufman was a true icon in the industry. His brilliant thinking and strategies inspired me every day. Together, we were an unbeatable team. We had the best partnership for thirty-four years, until he passed away. Sometimes I had to be extremely tough. In this business, I had to learn not to put up with any nonsense from anyone. I never did. I was never afraid of losing a job, being fired, or anything like that. I wouldn't let anyone run me over. I just wouldn't take any guff from people.

Through the years my intuition has gotten really good, and I know that comes from my relationship with God. The way I describe it is I just know things that I know because I'm told. It's not because Trudy Green knows. It's because God is telling me. He tells me if something's wrong and he tells me if something is right, and I know immediately if I'm doing something wrong. If I choose to do it and keep doing it, then I know bad things happen. I always know the difference between right and wrong and that it's a conscious choice. Whatever we do or don't do—every moment it is a choice. Each thing that comes up is a conscious decision. I know I have not always been conscious, and I've taken my problems in different directions instead of going all the way up. I've gone sideways a bunch of times and lost progress. But always I've known God has never left me, and I can always come back to Him again. I like to spend time every day talking to God. I do a lot of writing while I'm talking to Him. I've always used paper and pen to write down everything I am told. I try to stay in awareness and write what He is saying to me.

I do this every morning. If I've got a funny feeling inside me and I'm not feeling good, or I'm feeling like something's really wrong but I can't figure out what it is, I write those feelings to ask God what it's about.

Why am I feeling so much anxiety? Why am I feeling so much stress? Why am I feeling so much sadness or whatever it may be? Those are usually the questions I ask, and then I get the answers at the deepest levels. It's truly unbelievable. After I finish writing, I just feel completely free, and whatever that situation or the anxiety was—it's gone, and I'm calm again.

That's how I was guided to a different career than I thought I wanted. The opportunities kept coming up, and I kept taking them because I was told to say yes; so I did. I think music is so healing to people that God kept putting the opportunity in front of me, and I never questioned that. He just kept opening these opportunities, which were amazing, so I just kept saying yes!

It's always been my passion to be around conscious, spiritual people so I can learn and grow and keep developing to contribute more to this world. The worst experience for me is to let my connection with God grow cold. I have lost the connection at times and it's been horrible, and the only way I can get it back is by getting on my knees and being humble and saying, "I'm so sorry! You know I really want to come back! I've ignored you because sometimes I get so busy! I can forget to say prayers, or I forget to do my spiritual reading." We all can forget to do the important things that keep us conscious and grounded. I make excuses and say, "I'm too busy; I've just got to go get this done. I've got to get that deal finished." There is always something important that comes up and if you keep putting that first, then something happens, and you fall and then you come back up again. I think it's about staying disciplined and conscious every day, always remembering God comes first. He is what's truly important. Keeping a spiritual discipline and your spiritual practice every single day, I believe, is the most important thing we can do to stay happy and grounded.

"How can I contribute more to saving this world and all humanity?"
"How can I do more?" "How can I be more?" For me, those important

questions will continue to be there to guide me as I listen for daily guidance and answers.

Ask Gold Nuggets

- What is the purpose for living life, other than to love it?
- Who do you become if you act like this? Who do you become if you do this?
- Are you remembering the light of Creation that feeds your very existence each minute of each day?
- Why are you here, and what is your purpose for being here?
- How can you contribute more to humanity?

---

2. How to Approach God with Questions

And it shall come to pass, that before they call, I will answer;
and while they are yet speaking, I will hear.

—Isaiah 65:24

A Process for Asking God

When you remember who you are, you realize you don't have to desperately beg God to hear you, laden with fear and worry that you may be unworthy of an answer, there may not be enough to go around, or God simply won't hear you.

Like all couples and families, we have our challenging times. Times when problems are coming at us quickly and issues seem to pop up left and right, complicating our business efforts, relationships, and the way we feel about our life purpose. In those times our greatest gift is the awareness of who we truly are apart from all the noise and goings-on of the world. We know that the Creator, who created the Universe, also created us. Therefore, we are a part of Him. An individuated piece of God living in a body that He also created for us, in which to reside while we experience this earthly existence. Why would we ever have to plead, beg, and desperately seek God out in some faraway place? He's already inside us. Waiting lovingly and patiently for us to remember, acknowledge, and **ask**. Every question we need answered is already answered. Every problem we need solved is already solved. The direction we need to take is already available.

When we find our world getting a bit frenzied, and we're feeling out of sorts, instead of getting frantic, upset, negative, and fearful, we know our best decision is to do exactly the opposite. Stop struggling, worrying, and distressing, and just get very, very quiet. We have a special comfortable place in our home for our prayer and meditation sessions. It's a lovely comfortable spot in front of floor-to-ceiling windows where we're gazing at the natural beauty of the Sonoran Desert. The first thing we do is try to breathe more deeply and calm our bodies and our nervous systems, so they're better receptacles for God's wisdom and grace. Then we begin to put our focus on every positive thing in our lives, acknowledging every good that comes to our mind, and as we do so, we give thanks for each thing. As we continue this process, we feel our energy dramatically shifting. Instead of feeling the stress and tension we had when we started, we're feeling calm and present. We then become aware of a growing feeling of gratitude that deepens as we acknowledge more and more of our blessings. From our eyes that behold this beautiful world to the softness of our pillow as we lie down at night, we realize the importance of those small but valuable gifts we possess, which many people struggle without. At that point, we have changed our state of being from one of stress, lack, and confusion to one of deep gratitude and peace. And from that state, we deliberately remember who we are. That we are a Creation of the Creator, that He dwells with us always, and if we ask Him, He reveals the truth, the answers, and sometimes the patience and confidence we need to journey forward more happily, knowing that nothing will be hidden as long as we ask and remember.

> *...One God and Father of all,*
> *who is above all, and through all, and in you all.*
>
> —Ephesians 4:6

Two Young Actresses Accepted an Impossible Mission and Changed the World

Sara O'Meara and Yvonne Fedderson

Two young Hollywood actresses, Sara (Buckner) O'Meara and Yvonne (Lime) Fedderson, met playing the bubbly girlfriends of Ricky and David Nelson on *The Adventures of Ozzie and Harriet*. Little did they know, it was a friendship that would last a lifetime—one in which they would change the world together.

The year was 1959, and two rising stars, a stunning brunette and beautiful blonde, were picked from a possible cast of hundreds as part of a government-sponsored goodwill tour. They were flown to Korea, Okinawa, and Japan to entertain American soldiers stationed abroad after the Korean War.

A few days after they arrived in Tokyo, the entire city was shut down by a severe typhoon with violent winds. "Red flag" alerts warned locals to remain indoors, though a few desperate souls scavenged through the debris and wreckage looking for food and shelter.

Among these was a group of children huddled beneath a fallen awning, pressed together for warmth, but still shivering against the freezing wind. The children were barefoot, clothed in rain-soaked rags, and weeping.

After days trapped in their hotel room, the willful and daring actresses grew restless and decided to sneak out for a midday walk. They did not want to miss all the sights and sounds of this fascinating new culture. Propelled by youthful curiosity, they explored the side streets of Tokyo and strode right into the cowering orphans. Turning onto the side street, giggling as their shoes sank into the mud, the young Hollywood actresses must have looked like angels emerged from the terrifying storm to the children.

They immediately ran to the children and huddled as many as would fit under their billowing coats. Sara and Yvonne furiously flipped through the pages of their English-to-Japanese dictionaries to converse as best they could. They discovered the little survivors were orphaned, stranded, and homeless.

Sara and Yvonne did what any naïve, emotional young women might do and smuggled all eleven children into their hotel room. They bathed, fed, and played with the children before tucking them in for the night. After the children were fast asleep, Yvonne looked at Sara with a worried expression, "Now what?" as they realized they needed to face the reality of the situation they had stumbled into.

The next morning, Sara and Yvonne searched for orphanages to take in the rescued children, but none could oblige because of their own crowded conditions. There was also the fact that because the children were mixed blood—half-American and half-Japanese (many fathered by American servicemen)—they would receive no government funding. Neither country would accept the children because they had no birth certificates. At the time, they were called "throwaway children," unclaimed by the cultures of their origin.

They learned of a kind local woman named Kin Horuchi (lovingly known as Mama Kin) who lived in a one-room hut with several orphans. She agreed to care and provide shelter for the extra children with the promise that Sara and Yvonne would pay for these eleven orphans plus the ten already in her care.

They began their lifelong careers in fundraising by passing around a hat in the audience and collecting donations after singing to the servicemen. When our men in uniform learned about the children, they were eager to help. Sara and Yvonne decided there was nothing left to do but start their own orphanage, International Orphans, Inc.

When word of what was happening spread through the city, there were over a hundred extra children left on the doorstep of the modest dwelling within three short weeks. Mama Kin agreed to care for these extra children with Sara and Yvonne's commitment of financial help. Once again, the soldiers stepped up to help, and the hut was expanded into a comfortable home for the children in Mama Kin's care.

Sara and Yvonne returned to California and started fundraising. They implored friends, family, and contacts in the film industry to help the children they had grown to love. They collected enough money to build four orphanages in Japan for the throwaway children, who were now safe and secure.

Due to their great success, Congress later requested them to do the same in Vietnam.

Eventually the two women, along with volunteers, built and maintained five orphanages, a hospital, and a school. Through building orphanages with the dedicated oversight of the Third Marine Amphibious Force, Sara and Yvonne became friends and dedicated partners with Marine Corps Lieutenant General Lewis W. Walt, who was in charge of their entire orphanage operation in Vietnam.

After an event, General Walt, who appeared at many of their fundraisers, spoke with Sara and Yvonne privately. Over coffee he shared a history-changing secret. "Ladies, I have something to tell you—something that very few people know," he said in a hushed voice. "In a short time, I expect to receive orders from the president to pull our troops out of Vietnam."

Sara and Yvonne could not believe what they were hearing and immediately thought about their precious orphans. General Walt was tough but was a "teddy bear" when it came to the protection of the little ones. Still, he was committed to the safety of his men. He held up his hands before the ladies could speak: "I'm telling you right now—I don't want to hear a word about the children. There's absolutely nothing I can do. Do you understand? It's going to be hard enough to evacuate our men, so I don't want any problems concerning the children. I've got enough to deal with, okay?"

Sara pleaded, her eyes filling with tears, "You know these children will be the Vietcong's first targets because the orphanages are funded by Americans and the children are half-American!"

Yvonne began to cry as well and begged, "They won't survive with their mixed blood. They will be lined up and shot, just like we see on TV."

"There's nothing I can do," General Walt replied, clearly upset. "I'm sorry, but that's the way it is."

Sara and Yvonne wept most of the night, imagining the faces of the little children they had grown to care for as if they were part of their own families. In the morning, sadness was replaced by action. They called their ally Representative James C. Corman (D-CA) and boldly requested that he persuade Congress to acquire the planes to evacuate the boys and girls in peril.

Within twenty-four hours, the call from Congressman Corman came in. "If you can organize the children, I'll help get the planes."

Sara and Yvonne worked tirelessly for weeks, coordinated volunteers, and made miracles happen. The operation was dubbed by the media as "Operation Baby Lift." Sara and Yvonne cried tears of joy as the children were flown out of war-torn Vietnam and placed into the arms of loving adoptive parents. Through their orphanages, community efforts, and Operation Baby Lift, the Childhelp founders began their philanthropic careers rescuing thousands of babies and young children.

Word quickly spread of the wonderful things Sara and Yvonne were doing with International Orphans, Inc., and they were invited by the First Lady of California, Nancy Reagan, to speak about their life-saving missions. Their heart-wrenching story would be the perfect way to address what Mrs. Reagan called "America's best-kept secret"—child abuse in the nation.

Then Governor and First Lady Ronald and Nancy Reagan told Sara and Yvonne they were the perfect ones to begin the fight against child abuse in America, for they were brave in their actions where angels fear to tread.

Alerting the country of this horrible epidemic was the first step in helping the cause, and the ladies were eager to share the story of what was happening to American children.

Later in the year, the Senate Subcommittee on Children and Youth released a study that child abuse had become an epidemic in the United States and was the leading cause of death in young children. This horrific statistic showed the intensity of the issue in our own country and helped to convince many to join the cause. Unfortunately, this statistic is still true today.

After working endlessly, in April 1978 Sara and Yvonne opened the doors of the first pioneering residential treatment center for children traumatized by abuse. This month would later have national significance when they joined actress Sophia Loren to lobby President Jimmy Carter with the hopes of making April Child Abuse Prevention Month. (Eventually April was declared National Child Abuse Prevention Month in 1983 by President Reagan.) To this day, it's a month during which organizations throughout America pay extra attention to this critical issue.

The first Children's Village is located in Beaumont, California. This village treats severely abused children from ages four to fourteen and gives them a safe place to call home with therapy and structure. Since then, other villages, advocacy centers, adoption centers, and foster care placement/training programs have been added in locations around the country.

In 1982, the organization's name was changed to Childhelp. Decades later, Childhelp remains true to their vision. With prevention, intervention, and treatment programs in every state, this internationally respected nonprofit is the largest organization dedicated to helping victims of child abuse and neglect as well as at-risk children.

The Childhelp National Child Abuse Hotline, 1-800-4-A-CHILD, operates twenty-four hours a day, seven days a week, and receives calls from throughout the United States, Canada, the US Virgin Islands, Puerto Rico, and Guam. The service is staffed exclusively with degreed counselors and is pioneering text/chat research to keep up with emerging technology so they can reach the greatest number of youth in need.

Childhelp has also been a leader in prevention education, launching Childhelp Speak Up Be Safe and Childhelp Speak Up Be Safe for Athletes to protect youth in schools and sports.

Several of Childhelp's programs were firsts and continue to be studied by professionals worldwide as "models that work." The sixty years of successfully implementing best practices throughout the world has inspired Childhelp's next bold vision to create the Childhelp Global Campus to serve the entire world with the training and models perfected by Childhelp. Every step of the way, wonderful volunteers, many of whom participate in Childhelp chapters throughout the country, lend a helping hand. Though it has grown beyond their wildest dreams, Founder, CEO, and Chairman Sara O'Meara, and Founder, Vice Chairman, and President Yvonne Fedderson, who still work every day for this critical cause, have never forgotten those eleven little orphans in a storm who inspired their mission of hope.

Ask to Find Your Purpose: Yvonne Fedderson's Story

I definitely think the way you understand something, if you want things to work out in life, is that you have to learn to ask questions. It's a very important life skill.

I was very inquisitive when I was young. I was very active in school and my church. I asked many questions and fortunately had people who answered them in a meaningful way that I could understand at that time.

The questions I asked and the answers I was given, especially about spiritual matters, helped me to get on a spiritual path that has guided me my entire life. Even when I entered the film industry, I would always pray when I was going on an interview and ask if it was right for me to get the part. I wanted to feel good within myself if I was going to make a decision. I'm sure I made mistakes. Many of them I remember vividly, but you learn through those challenges. That's the beautiful part about life.

As a young child, I was always a movie buff, and I would write to various famous stars and ask them for pictures, autographs, and things like that. I was always interested in that, but I never thought it was something I would be a part of. The amazing thing was, most of the stars answered my letters. It was really special to have those requests answered.

One summer after graduation, my parents allowed me to go to the Pasadena Playhouse, which is a place many people go to learn how to act but also to be "discovered." They had one main stage and several smaller stages. Usually family or friends would come to see actors perform if they got on one of the stages. I did plays in the smaller venues, but one day in class a man sitting next to me asked, "Would you go with me to read for main stage?"

He was nervous to go alone, and we had connected, so I said, "Sure, I'll go with you."

We were sitting in the audience at the main stage, and the director suddenly looked up at me and asked, "You up there...would you please come down and read for this part?" I went down, read, and ended up getting the part! It was a famous play called *Ah, Wilderness!* with Will Rogers Jr. and Bobby Driscoll.

Right after I got the part, several agents came up to me. They each said they would like to represent me if I did not have an agent. I thought that sounded like fun, so I said, "Okay!"

You had to be a card-carrying member in the union, and it was kind of tricky. I picked the agent who could get me in. Right away I got a part on *Father Knows Best* with Robert Young and Jane Wyman. I only had one line, but right after that show, the producer said, I'd like to have you as a regular, and I thought, *Oh my gosh!* I ended up with a running part for four more years. My career started, and it just took off!

I did some popular movies at the time like *Dragstrip Riot* and *High School Hellcats*, as well as a few classics like *The Rainmaker* with

Katharine Hepburn and *Loving You* with Elvis. I also appeared in many TV shows like *Father Knows Best*, *The Adventures of Ozzie and Harriett*, *Gomer Pyle*, *Family Affair*, and *My Three Sons*. I just would go from one show to another. I was very fortunate and blessed, but it all played a part in my future destiny.

Sara had come to California from Knoxville, Tennessee. We first got to know each other because we were both Sunday school teachers at the Hollywood Presbyterian Church. We were active in the Hollywood Christian group. In addition, I was involved with a group of actors who would do a show every weekend for the servicemen somewhere in the United States. The group was championed by an actor named Charles Watts. Charlie would get the older actors and actresses and I would get the young ones, and we would entertain servicemen on the weekends. One day when I was working on *Ozzie and Harriet,* Sara was there working as well. I recognized her from the other places we'd run into each other. We started talking, and I invited her to be on the show for the troops the coming weekend. She thought it sounded like fun and said yes.

We shared a room together that weekend and really started to get to know one another. We realized how close our beliefs and values were, and because of that we grew close very quickly. Shortly after we had gotten to know each other, she had to move out of the apartment where she was living and find another. I was living at home with my mother in Glendale. "It's a waste of time to drive so far to the studios," Sara said to me. "Would you like to get an apartment together?" I knew it was a great idea, so we got an apartment Hollywood.

Through our work with the military, we learned that they were looking for two actresses to go overseas to entertain the servicemen. When we entertained at home in the US, the military paid only for bare basic accommodations, but overseas on this particular trip they were going to have actors travel GS-16 class, which meant you would go first class all the way, as you had the same status as a general. When we got the information, we asked each other, "Why not try out?" We each went on interviews two different days. They did not know we even knew each other, let alone that we were close friends. Miraculously, out of all the applicants, we were the two selected to go!

We were told they had interviewed five hundred young women for the assignment. When we got the phone calls, we looked at each other and said, "There must be a reason that we were chosen because this is just unbelievable! For us to be selected without them knowing how connected we are...my goodness...God must have had his hand on this!" And, of course, that's how we found the children we saved and ultimately started Childhelp.

You live life and one thing leads to another, but sometimes after you live a few years, you look back and realize all the pieces of the puzzle of your life come together. That one question that led to an answer that led to a complete pivot of your life and your purpose. It's all for a reason. It's truly incredible and amazing when you look back and you get it.

Being Hollywood actresses is what brought it together for us, and we enjoyed those years in show business. During that time, we made a lot of friends and it was fun, but it led to something bigger and better for our lives. Having been sent overseas to entertain, we found the orphaned children. That was the thing that changed both of our lives completely. It changed what we were going to do forever. Sixty years later, we're still rescuing boys and girls in need, and we've loved every minute of it.

We've met so many wonderful people through our work. I think that if you really do something you love, you don't mind the time and energy you put into it. Some people ask us, "Don't you get tired? Aren't you going to retire?" Just like every other question, the answer comes from our purpose-driven mission. We'll never retire because we feel so good about what we're doing. We know we're in our sweet spot, so this is where we belong. This is our mission for life. What's really beautiful is that it's become the mission of many of our volunteers as well. We have many volunteers who have been with us thirty, forty, fifty, or even sixty years. These volunteers are all over the country. They work so hard and raise millions of dollars every single year because they see how many children's lives they change for the better.

There are so many children out there who need our help and our love to turn their lives around. It's just so sad when you see a child who arrived at one of our villages so scared, feeling like it's their fault. But it is so wonderful, such a good feeling, when you go back a few months later and see a huge difference after they've been living in the security of our villages. They learn how to live in a family-like environment, from setting the dining table and having a normal meal to having responsibilities and rewards for their achievements.

Our pioneering animal program ranges from the skill-building and caretaking of our equine therapy to the comfort a child feels in revealing his or her heart while cuddling a specially trained therapy dog. Often, they've been so violated by those who were supposed to care for them, including their own parents. In our nondenominational chapel, they learn about God, how valuable they are to Him, and how His love transcends all things. With all those positive possibilities available to them, they begin to heal, trust, and dream again.

If you are purpose driven, you come alive again every day. It's so vitally important to love what you're doing, and we do. I think if everyone would find something that they love to do, then they would never want to quit.

When it comes to knowing the right way to keep asking the right questions that move you toward your purpose, there are some important things to keep in mind. You must get your ego out of the picture as much as possible and really focus on your purpose. In our case, we have to think of the children. We need to remember we're not asking for ourselves, we're asking for the children. They need us to ask because they have no voice. They're too young or too scared or beaten down to ask. We've had to learn that even though it's hard to seek donations, it must be done to support this critical cause for the children. When you are really sincere and speak from the heart, you learn to just put it out there, knowing you're doing it for God's little children. You're working for something so much bigger than yourself. I think people can feel when your request comes from a place of phoniness or when you really mean it and it's sincere. We always ask with grace and gentleness.

The most important thing, always, is to ask yourself and God to understand what your talent is and use it for something good: something that will bless you and others. When you know your mission, you never give up. Every time we started a new program for Childhelp, it was a challenge, but with God's help, we withstood the storms and have received many beautiful miracles for the children we all love.

To Save the Children, We Never Stopped Asking: Sara O'Meara's Story

I think about questions all the time. The most important questions I have asked forever are, "What is my mission?" and "What does God really want me to do with my life?" Most people, whether they know it or not, have that question in their hearts because we want to be guided. My question was always, "Please, will You show me, God, exactly what You would like for me to do? What Your plan is for my life? Not my own plan but *Yours*. God, please show me that."

One of the gifts that God gave me is courage. I'm an overcomer. It's important that we do not let the opposition of the world take charge of our lives. There are so many ways life pulls at you. People giving you advice, telling you what's best for you, and pushing you toward what they think you should be or do. In my life, I've found that I've had to give up a sure thing sometimes to do the right thing. God gave me some-thing that I would get nothing in return for, except the joy of helping people. I know that was important for me to understand and accept as my work for the children grew because we've helped so many children now. There are many of those children whom we will never meet. We may never look them in the eyes and receive their gratitude. But that's where His guidance to do it for the joy of giving, not for our own glory, has been a pillar for both Yvonne and me to hold on to. We know we're working for the children and God, not for our own praise or power. We are all God's children.

Questions really matter in life. If you question yourself, asking, "Am I on the right path? Which is the path that God wants me to be on?" you're likely to get important answers that are tied to your highest destiny. Sometimes you get a big calling—something so much bigger than your-self, like the one Yvonne and I took on. When you answer the call, often you're going to find yourself in a spiritual battle with opposition and ego. You can't let yourself be worn out by that. You have to go forward and just do what you know you've been guided to do and put your total reliance on God. I believe that every battle worth fighting is a spiritual battle between what you're destined to do and the things that get in the way of that.

We all are faced with that in our lives. We have decisions to make, and making those decisions raises questions in our mind. Questions like:

"Am I doing the right thing?"
"Is this my mission?"
"Am I doing it in a humble way or not?"
"Am I doing it only to please myself or to please God?"

I think we have to be fearless and graceful about that. It's really important to ask ourselves questions all the time. In fact, I think the most important ones for us to ask are the questions we have within ourselves. When we get answers from the Holy Spirit, that's the highest answer. And that's available for anyone. You just need to know and believe that God is always there to guide you. You learn to get secure when you get that direction, trust it, and walk through it. It may look crazy to other people, but that's when you have to adhere to your guidance.

We had so many naysayers along the way. People who told us, "You can't do that. Return those children to where you found them. You'll never find a home for them. You can't build orphanages in another country. You'll never get support for this. You cannot solve the problem of child abuse. It's too hidden. It's too big." I'm glad we tuned out those voices and followed what we knew was our divine mission.

We have helped save over ten million children from the darkness of child abuse and neglect, and we're working to bring in funding for the largest child-protection project ever called Childhelp Global Campus. We will have all of our sixty years of best practices there, but it will be like an entire city where a child can come at birth and stay through emancipation if they need to. All parts of the ecosystem of prevention, healing, and therapy will come together to keep children safe. We will have an International Training Center to share best practices with every state, city, and country in the world. This is how we can reach all children and keep them safe from abuse. Looking back, I know we found the answers to our questions from the right source. Had we relied upon the many naysayers throughout our lives, none of these miracles could have happened.

In our sixty years of running our organization, we've had many times when asking an important question meant literally everything to us and our survival. One specific time that stands out so dramatically in my mind is when the housing market crashed. The economy, and every business imaginable, was struggling to stay afloat. The donations to Childhelp slowed enormously. Everyone was economically burdened. We were up against a wall and were just an hour away from closing our doors because we couldn't meet payroll.

We had to ask one of the hardest questions ever, and we had to ask it of someone we did not even know. It was friend of a friend, and we asked if she would give us the funding just to see us through. We needed a million dollars, and we had to have it in an hour.

We had met the daughter of the woman at a spiritual conference a few months earlier, and she had mentioned that they had a foundation that might fit with our mission. It was a small foundation, and the mother was in charge of it. She had never met us, and it took a lot of courage to get on the phone with her and talk about our desperate predicament. After hearing us out, she said, "Well, our foundation couldn't give you the money that quickly even if we wanted to because we couldn't get together to vote; we don't have the time. I'd have to do it personally. If my daughter will give five hundred thousand, I'll give the other five hundred thousand. How do I get it to you? I could wire it." She wired the money within the hour.

If we had not been bold and courageous enough to ask that question at our most desperate hour, Childhelp was in danger of not surviving. I think of where that would have left all the children we serve. That was a very hard question to ask, especially of someone we didn't even know. That she said yes to our desperate request is truly incredible. It's an amazing example of how important it is, and how much courage it takes, to ask hard questions.

Another question that was a hard one for me was one I asked of the late actor Merv Griffin. I asked him if he would consider giving us his resort, a dude ranch, in order for us to make it into a residential facility for abused children because we really needed one. To our delight and surprise, he said yes. But his answer was even better than that. He not only gave us the ranch, he gave us the horses, the equipment, and every single thing on this guest ranch down to the dishes. He just walked out of a five-star resort in order to give us the whole thing. Had we not been strong enough to ask him, we may never have had that. It was amazing! The point is, you have to get over your fear of asking and stay focused on the things you've been given to do in this lifetime.

One thing I've learned through the years is that you have to be smart enough, before you ask the question, to think about *how* you're going to ask your questions. It's the wisest thing to do because sometimes when you ask people questions that may be a little bit personal, intrusive, or uncomfortable, you have to pray that you'll do it in a certain way that won't embarrass them or you. Each and every time you ask, you have to be cognizant of the question you're asking and ask it so artfully and gracefully that they say yes.

I don't have a doubt that Childhelp will grow and flourish for decades to come because God's hand is upon it; Childhelp belongs to Him. God is the real Chairman of the Board, and we are honored to play a part in healing His most vulnerable children so they may grow up safe and secure, inspired to ask their own questions and find the answers within their hearts.

Your Role in the History of the World

No matter what, each person on Earth plays a role in the history of the world. Normally, we don't know what that is, so **ask** what your role is in the history of the world. Open your heart to the questions that create the path to your destiny, purpose, and fulfillment of your life.

Judge a man by his questions rather than his answers.

—Voltaire

Ask Gold Nuggets

+ What is your mission and what does God really want you to do with your life?
+ Is your mission driven with a higher purpose?
+ Are you doing the right thing?
+ Are you doing it in a humble way or not?
+ Are you doing it only to please yourself or to please God?
+ Are you willing to overcome life's storms and challenges?
+ Are you courageous enough to ask the hard questions?

3. Ask Like a Child

Truly I tell you, unless you change and become like little children, you will never enter the kingdom of heaven.

—MATTHEW 18:3

What is Jesus trying to tell his listeners here? Clearly, he wants us to understand that not only does God love us as a father loves his child, He also wants us to become like a child, because children are innocent and trust with a pure, uncorrupted heart.

Ask Free of Cynicism

The beautiful thing about a child is that he/she hasn't lived enough to be influenced by the concerns of the world—a far cry from the cynicism that develops within most adults. Unfortunately, the older we get, the more emotional and mental hurdles we allow to get between us and our destiny. We allow these hurdles to knock us down or stop us in our tracks, giving up on the rewards that await us if we keep moving forward across our Destiny Bridge. If we can become more like a child, and trust with childlike abandon in all things good, it frees our hearts and allows us to become more of a positive magnet for all the things we desire.

The Qualities of a Child

- A child is humble.
- A child is pure.
- A child is innocent.
- A child trusts purely.
- A child believes with simplicity.
- A child is free of prejudice.
- A child is lighthearted and joyful.
- A child marvels at the little things.
- A child has the faith that he/she will be taken care of.
- A child notices the world's splendor.
- A child feels deserving of God's love.

Because of their innocence and purity of heart, children have no problem asking. They trust at such an uncorrupted level that they believe it is the pleasure and duty of their parent to take care of their needs and to love and cherish them. We can learn so much from the faith of children as we approach life knowing that God loves us like a devoted parent and wants all good things for us.

> *Jesus said, "Let the little children come to me,*
> *and do not hinder them,*
> *for the kingdom of heaven belongs to such as these."*
>
> —Matthew 19:14

What a beautiful thing Jesus said when he declared *the kingdom of heaven belongs to such as these.* He is telling us that, as we live with the same simple faith and trust in our hearts as children, the kingdom of heaven is ours! We're not talking about some faraway place. We're talking about your life right here, right now. We can all probably relate to the feeling that life sometimes feels like heaven and sometimes like hell. We all have the ability to create heaven on earth with new levels of awareness. Challenge yourself to have childlike faith and to know that all good things are there for you—if you ask and believe you are worthy of the abundance of the Universe.

Sylvia Alice Earle, DSc, is a world renowned American marine biologist, explorer, author, and lecturer. She has been a National Geographic explorer-in-residence since 1998. At age eighty-three, she is still diving all over the world and leading the charge to clean up our beautiful oceans, which are being polluted by plastics and chemicals as our planet's population and industrialization increase. We have spent wonderful times with Sylvia conversing at various events and can vouch for the fact she is as energetic and enthusiastic about life as any thirty-year-old! Within the same vein of wonder and innocence Jesus referred to, Sylvia also believes you need to become like a child to become a great explorer or scientist!

The best scientists and explorers have the attributes of kids! They ask questions and have a sense of wonder. They have curiosity. "Who, what, where, why, when and how?" They never stop asking questions, and I never stop asking questions, just like a five-year-old.

—Sylvia Earle

Sylvia's prize-winning TED Talk urged people to help clean the oceans: "I wish you would use all means at your disposal—films! expeditions! the web! new submarines!—to create a campaign to ignite public support for a global network of marine protected areas, Hope Spots large enough to save and restore the blue heart of the planet."

With TED's support, she launched Mission Blue, which aims to establish marine protected areas or "Hope Spots" around the globe. Mission Blue's vision is to achieve 30 percent protection of the ocean by 2030. Over two hundred organizations have supported them in this mission to date. These supporters range from large, global companies to small, bespoke research teams.

Sylvia is an absolute marvel and is making magnificent, positive change for the world because of the childlike hope, wonder, and idealism she has embodied her entire life!

True wisdom comes to each of us
when we realize how little we understand
about life, ourselves, and the world around us.

—SOCRATES

My Brilliant Lifetime Friend

Byron Tucker and I (Mark) met as young undergraduate students, among the few selected to be Student Ambassadors to India, considered a less-developed country. When we first met in Putney, Vermont, to train for the Experiment in International Living assignment, I was a bit put off by Byron's Southern aristocratic demeanor and his big Ivy League status from Amherst College. He talked about how in high school he rode his favorite Tennessee walking horses. As a kid from a blue-collar family, the only thing I rode to high school was my little Suzuki motorcycle, which I bought used from a friend. But that changed when we got to India, and he needed my help.

Byron unfortunately got into a yoga posture/asana that injured his knee. The local medical doctors could not fix his injury quickly. I felt compassion for him, so I went into the black market and bought him a pair of crutches. We both tower over six feet, so I used my size to get the right size crutches. From that point on, we became friends. Ultimately, after the Experiment in International Living home stay was over, we independently decided (against our signed agreements and the conventions of our Ambassadorial status) to travel independently throughout India. Such travel around India was pretty much unheard of in the late sixties. We went from Chikmagalur, Mysore State, to Bangalore to Madras to Calcutta to Kashmir to New Delhi and on to a university stay in Bombay, where we rejoined the group.

Every minute was thrilling. We were two strange white giants in a strange land that was extraordinarily multidimensional, complete with 325 different dialects and 18 full languages with their own alphabets and literatures. It was a once-in-a-lifetime experience worthy of penning a Hemingway-like story. It cemented a friendship that has lasted a lifetime.

Byron, when not doing business on Wall Street, is an accomplished poet and voracious reader. Each of his six homes overflows with libraries that would make most librarians envious.

Byron is one of the wisest men I have ever met. He has over a 90 percent comprehension of all of his various and sundry inputs—whether people, places, things, business, academics, spiritual studies, history, or travel. We and our wives love hanging out and traveling together. Last year we traveled together to Majorca, Portugal, and Spain, and have more exciting, life-enriching trips planned in the future.

At dinner one night, I asked him, "Who is the best question asker ever?"

Smilingly, he spontaneously answered, "Why, I am." He proceeded to enrich my evening with his reflections and wisdom on life, questions, and answers.

Questions to Understand Belief Systems: Byron Tucker's Story

Frankly, I don't know anybody who has asked as many hard questions as I have. I used to drive my parents, sister, teachers, and strangers crazy as a kid, asking why and needing real explanations. My parents were occasionally impatient, but they responded as best they could. My father was well-read with an extraordinary vocabulary. He traveled solving the interface problems for AT&T and local telephone-operating companies, and my mother was a nurse and a good businesswoman and manager.

When I was seven or eight, I asked my decade-older sister who brought home some graph paper what the lines were for. "Nothing," she answered. She should have said they have no specific meaning until you assign meaning to them. They help you understand spatial relationships and value make them visual and quantifiable. Even at that age, "nothing" seemed like a ridiculous and unacceptable answer to my question.

I have a profound curiosity that started with my early questioning of my parents. I read a psychological study thirty years ago that said that children in homes full of books tend to become good readers and motivated to curiosity and higher studies. My dad was a voracious reader, as was my aunt. Both were positive influences on me. Reading has been a hobby and a passion to me for as long as I can remember. Reading makes you more aware and available and deeper as a person. I can talk to anyone, anywhere in the world, because I am well-read and know a little something about almost everything. We each perceive the world through the filters of our own lives and experiences. I wanted to know and understand everything and come to an unmitigated view of "reality" and be able to discuss it.

I believe we each need to define ourselves and not be constrained by some parent's, teacher's, or other person's point of view of what we call reality. So, I launched myself into a lifelong self-educational pursuit using the questioning to be able to understand all belief systems. My initial serious questioning was of religious beliefs.

For example, I was sitting in church one Sunday as an eight-year-old, and I had my first "peak" experience, essentially a mini-mystical experience of expanded connectedness. It was not because of the church or the pastor; it just happened. I think many, if not all, people have such experiences but are afraid to talk about them because they are concerned others will think they are crazy or not living in reality, or fear they will get shut down for talking about such experiences. My experience was beyond words. I was spiritually overcome in a new opening, impossible to fully articulate. My mother did not know what to do with me, so at the end of the church service, she asked the minister to pray for and over me. The praying was nice, but I was in an Awareness beyond the minister's understanding. As I have traveled through these portals occasionally and often unexpectedly, I have invested much of my life thinking about them, reading and exploring esoteric literature and practices and studying with the masters seeking entrainment. Entrainment actually transcends normal human consciousness and takes us to alternative perceptions—doorways into greater understanding. Entrainment is the subtle, harmonizing vibrations that one telepathically receives from a master teacher or greater Awareness. Many master-disciple relationships rely on this as a method of training and transmission of insight. We could say that Christ clearly experienced entrainment and entrained his disciples since they were able to do many of the things He could.

My parents wanted me to pursue a higher education. I was accepted at great schools like Vanderbilt University, University of Tennessee, and University of Virginia, but the South in the sixties was constraining in its point of view and had what I thought of as limited thinking. I knew there was more in the world.

Fortunately, right at that time, a girlfriend asked me to visit her at Smith College. She had me stay nearby at an Amherst College fraternity. Amherst really spoke to me. I loved the school, the professors, the students, and the geography. It was mind-opening in every good way. I decided to apply. On my next visit to my girlfriend, I went in for an interview. When I sat down to be interviewed, I was "on!" I was self-clear, extraordinarily articulate, and in the moment. To the depth of me, I could really hear and answer what the dean was asking. I crafted my answers to his real questions as opposed to the superficial appearances. Being super present and in the zone really worked! I was admitted! Ultimately, going to Amherst opened up a world for me of connections, ideas, and yet more questions. Years later, before I graduated, the same dean showed me his interview notes. I learned then that interview was the *key* to my admission.

From there, I was chosen to go to India to participate in Experiment in International Living. I always had a taste for the bigger world. In the fifties my father drove us all over the country. I loved it. There were no jet airplanes for long-distance travel until 1959. Dad was knowledgeable about much of the world, and a lot of our dialogues let me know what was out there to experience.

Later, after finishing graduate school at the University of Chicago with an MBA, I began working on Wall Street in investment banking and later at Goldman Sachs in the commodity department. But after a few years, because of my questioning, I decided to pursue my own path and interests rather than the path of an investment banker. I am into self-questioning. I asked myself, "What's the highest and best use of my life, talents, and gifts and my happiness?" It was an internal struggle to leave, and then, once I left, I could not look back. I went on to create my own business in various areas and engage in active trading, which I still do to this day.

Questioning is an iterative process that requires repeated pursuit. I have learned that the whole Universe conspires to give us the answers we need. If we listen quietly in meditation and surrender our ego, we will hear answers curated just for us. Inside my mind and spirit, I have come to realize profound inner guidance that is true and clear. It takes quiet patience and intuitional listening to hear those subtle whispers of guidance. Higher knowing or Awareness does not shout. We must ask and then patiently listen with faith.

My view on questions is that you can give somebody fifty answers and they will go over them like water on a raincoat. But if they ask one question, they become open to receiving insights and understanding. Questions are, therefore, far more important than a slew of solutions. Questions asked lead us onward. Our biggest questioning challenge is to ask how we individualize the right questions to bring out wisdom in the right answers. With faith in a supportive Universe—impersonal but not indifferent—we will ultimately get exactly what we need, though perhaps not what we think we want.

Quite recently, a man who was in real pain and suffering came to talk to me. His question caused a profound answer to come through me. The answer inspired him to become a different human being because he listened to insights that came, through me, for him. I have spent my whole life cultivating real insight and seeking to *wake up*—the word "buddha" means awakened. This leads to service to others when it is needed and asked for. It is important not to try to help unless it is requested, for if we do, it can lead to undesirable consequences.

Life is like a piece of cloth, one whole that is all connected. I, like everyone else, am just one of the expressers of consciousness in the magnificent expression of Awareness. Awareness permeates all and everything; it *is* all and everything. It is not specific to me or any one individual. We are not containers of Awareness; we are its instruments. As Awareness seeks to experience itself, we provide the uplink, the data of experience in this dimension. But since we are Awareness also, we have access to the knowing and guidance that reside there, coming to us in subtle, quiet expressions. Though occasionally we do need to be hit on the head both physically and symbolically—often in the form of a crisis or serious illness. The barrier is the self-imposed limitations of the ego, which thinks it has godlike powers and wants control without realizing its inherent limits and self-referential perspective. Thus, suffering comes into the world. When we accept our role as connected beings, we move into harmony with life, forgiving all completely and loving without an object.

The first step in *asking* that seems self-evident is asking yourself: "What do I really want?" When you figure that out, pose your next question and your next, such as: "How do I do that?" "How do I make it happen?" Each question reveals the following questions and, in this way, like a path to your destiny and fulfillment, your questions become self-revealing as to the next step in that path.

Ask Gold Nuggets

- Can you ask with the innocence and purity of a child—trusting you will be answered?
- Do you feel deserving of every gift—like a child?
- Like a child, never stop asking who, what, where, why, when, and how.
- You can only understand belief systems by questioning everything.
- Life has endless gifts to offer if you have profound curiosity.
- Asking questions with faith will ultimately get you exactly what you need.

4. A Lifetime of Asking

Be a Grantor of Wishes

Throughout this reading journey, we have learned much about perfecting the art of asking and have come to understand the science that explains the transformational power of asking. Now we want to shift perspective to the other side of the asking equation. On that side is the person who answers the call when someone is in need. The friend or stranger who gives help when asked. The coworker who shares an important illumination where it is requested. The one who opens up when a relationship calls for more openness and more transparency. That person who fulfills another's appeal or petition to fulfill an essential necessity. The individual who sees an opportunity to respond to make someone else's life better in some way. We call that person the *Grantor of Wishes*. Being a Grantor of Wishes inherently elevates you to a status of human existence in which you have transcended the need to be only self-serving and, in doing so, have discovered the joy of expanding your good beyond yourself. The greatest Grantors of Wishes are those who understand that by sourcing, serving, and giving, they are opening up the cornucopia of the universal abundance to be poured out in their own lives. The law of attraction teaches us that we are truly like magnets of experience, intention, and states of being. What you put out—good or bad—comes back multiplied and magnified and gives compounding returns. As we are more giving in every way, we draw gifts in every form right back to us.

> *He who receives an idea from me,*
> *receives instruction himself without lessening mine;*
> *as he who lights his taper (candle) at mine,*
> *receives light without darkening me.*

> —President Thomas Jefferson

Jefferson's epistle imparts the idea of giving without giving up or losing anything. The sharing of ideas, friendship, kindness, and love has the power to create goodwill, often igniting a spark for change. Changes that might makes someone's day so much better or changes that make the entire world a better place. Often, these important gifts we give have no price tag attached to them other than a bit of deliberate time and effort.

We find that people who give more of themselves are more fulfilled, happier, and expandingly useful. Many times, wishes are easy to grant; they just require a little bit of thoughtfulness.

Each time you give, you expand yourself in some way. That expansion of your mind, heart, and soul, inexorably and inevitably, will serve to make your day and even your future better in every way. The Eastern religious philosophies talk about this principle as Karma. Christianity talks about it in terms of reaping what you sow. It is the same idea expressed in different ways.

Just as we were contemplating how embracing a spirit of generosity makes us happier human beings, a friend of ours sent us an irresistible animated video. The cartoon animation starts with a puppy happily jumping onto a fisherman's little dinghy early in the morning. As the fisherman is busy at one end of the boat casting his line into the lake, a mother stork lands on the edge of the dinghy and starts stealing earthworms out of the fisherman's can of freshly caught earthworms. The puppy ferociously starts barking at the thieving stork. The fisherman, not cognizant of the reason for the incessant barking, shushes the puppy. The fisherman thought his barking puppy was scaring away the fish he planned to catch. When the stork returns again, the puppy again barks and again gets silenced by his unsuspecting master. The mother stork revisits a third time, and this time, the puppy fights to keep the worm from the stork—each tugging on either end of the worm. Finally, the puppy pulls it away from the stork.

Feeling victorious, the puppy watches the stork fly away in defeat and land at her nest, where there are three baby storks. She stares down at them sadly because she has no worms to give her hungry babies. The puppy watches this for a few minutes and looks down sadly as he realizes he has deprived the baby storks of their nourishing sustenance. Suddenly, he jumps up, wagging his tail toward the stork, and makes sure she sees him tip over the entire can of worms on the boat floor for her. The mommy stork flies back and scoops up all the worms to deliver the feast to her babies. The puppy settles down contentedly in the boat, knowing happily that the baby storks have been well fed. As he rests contentedly, a shadow is suddenly flying over him, and the puppy looks up once again to see the mother stork returning. This time, her mouth is brimming full of fish, which she dumps on the deck of the boat. The puppy barks enthusiastically, and the fisherman is amazed at this surprising spectacle. Beholding this huge catch, his face is grateful and pleased as watches the stork fly away.

Such a lovely metaphorical story of how depriving others of something can result in a heavy heart. How giving of ourselves to make someone else's life better can bring us joy. And beyond that, how being generous and unselfish attracts back greater abundance than we could have achieved by being stingy.

Who suffers the most when you reject someone's heartfelt request?
Extraordinary international speaker and motivator Jim Rohn would say withholding generosity causes pain to a heart and soul! Jim and I (Mark) toured the world nonstop, speaking to tens of thousands per

month and sometimes in seven different countries in one month. We were on platforms everywhere together with most audiences in the size of six to ten thousand people because we were being featured on satellite TV, when it was brand new, on a program called *The People's Network*. I respected and admired Jim and will never forget some of the amazing stories he told that presented life lessons never to be forgotten. One such story was of a sweet little Girl Scout.

When Jim was down on his luck and financially broke, a Girl Scout knocked at his door one Saturday. She asked him to buy Girl Scout Cookies. He lied to her and told her his pantry was full of Girl Scout Cookies and gently dismissed her. She asked, he rejected her request, and when she left, and the whole encounter was over, it hurt his soul. Jim said it was a turning point in his life. After she left, he slumped against the door in grief, shame, and regret. He announced to himself at that moment, "This will never happen to me again; I am better than this!" Jim quickly started earning money again and grew quickly in business. He promised himself to always carry two thousand dollars cash on his person. Whenever he saw Girl Scouts selling cookies in front of a grocery store, he politely asked how many boxes they had. They would tell him, and he would buy them all on the spot and give them away to friends.

We both adore being Grantors of Wishes, and conversely, we have been blessed by generous grantors over and over again throughout our lives. One of my (Crystal) dear friends, Olivia Newton-John, has been such a beautiful example to me of letting kindness and generosity rule her decisions. We love hanging out with Olivia and her husband, John Easterling, who are both such special and amazing people. Olivia, of course, has had an iconic career as a singing star, and John created the fabulous Amazon Herb cosmetic and nutraceutical line, of which I was a superfan! Any time we had to be in Las

Vegas when Olivia was performing there, we would let them know ahead of time and plan to get together. We would spend time cruising through the fabulous shopping malls, finding fun goodies to buy, have wonderful meals together, and just enjoy a special time of rich friendship as the hours would slip away. One such time, Olivia and I were walking along chatting together while the guys talked business. I told her I was so disappointed that after John sold his Amazon Herb Company to a new buyer, they had eliminated the fabulous vitamin C serum called Camu-C, which came from a plant in the Amazon. I was saying to Olivia that I wished they would bring it back. She mentioned that she had found another vitamin C facial serum that was really good—not as good—but a close second to John's earlier formula. She gave me the name of it, and I was thankful. When we showed up the next day for lunch together, she handed me a bag from a shop. I opened it and, lo and behold, she had gone out and gotten the vitamin C formula for me. A very expensive bottle, I might add. I was so touched by her kindness and thoughtfulness. Right in the midst of her months-long Vegas booking, she took the time to thoughtfully grant me my wish.

Later that year I was finishing my book *Skinny Life*. I asked both Olivia, who has a health clinic in Australia, and John, with his health background, if they would consider giving me an endorsement. They said they would be honored to do it, but they'd like to read the book first. They each took a copy with them on their flight out to Australia. Olivia wrote me a few days later with the most beautiful endorsement. She said they had spent the entire flight reading my book! I was blown away at the generosity of time they were willing to give to serve me! Another time, Mark was booked to speak at a mega-church in Vegas. Olivia happened to still be there, so he asked her if she would like to come and sing to the congregation.

She looked at her calendar, realized she wasn't booked that Sunday morning, and even though she had a show that night, she said yes. She attended church with us and performed her beautiful song, "Grace and Gratitude." Again, most people with the commitments and nonstop schedule Olivia has carried for so many years typically make themselves very unavailable to people and requests. I saw other ways Olivia gave to others, including dedicated fans, staff, and helpers, with great kindness and generosity. One time I asked Olivia how she manages to be so kind and giving to so many people. She said, "I made a decision a long time ago that, whenever someone asks me for something, I will try to give them what they want or need if there is any possible way that I can do so." It was that simple. Olivia finds joy through the beauty and grace of being a Grantor of Wishes. She has an amazing heart and soul through and through, and I'm honored to call her friend.

Bill Gates and Warren Buffett are two of the richest men of all time and phenomenal best friends who regularly play bridge and travel together doing good and having fun. Bill Gates co-founded Microsoft, and Warren Buffet is called the "Oracle of Omaha" and considered the world's best value investor. Bill and his wife, Melinda, created the Gates Family Foundation, launched with $26.2 billion. Buffett, who said he was exemplary at creating wealth but not good at philanthropy, decided to put a huge amount of his massive wealth through the Gates Foundation.

Meeting with great regularity, Bill and Warren decided more needed to be done to solve the needs and problems of the world. Most people know the story of Jesus and the *Last Supper*. So, these two cleverly and wisely created the *First Supper*. At the First Supper, forty attendees who were worth a billion dollars or more were invited to sign the Giving Pledge and encouraged to gift half of their massive wealth away, preferably while alive, to good causes of their respective choice. A mind-boggling $122 billion was committed by the rich to tackle some of the world's most pressing needs. The list of First Supper invitees included people like Oprah Winfrey, Steve Case, Jon Bon Jovi, Marc Benioff, David Rubenstein, and Marc Andreessen.

The Giving Pledge has since taken on a life of its own. Charities have never been more thankful than to have Gates and Buffett as their seminal wish-granting stimulators. I (Mark) was invited to attend a poker night with a very selective group of people held at the Las Vegas Wynn Hotel a few years back. Warren was there speaking live to a small group and delighting the crowd with his intelligence, wit, and humor. He was recounting to us the experience of the First Supper. He said he was quite astounded that with all their excess wealth, about 20 percent of attendees were not willing to commit to any giving. In jest, he said that experience made him decide to write a book called *How to Get By on 500 Million Dollars!*

This year we were asked by one of the greatest nonprofit organizations, Childhelp, if we would consider cochairing their sixtieth campaign to help raise two hundred million dollars for the new Childhelp Global Campus. We did not need another thing to do. In fact, just the opposite; we were already scheduled to the max. We considered this big request carefully, knowing it would require a lot of time, energy, relationship capital, connections, and endless thinking and strategy. We use meditation and prayer, always, when faced with a big decision such as this one. After a day or so of contemplation, we felt so moved by this calling that we knew we just needed to trust it and say yes, not really knowing everything ahead of us. The founders of this wonderful organization, Sara O'Meara and Yvonne Fedderson, who have given sixty years of their lives working to prevent and treat child abuse, told us in their experience that when people have stepped up to answer the call of serving these children in need, they begin to notice increased blessings in their lives. We weren't sure what to expect, only that we knew if we truly dedicated ourselves to this profoundly important cause, we could make a positive difference in advancing the cause of prevention, treatment, and long-term solutions for abused children. Because of that, it was a must for us to say yes.

Now that we are half a year into the journey, we reflect back and can say, without equivocation, blessings have been coming out of the woodwork. Not only have we been very successful about engaging high-net-worth, creative people to join in our mission, we have also had our own personal surprises of abundance fall into our laps. Out of the blue, decades-old audio programs and books done by each of us have been sought out by new publishers, who are willing to pay signing bonuses for the rights to re-release them. Large companies have sought our advisory services and want to compensate with stock and cash. New companies have given us large percentages of the company to be the marketing maven in the nutraceutical space. We didn't agree to help the children because we expected something in return. We just knew it was something that called to our hearts and made us happy to do. But God's perfect Universe has a magnificent accounting system. When you deposit goodness, favors, help, and kindness into your universal bank account, that goodness will show up for you in all sorts of surprising ways!

It's a wonderful exercise to take a few moments and think of those times you've helped someone in need: how you might have made someone's day or even set someone on a new path to become their best. When opportunities arise to be a **Granter of Wishes** in some way—large or small—we encourage everyone to imagine for a moment what it will feel like to reject someone versus what it will feel like to say yes, and then make the decision deliberately and thoughtfully.

We Need One Another (by Jim Stovall)

The idea that none of us is an island, in that we are all interdependent upon one another, is a foundation of human existence.

At a critical point in my life when I found myself at the intersection of my hopes and my dreams, Mark Victor Hansen was there to provide me with the inspiration and boost I needed.

I had written seven business/success books before I had the inspiration to write my first novel, entitled *The Ultimate Gift*. I could have wallpapered my office with rejection letters from publishers until I found one independent publishing group willing to take a chance on my little story. I needed credibility desperately, so I reached out to what, at the time, was a distant acquaintance, Mark Victor Hansen, to humbly request his endorsement for my new title. Mark enthusiastically wrote, "I love this book. I see this book becoming one of the great and inspiring movies of all time. It touches my heart and soul deeply, profoundly, and permanently, and it will yours too. Happy reading of *The Ultimate Gift*."

Those powerful words from a powerful force in the publishing industry like Mark Victor Hansen created the groundswell that changed my world. That little book and three sequel titles, along with the movie trilogy—*The Ultimate Gift, The Ultimate Life,* and *The Ultimate Legacy*—have grossed in excess of one hundred million dollars and have impacted people around the world.

Today, when aspiring authors reach out to me for an endorsement, I respond eagerly and quickly because if I live to be a hundred, it will take all those years to repay the positive influence that Mark Victor Hansen created for me.

My Devastating Setback Was a Setup to Help Millions: Jim Stovall's Story

As a young man, my goal was to become a professional football player. I had the size, speed, and courage, and all the coaches and scouts wanted me and assured me I had a future in football. Then everything in my life turned upside down. During a routine physical, I was diagnosed with a condition that would cause me to permanently lose my eyesight, at nineteen years old. I went into a depressing tailspin with everyone telling me what I could not do. The loss of my sight quickly progressed. It was scary and embarrassing to be bumping into things and not be able to see where I was going. As it got worse, I stopped going outside much. I was stuck sitting alone and lonely in a little nine-foot-by-twelve-foot room, which I feared I would never leave. I couldn't accept it. I had to figure out something better, so I started asking myself, "What can I do with my life now as a blind person? Where can I make a difference in the world living with this handicap?"

I went to my father and said, "I'm not going to be able to get a job; I'm going blind too fast. I'm going to have to go into business for myself." Dad introduced me to my mentor. The man was a self-made millionaire. He made ten million dollars during the Great Depression and gave 90 percent of it to charity. He then worked for the rest of his life for a dollar a year for a nonprofit and lived off his investments. I learned so much from this man. He was the one who got me to read *Think and Grow Rich*, and it changed my thinking and my life. I learned that no one can get out of poverty by impoverishing you and me. They can't get others out of poverty by taxing you and me into oblivion. I learned that when people become entrepreneurs, they get themselves and many others out of poverty.

Sitting in sheer boredom in that room—it was just me with a TV, video player, radio, and telephone—one day I put on an old John Wayne movie. Frustrated and depressed, out of nowhere, I uttered the magic words—disguised as a problem—"Somebody ought to do something about blind people not being able to see the action and only hearing it on TV."

I went to a support group for the blind. There, everyone was complaining and bemoaning their blind fate. I knew intimately that experience. Fortunately, I sat next to a blind lady and single mom named Kathy Harper, who was a legal assistant. I told her my frustration about not being able to enjoy movies because I couldn't see the action and that somebody ought to do something about that. Kathy's poignant question to me was: "When are *we* going to do something about this?"

That question kick-started our co-partnering on the creation of Narrative Television Network (NTN). Kathy left her position at a prominent law firm, and we started to work immediately. We created a network that would provide a verbal description of every single piece of action, small or large, so that a blind person could have a rich, enjoyable experience watching TV. Most people who learned what our plans were said, "I hope you don't mind my laughing, but this is a joke, isn't it?" Once I figured it out, I co-created Narrative Television, which opened up the world of movies and TV to millions of blind Americans and millions more blind people around the world. I gained valuable wisdom when I discovered that the problem is the solution and the question can provide its own answer, which creates another question to be answered.

Kathy and I were literally the two blind people running this company, as in the "blind leading the blind." When I first started Narrative Television, I would do any publicity I could, because I could not afford to advertise. I actually did *The Howard Stern Show*. Howard asked me: "What's the best thing about being blind?"

I had never been asked that question before, so it passed all my filters. It was a beautiful question. "There are no ugly women," I answered. "There are no cloudy days."

In Philly, where the TV station started airing our programming, we were given time and told that we had to fill all the blank time with interviews. So I called up and scheduled fantastic interviews with Katharine Hepburn, Jimmy Stewart, Frank Sinatra, and Michael Douglas. We had dozens of these famous and interesting people to wrap around these movies we were showing. The funniest ever was Tim Conway who, upon commenting on the irony of TV for the blind, said, "Great idea, Jim. You could expand and do a radio show called *Dad's Shoes for Amputees*," and he went on to rattle off about ten similar and hilarious paradoxical ideas.

One of the outstanding interviews I did was with Academy Award–winning actress Kate Hepburn. "What would you have done with your life," I asked her, "if you hadn't become an actress?"

"I would have had to have found another way to support my habit, Jim, because I do this out of an innate need to be an actress," she replied. "It's the passion that makes the difference. It's not being a star making the money. It's that I have a need to do this, and the fact that I make a living doing it is convenient. But, if I had to feed myself another way, I would I still do what I do; it's my passionate purposefulness."

Once my business and book sales were up and rolling, my assistant came to me and said, "John Wooden is on the phone for you." I thought she was kidding or mistaken; perhaps it was a common name, or someone was mimicking his voice and playing a trick on me.

To my delight, it was *the* John Wooden. Wooden had read my books and become a raving fan, and he wanted to talk. We became great friends. Wooden was ninety-five years old at the time and lived to be a hundred. I loved asking John the most perplexing questions. We spoke weekly from then on. At a turning point in my life, when I asked him for advice, Wooden responded, "Always ask yourself this question: *'What would I do now, if I were amazing?'*" That question has guided me ever since he uttered it. I am always trying to be, do, and have the amazing.

I think if William Shakespeare, the Apostle Paul, and Dr. Napoleon Hill were alive today, in addition to writing books, they would be making movies. Because no matter how many books you and I sell, there are a whole lot of people who are never going to crack open one of those books. But they'll go to the theater this weekend, and you can reach them in amazing ways.

Today, I am a bestselling author, and some people find it hard to imagine that there was a time in my life when I had never read a book, much less written one. As a young man, I was an athlete and never focused on books or any other intellectual pursuits. Only after losing my sight did I discover audiobooks through the National Library for the Blind. Now, thanks to high-speed listening via compressed digital audio, I read an entire book every day.

Right now, I'm doing a series of books destined to become movies: the series is called *Homecoming Historical*. The books all take place at modern-day high schools. The first one's called *One Season of Hope*, and it's about Harry Truman. Number two, *Top of the Hill,* is about Napoleon Hill; and the third is *Will to Win* about Will Rogers. All three have been optioned for movies. I'm excited about working on this series, you know, because for me, my life has taken an amazing turn: to write a book and then turn it into this visual medium!

As a blind guy, I started with nothing. I was broke and scared to death to start with zero. Now I have in excess of ten million dollars. At Oral Roberts University, my wife, Crystal, and I just gave one and a half million dollars to the Stovall Center of Entrepreneurial Excellence. We want to get everyone educated into entrepreneurship. I want people to know that opportunity exists inside each of us to overcome whatever adversity besets us.

When my Narrative Television co-founder, Kathy Harper, died of breast cancer, Crystal and I became guardians of her thirteen-year-old daughter. Then we lovingly adopted her. I did not have a clue about how to raise a daughter. She just became a National Merit Scholar, so it appears we did okay.

Asking takes the fruit off the tree and multiplies it. Great questions are the key to all knowledge. Questions are the key to everything. When I was incarcerated for three years in the small room, I learned to focus on three questions:

1. "How do we know who created us?"
2. "Why am I here?"
3. "What am I supposed to do?"

My seemingly devastating sudden onset of blindness and the changes it ultimately caused in my life remind me of the story of *Joseph and His Coat of Many Colors* that says: "What you meant for my harm, God meant for your good and advantage."

Now I'm proud to say, "I write books that I cannot read that are turned into movies that I can't watch."

God Loves Bucket Lists

For what big and small things have you asked? Perhaps you wanted to get picked for an athletic team, win an award, get a medal, become an Eagle Scout, go to college, become a doctor, or something as simple as do a cartwheel or climb a tree. Some call this their bucket list, want list, or wish list—note the critical word is *list*.

Our goals can only be reached through a vehicle of a plan,
In which we must fervently believe,
And upon which we must vigorously act.
There is no other route to success.

—PABLO PICASSO

By recording your dreams and goals on paper, you set in motion the process of becoming the person you most want to be. By doing so you put your future in good hands—your own. Our vision is that you catch the spirit of asking for all that you want and maybe heretofore have denied yourself. It's our desires, dreams, and hopes that keep us happy and focused on the joys of living. Now we're challenging you to write down all that you desire; everything that would make up your perfect bucket list. When you write your list down, you can keep looking at it and rekindling joyous enthusiasm that comes from hoping for and experiencing the bounty of life.

I (Mark) was inspired and befriended by Dr. John Goddard, World's Best Goal Setter, with 127 goals that he asked for, and mostly got, by writing them all down when he was a lad of only fifteen.

Thusly inspired, I wrote more, and here is a small sample of what I have asked for in writing. We hope it inspires you to write down all your goals and forever keep asking and adding more. When you achieve them, as you surely will, do not cross them out like a grocery list of milk, eggs, and butter. Rather, write down *victory* next to each achievement because all our lives pulsate up and down. On a down day, remember to look at all your many victories, and you will feel good about yourself again and move forward to better and bigger asking and more victories.

- Become an Illinois Counsel Recovery Team Scuba Diver—**Victory**
- Start my own rock and roll group, The Messengers—**Victory**
- Milk a cow—**Victory**
- Work with a genius—**Victory**
- Wear only comfortable shoes and boots—**Victory**
- Take a spur-of-the-moment vacation—**Victory**
- Own my dream home—**Victory**
- Smell the freshness of the desert after rain—**Victory**
- See the lava flowing out of Kilauea, Kona, Hawaii—**Victory**
- Vote in every election for which I am eligible—**Victory**
- Assist in the birth of a foal—**Victory**
- Vacation on a beach reading my favorite selection of books—**Victory**
- Hang with truly interesting, brilliant, and inspiring people of achievement—**Victory**
- Win the book of the year award—**Victory (1999)**
- Become world's bestselling author, *Guinness Book of Records*—**Victory (2000)**
- Win Horatio Alger Award for Distinguished Americans—**Victory**
- Learn jokes that get laughs—**Victory**
- Take part in a new archeological find in Guatemala—**Victory**
- Climb Mountains Whitney, Fuji, Kilimanjaro, and Machu Picchu—**Victory**
- Watch the Ball Drop on New Year's Eve in NYC—**Victory**
- Do a cattle drive on Parker Ranch on the Big Island of Hawaii—**Victory**
- Find a great and inspiring teacher for my daughter when she went to kindergarten—**Victory**

- Learn to speed read—**Victory**
- Become a philanthropist and inspire others to do the same or more—**Victory**
- Give leadership, money, and muscle to Habitat for Humanity—**Victory**
- Attend Calgary Stampede—**Victory**
- Fly in a Concorde over Earth and see its curve at 60,000 feet at Mach two—**Victory**
- Learn to ski—**Victory**
- Go to a red-carpet movie and play opening—**Victory**
- Make the cover of *Time* magazine—**Victory**
- Learn a new word or more every day of my life—**Victory**
- Be debt-free—**Victory**
- Travel everywhere in India, China, Thailand, and Vietnam—**Victory**
- Attend a national political convention—**Victory**
- Shop Rodeo Drive and Fifth Avenue—**Victory**
- Give away everything I haven't worn in three years—**Victory**
- Swim with dolphins—**Victory**
- Safari across Africa's Serengeti Plain—**Victory**
- Eat tapas in Spain on the street—**Victory**
- Visit and vacation in Sedona, Arizona—**Victory**
- Read the Bible cover to cover—**Victory**
- Bring flowers to my wife for no reason—**Victory**
- Visit and tour the White House—**Victory**
- Keep all my journals for life—**Victory**
- Study dialogues of Plato—**Victory**
- See our children happily married—**Victory**
- Work out six days a week vigorously to be totally fit—**Victory**
- Fall in love with the right woman, at the right time for both of us—**Victory**

We all have those day we feel we haven't done enough, lived enough, or been enough. When those days come up for you, pull out your bucket list and see the things you've experienced, accomplished, or conquered. Focusing on what you've done—not what's missing—will keep your spirit positively focused so you become a magnet for experiencing ever-more-wonderful things!

Ask Boldly

These bold askers have changed the world and fulfilled their destinies. May their destinies inspire and trigger and help you release your destiny.

- "**What are you going to do to positively affect one billion people in the next decade?**" Creators of Singularity University, Drs. Ray Kurzweil and Peter Diamandis, challenging each attendee to think of their own idea to positively change the planet.

- "**Ask not what your country can do for you, but what you can do for your country.**" Immediately after reciting the oath of office as the 35th President of the United States, John F. Kennedy delivered these powerful words in his inaugural address. This speech, the first delivered to a television audience in color, is considered among the best inaugural speeches in presidential history.

- "**Is there a God? What is my purpose in Universe?**" These are the questions Dr. R. Buckminster Fuller asked when he was ready to jump into Lake Michigan to drown himself, because he felt he let his four-year-old daughter die of spinal meningitis while he attended the Harvard-Yale football game. The answer that came to him changed his life and the world forever. It was for him to show what one average man can do, and to help find the solutions to make humankind 100 percent economically and physically successful. "Bucky" was an American architect, systems theorist, author, designer, inventor, and futurist. In his lifetime he published more than thirty books, coining or popularizing terms such as "Spaceship Earth," "Dymaxion" house/car, ephemeralization, and "tensegrity." He also developed numerous inventions, mainly architectural designs, and invented and patented the widely known geodesic dome. Carbon molecules known as fullerenes were later named by scientists for their structural and mathematical resemblance to Bucky's geodesic spheres.

- "**What do you want us to do with these kids, God?**" asked two young starlets, Sara O'Meara and Yvonne Fedderson, who stumbled across eleven forlorn and forsaken children in 1959 war-torn Japan and courageously took them in. The answer they received was to take care of these children before they left Japan. Years later, after forming several international orphanages, they ultimately started Childhelp, which has now asked for and received help for over ten million abused children.

- "**What is the best gift given to any community?**" His answer: "I will spend the first half of my life earning the money and the second half of my life giving it away to do the most good and the least harm with it." Andrew Carnegie, the benefactor to 2,509 American libraries, Carnegie Hall in New York City, and Carnegie Mellon University in Pittsburgh, Pennsylvania, at the time the richest man in the world with four hundred billion dollars in wealth.

- "**Are women persons?**" asked Susan B. Anthony. Anthony was the bold suffragist of her generation and became an icon of the women's suffrage movement. Anthony traveled the US to give speeches, circulate petitions, and organize local women's rights organizations. In one of her famous speeches, she laid out the facts and posed that ultimate question that all citizens had to face. She went on to say: "**And I hardly believe any of our opponents will have the hardihood to say they are not. Being persons, then, women are citizens; and no state has a right to make any law, or to enforce any old law, that shall abridge their privileges or immunities.** It was we, the people; not we, the white male citizens; nor yet we, the male citizens; but we, the whole people, who formed the Union. And we formed it, not to give the blessings of liberty, but to secure them; not to the half of ourselves and the half of our posterity, but to the whole people—women as well as men."

· **"How can I help solve the world-wide issues of poverty and hunger?"** Dr. Muhammad Yunus asked himself. As a Fulbright Economics Scholar, he had studied at Vanderbilt University in Nashville, Tennessee. He returned to his home city of Chittagong, Bangladesh, and saw starvation and poverty—making people look like the walking dead. He pulled money out of his own pocket and lent money to women to become entrepreneurs. His answer to his big question was to create micro-credit, micro-finance. Yunus became banker to the poor in his home country of Bangladesh. Ultimately, he launched Grameen Bank and created micro-lending to battle against world poverty. His micro-financing model is serving loans of over one hundred billion dollars. Grameen Bank is owned 5 percent by the government of Bangladesh and 95 by the borrowers. They have given loans of over two hundred and fifty billion dollars to date.

- "Why can't I make a mobile X-ray to save lives on the spot?" asked French physicist Marie Curie. At the start of World War I, X-rays were still found only in city hospitals, far from the battlefields where wounded troops were being treated. Curie's solution was to invent the first "radiological car"—a vehicle containing an X-ray machine and photographic darkroom equipment—which could be driven right up to the battlefield where army surgeons could use X-rays to guide their surgeries. Curie solved the problem of electricity needed for the machine by incorporating a "dynamo"—a type of electrical generator—into the car's design. The petroleum-powered car engine could then provide the required electricity. Curie was also the first woman to receive the Nobel Prize in Physics in 1903, which she shared with her husband Pierre Curie. She is also the only woman to have received multiple Nobel Prizes, when she received a second one in 1911 in Chemistry.

- "Will you please help me find my way in life, and I will l build you a shrine?" Danny Thomas, who was a struggling entertainer, down on his luck, promised while praying to St. Jude Thaddeus, the patron saint of hopeless causes. With that prayerful request, he got a gig in Las Vegas for thirty-five thousand dollars a week. It launched a star-studded career in television and movies. Danny then went on to create St. Jude Children's Research Hospital in Memphis, Tennessee, devoted to curing catastrophic diseases in children. The hospital provides free treatment and shares all research freely with the world. It has become an international beacon of hope. Danny is gone, but his dream lives on and is serving more than ever, led by Marlo Thomas, his daughter.

- **"How did you get rich?"** Napoleon Hill asked the richest man in the world, Andrew Carnegie. Carnegie answered over three days, and asked Napoleon to invest the remainder of his life to learn, teach, and write about the principles and philosophy of personal success and achievement. Hill agreed. Carnegie introduced him to the five hundred most successful people of his time. Hill wrote the book that has inspired more individuals to become millionaires than any other book, *Think and Grow Rich*.

- **"Could I take an unknown kid off the street, have him or her go through the process—with songwriters, choreography, masterful studio musicians, voice training, wardrobe, grooming, and diction coaching to create musical stars?"** asked Berry Gordy, founder of Motown Records. His previous work in a Lincoln-Mercury assembly line for $86.40 a week helped him appreciate the plant's precision and efficiency. Raw metal started on the assembly line, and a brand spanking new car rolled out. He converted that great idea to the music industry. He created what everyone called Hitsville with stars that included Michael Jackson, Diana Ross, Gladys Knight & the Pips, The Temptations, and Smokey Robinson.

- **"Will you taste my finger-licking good recipe?"** Colonel Sanders asked one thousand and nine restaurant owners this question until one was willing to invest in his idea and franchise. The deal he struck to get a nickel for every piece of chicken sold in the Kentucky Fried Chicken restaurants made him a wealthy KFC legend.

- **"I knocked on eighty doors and asked them for their business. All of them turned me down until I got to the eighty-first one, which bought a four-million-dollar system."** Ross Perot had a brilliant idea to form a start-up company called Electronic Data Systems. His positive, can-do attitude kept him going through a lot of rejection all the way to success. Ross cheerfully explained, "The way I see it, I got paid almost fifty thousand dollars each time I asked, and someone said no."

- **Jack Canfield and I got turned down 144 times by publishers when we asked them to publish our book, Chicken Soup for the Soul.** Because we continued to ask and didn't stop asking, we prevailed and have to date sold two billion dollars' worth of books and created one billion dollars in licensing sales. Those are results worth the rejections we painfully took.

God is the master Creator, and we are expressions of his great Creation. We are here to ask, create, and contribute. When you begin to have a natural internal flow of curiosity and communion with your Creator, you discover that you, as the expresser, are greater than any individual expression. Your inward desires and requests in consciousness become your most glorious manifestations.

Powerful Spiritual Asks to Consider

I ask to awaken my soul to serve greatly with love.

I ask angels to work on my behalf.

I ask to facilitate my greatest contribution(s) to the world.

I ask to help to overcome my deepest fears.

I ask to discover my full talents and abilities.

I ask to discover the greatest possibilities for my life.

I ask for robust energy and excellent health.

I ask for wisdom and illumination.

I ask to stimulate my imagination and intuition.

I ask for complete blessings over my entire life and future.

I ask for financial abundance and prosperity.
I ask to make my great dreams a reality.
I ask for the highest-quality life I can live.
I ask to be creative and original.
I ask for passionate purposefulness.
I ask for great plans for my future.
I ask to discover my destiny.
I ask for the fulfillment of my life purpose.

Ask wisely, prayerfully, acknowledging with humility, that the beautiful power with which you were perfectly created can be joyfully expressed through your pursuit of an ever-better life.

Nothing about you or your destiny is set in stone, but you must continue to ask so that your destiny will continue to unfold before you.

If you ask for little, you will get it. If you ask for a lot, you will get it. The choice is, and always has been, yours. The world is your oyster, and it is there for the asking. So ask fearlessly!

Ask Gold Nuggets

- Be a Grantor of Wishes.
- Fill your own heart by giving to others.
- A devastating setback can be a setup to help millions.
- What were you created for, and what are you supposed to do?
- God loves bucket lists. Make sure yours is written and clear.
- Asking boldly releases your destiny.
- Know and review daily—your powerful, spiritual asks!

Epilogue

Like Micaela, you can see there is so much more to your life than that which is immediately visible. You have been given the vision of the Destiny Bridge, which is always shimmering, beckoning you to step across it. As you enter that bridge with your hopes and dreams alive, remember to ask and never stop asking. As you do, your magnificent journey will begin to magically unfold before you, your gifts will continue to be revealed to you, and most certainly, your destiny awaits you.

We want to hear about your unique successes, achievements, and transformations as you embark on the asking journey. Please write us at: share@asktheaskers.com.

Acknowledgments

We want to deeply thank and appreciate the following individuals for going above and beyond the call of duty to help make this book happen:

Our amazing friends and contributors to this book. They are the bold askers of the world who have generously shared their journeys so that others could benefit and learn. We are vastly blessed with true-blue, wonderful, giving friends. Each person was kind, considerate, and comprehensive, and went deep with their personalized answers to make this book the ultimate book of asking. Loving thanks to all these special humans for their contributions to this book: Bob Proctor, Peter Guber, Trammell Crow Jr., Trudy Green, Rita Davenport, Jim Stovall, Meredith Walker, David Webb, Wyland, Deborah Rosado Shaw, Dan Clark, Dr. Nick Delgado, Ken McElroy, Brad Rotter, Mayor Brad Cole, Mayor Rex Parris, Greg Hague, Janet Davis, Preston Weekes, Audra and Aren Hansen, Sara O'Meara, Yvonne Fedderson, Lyn Marquis, Pat Burns, and Margo Stanley.

Thanks to our agent, Dan Strutzel, who has been a great, true, and helpful friend for years. He is wise and dedicated to bringing forth the best in everyone. Once we discussed our idea for the book, his commitment to it never wavered.

A big thanks to our publisher Anthony Ziccardi, of Post Hill Press, who trusted us to deliver our craft with our personal style and wisdom. He has been a true partner in making this happen. He is a gem in the world of publishing.

Thanks to our beloved families, who always cheer us on through each and every project. Their love and support give us purpose each and every day.

Most importantly, we want to thank you, the reader, for reading this book and asking your friends to get a copy. As we all become better askers, we vastly improve our lives, purposefulness, destinies, and the future and our world.

If we neglect to thank someone, please forgive us, as we are extremely excited to get a much-needed book in print as soon as possible. Know each person who has been a part of this project is very dear to us, so we thank you.

About the Authors

Mark Victor Hansen is probably best known as the co-author for the *Chicken Soup for the Soul* book series and brand, setting world records in book sales, with over 500 million books sold. He is also a prolific writer with 307 books authored or co-authored, including *The Aladdin Factor, The Power of Focus, The Richest Kids in America, The Miracles in You, You Have a Book in You,* and the *One Minute Millionaire* series. Mark also worked his way into a worldwide spotlight as a sought-after keynote speaker and entrepreneurial marketing maven. He is a charismatic speaker having spoken to 7,000 audiences in 78 countries.

Crystal Dwyer Hansen is a business strategist and successful entrepreneur, speaker, and author in the US and China. Crystal, also known as the "celebrity coach," is a certified life coach and wellness/nutrition expert, whose personal coaching, speaking, CD and video programs, books, and articles have helped people all over the world. Crystal is a Member of the International Coaching Federation and the founder of Crystal Vision Life, Ltd, (crystalvisionlife.com) and Skinny Life®, a wellness company (skinnylife.com). Crystal is also the author of *Skinny Life: The Real Secret to Being Physically, Emotionally, and Spiritually Fit.*

Mark and Crystal are heavily engaged and invested in clean, renewable energy through ownership in two companies, Metamorphosis Energy and Natural Power Concepts, based in Hawaii.